The Church of Christ

BY

THOMAS W. PHILLIPS

"A LAYMAN"

THE STANDARD PUBLISHING FOUNDATION
CINCINNATI, OHIO, U. S. A.

Printed in U. S. A.

DEDICATION

This book is respectfully dedicated to believers in Christ, to strengthen their faith "that they may be ready always to give an answer to every man that asketh a reason of the hope that is in them" (1 Pet. iii. 15). It is dedicated to those who seek the kingdom of God, answering the question, "What must I do to be saved?" It is dedicated to unbelievers, to convince them that Jesus is "the Christ, the Son of the living God," and the Saviour of the world.

CONTENTS

BOOK SECOND.—EVIDENCE OF PARDON AND THE CHURCH AS AN ORGANIZATION

INTRODUCTION

In presenting this book to the public as a layman, we have no apology to offer, as the early Christians when they were "scattered abroad went everywhere preaching the word." The Young Men's Christian Association, of which the writer is a member, the Young Women's Christian Association, and the Young People's Christian Endeavor Society are all doing most effective work for the cause of Christ, yet without title, ritualism, or robes.

In telling the story of Christ's Church we are entering a field open to all—not limited to a chosen few or confined to a class—for Christian revelation was given to all mankind.

Teachers in the Sunday School, Bible Class, and various Christian organizations have made a deep and lasting impression upon the world. Jesus preached to the multitudes. "The common people heard Him gladly";[1] and He said, "The poor have the Gospel preached to them."[2] The apostles and evangelists preached to the people, and the people, hearing, believed. The inspired history of Christ and His religion is adapted to man in all the varied walks of life. Even prophecy of Scripture is not "of private interpretation."[3]

[1]Mark xii. 37. [2]Matt. xi. 5. [3]2 Peter i. 20.

When Christ was first preached multitudes "gladly received the word." If we can not now understand as they did then, what God willed, what Christ said, and His ambassadors taught, the Christian Scriptures are not a revelation to man. The will of God is plainly revealed, showing all that man is to do, to be, to suffer, and enjoy. All Christians, without distinction, are called "a royal priesthood," and are made "kings and priests unto God," and may understand and teach His word.

The writer, believing that in Christ and His church the mystery of life and death is solved and man's duty and destiny revealed, deems it most important that the teachings of Christ and His ambassadors be properly presented to the world. When we observe the divided condition of Christendom, we feel assured that there must be something fundamentally wrong in the presentation of Christian truth, because parties and sects of Christians, while differing can not all be right.

We are largely creatures of environment. The rule is that the child follows the faith of its parents. Demonstration of this is seen in both politics and religion. If a child's parents are Republicans, the child will be a Republican; if Democrats, the child will be a Democrat; and so with the various political parties, no matter how divergent and contradictory in sentiment or principle such parties may be. The same is true in religion; a child born of Roman Catholic parents becomes a Catholic; of Episcopalian parents, becomes an Episcopalian. The same is true of the Baptists, Methodists, Presbyterians, and the multitude of different denominations; all have observed these influences of environment which appear on every hand; and yet many people believe that those who differ from them hold the most untenable and absurd views upon social, political, and religious subjects. We may well ask the question, Are we following blindly in opinions or faith because of our early training? Recognizing these facts the writer decided to reinvestigate his accepted religion, and, if possible, to make an original and impartial investigation of the subject pertaining to religious truth, considering it from the Heathen, the Jewish, and the Christian standpoints, the result of which is here given.

It is obvious that several hundred churches, denominations, sects, and parties in Christendom can not all be right. They may all be wrong, but no two of them can be right, if Christ's Church was a unit and divisions were forbidden by the statement "That there be no divisions among you."[1] Two men can not differ about any fact or truth and both be right; about any inspired command and obedience to it; about any divine ordinance and its observance, about officers under Christ and their duties, and both be right, any more than they can differ about the fact that the sun shines by day and the moon by night, and both be right. It is, therefore, the design of this volume to unfold the simple truth in regard to the Church of Christ, both in faith and practise. In

[1] I Cor. i. 10–13.

doing this we place emphasis upon the completeness of the Christian religion as being adapted to all men everywhere and in all time.

Christianity is a new or an original religion. The proffer of absolute pardon to a world lying in sin was promised only through Christ. This great fact being of such importance, we have passed in review, in the order in which they occur, all the cases of forgiveness or pardon recorded in the New Testament, comparing one with the other in order to learn if the same terms were required of all, if there is one universal law of pardon, and if all persons come into Christ's Church upon the same terms. We know of no book covering this ground, which alone is deemed sufficient reason for presenting this volume to the public.

Again, reasons are given to show that all who come into the Church of Christ have the full assurance of pardon and acceptance with God.

Again, the Church of Christ is a complete organization, divinely constituted, without any authority given to any man or set of men or ecclesiastical body to change any of its rites, its officers, or its ordinances.

Also, the church was a unit, Christians were one in Christ, being "complete in him," "There shall be one fold and one shepherd."[1]

The conclusion shows the superiority of Christ and His own infinite greatness in the revolutions He wrought in society and the world.

[1]John x. 16.

BOOK FIRST

THE HISTORY OF PARDON

CHAPTER I

NEWNESS OF CHRISTIANITY

Christianity, an Original or New Religion. Adapted to All Mankind. The Only Religion Promising Forgiveness of Sin. New, in Promising Eternal Life. New, in Teaching the Fatherhood of God. New, in Being Positive. New or Original in that It is Missionary.

CHRISTIANITY is an original religion. It was not handed down by tradition; it was not the outgrowth of human philosophy or reason; it was not compiled from preceding religions, but it was new.

All the greater religions are historical, whether of divine or of human origin, and are to be judged in the light of history. Having considered the Pagan, Patriarchal, Jewish, and Christian religions, we are assured that the facts of history fully justify the following conclusions:

First, Christianity is the only religion thus far developed in the world that is adapted to all mankind, to every individual, race, and nation. It commands all that is for the best good of man; it forbids all that is injurious and wrong. It promises all that is good, both in the present and in the future. It is the one religion that promises the full pardon of sin. Of all the recorded Pagan religions there is nothing embraced in them looking to or promising the forgiveness of past sin. They offered sacrifices to their deities to propitiate their anger, to turn away their vengeance, and for aid in time of trouble or time of war, but nothing in their systems proposed the forgiveness of sin.

Even the Patriarchal and Jewish religions, which were the only revealed religions prior to the Christian, did not promise complete or full pardon for sin. There was a carrying forward of sin under the Jewish economy until the promised Messiah should come. "There was a remembrance of sins year by year"; "sacrifices which can never take away sins." [1] He was "the Lamb of God who taketh away the sin of the world." Such wondrous words were never spoken of any other being. This new religion lifts up the fallen, cleanses the vile, makes the sinful holy. "If any man is in Christ, he is a new creature." [2]

Second, Christianity is new or original in that it directly promises eternal life—an individual, personal, immortal spirit clothed with an immortal body. The question, asked by Job in the dawn of history, "If a man die shall he live again?" [3] and anxiously repeated by the wisest and greatest of earth in succeeding ages, remained unanswered until Christ. Heathen religions taught the transmigration of souls, the embodiment of the human spirit in various animals. Their highest idea was that the human spirit would finally enter Nirvana or be absorbed in the sun, or deity, but they did not teach a personal, individual immortality.

When we come to the Jewish religion and its legal system we do not find the promise of immortality or eternal life in the five books of Moses, but in its stead we have a chapter of curses and blessings, all tem-

[1] Heb. x. 3–11. [2] 2 Cor. v. 17. [3] Job xiv. 14.

poral, both as to punishment for disobedience and reward for obedience. The people were to be blessed in basket and in store, in their outgoing and incoming, were to have fruitful seasons, and, in fact, all temporal blessings were to follow them if they were obedient unto the law. If not, they were to be punished by war, by famine, by pestilence, by all manner of evil on account of disobedience to their prescribed law.[1] In the prophets and in the Psalms there are references to life after death, but nowhere in the Old-Testament Scriptures is immortality or eternal life promised for obedience to any commands therein given. Christianity, therefore, alone promises a future and an immortal existence. Christ says: "I am the way, the truth, and the life. No man cometh unto the Father but by me." No one before or since claimed the power over life and death. He said, "I am the resurrection and the life: he that believeth in me tho he were dead yet shall he live, and whosoever liveth and believeth in me shall never die." "I go and prepare a place for you, . . . that where I am there ye may be also." "Be thou faithful unto death and I will give thee a crown of life." Paul says, speaking of this mortal body: "It is sown in corruption, it is raised in incorruption; it is sown in weakness, it is raised in power; it is sown a natural body, it is raised a spiritual body."[2] Here, therefore, we have specific and definite existence, a spirit clothed with a glorified and immortal body, a wondrous revelation when we consider it in contrast with all preceding religions.

[1]Deut. xxviii. [2]1 Cor. xv. 42–57.

Third, the Christian religion is new or original in that it teaches the fatherhood of God and the brotherhood of man. There is nothing in heathen religion that teaches this relationship. Max Müller states, in his "Chips from a German Workshop," that no such word as "mankind" is found in human language before Christ—that there is nothing in language to express the kinship of the race. Before Christ it was Egyptian, Mede, Persian, Grecian, Roman, Scythian, barbarian, bond and free, but no word to express the kinship of man. Paul said, in his address on Mars Hill to the Grecian philosophers, that "God had made of one blood all nations to dwell on the face of the earth." The Grecian people, notwithstanding they were the most advanced of all others in reason, philosophy, and art, had no word in their language to show that they were related to any other peoples or nations; in fact, all other nations were considered barbarians by them and so called. Christ says: "Neither knoweth any man the Father, save the Son, and he to whomsoever the Son will reveal Him."[1] He was the first on earth who taught to pray, "Our Father who art in heaven." The Christian Scriptures everywhere bear testimony to the fatherhood of God, and exalt believers by calling them sons and daughters of the Lord Almighty, "heirs of God and joint heirs with Christ." Other religions require priests, sacrifice, ceremony "in temples made with hands,"[2] but individual Christians are both "a temple of God,"[3] and "a royal priesthood," "an holy priesthood to offer up spiritual sacrifices, acceptable to God, by Jesus

[1]Matt. xi. 27. [2]Acts xvii. 24. [3]1 Cor. iii. 16; 2 Cor. vi. 16.

Christ,"[1] and these Christians have access to God anywhere on sea or land.

Fourth, the Christian religion alone teaches humility as the road to greatness. Christ says: "He that is greatest among you shall be your servant." From that time on the greatest of earth have been the greatest servants. "He that shall humble himself shall be exalted."

Fifth, the Christian religion is original in that it is positive. Other philosophies and religions were negative. Jesus said thou shalt, they said thou shalt not. He, while restraining wrong, taught active goodness. He says: "Every tree that bringeth not forth good fruit is hewn down and cast into the fire." Man must bear fruit. "By their fruits ye shall know them." By restraining all that is evil or sinful in man he could not be made positively good. He must do good in order to be good. Like a fruitless tree a man may be negatively good in society, or selfishly exclude himself from it, yet he, according to Christ, is only fit for the ax and the fire. Instead of the injunction "Oppress not the widow and the fatherless," the command is to "visit the fatherless and widows in their affliction." While caring for such, no one would injure them. So along all lines of duty, while engaged in benefiting others, no one will wrong them. While blessing, they can not curse. Do unto others as you would have them do unto you banishes all moral wrong as light banishes darkness. And Jesus says, "Let your light shine."

All the lessons taught by Jesus in His parables are positive. The miracles of Jesus were all character-

[1] 1 Peter ii. 5–9.

ized by positive good. On earth He "went about doing good," and in the final judgment He says, "Inasmuch as ye did it unto one of these my brethren, even these least, ye did it unto me."[1]

Sixth, Christianity goes beyond all preceding law and religion in that its author makes the intent to commit sin a crime and lust a sin,[2] and in that He teaches "on earth peace among men." The religion of Jesus is original in its entire sweep, in its facts, precepts, and promises, in not resenting wrong and in doing good to enemies. It required the death of its Founder for its completion. It is the only religion that has a Gethsemane and a Calvary on the road to life, and that embraces the entire duty and destiny of man.

Seventh, the Christian religion is new or original in that it is missionary.

J. Freeman Clark, in his book entitled "Ten Great Religions," states his conclusions as follows: "All the great religions of the world, except Christianity, are ethnic religions or religions limited to a single nation or race. Christianity alone is the religion of all races. The religions of Persia, Egypt, Greece, Rome, and Scandinavia have come to an end, having shared the fate of the national civilization of which each was a part. The religions of China, Islam, Buddha, and Judea have all been arrested and remain unchanged and seemingly unchangeable. Like great vessels anchored in a stream, the current of time flows past them and each year they are further behind the spirit of the age and less in harmony with its demands. Christianity alone of all religions seems to possess the

[1]Matt. xxv. 40. [2]Matt. v. 21-28.

power of keeping abreast with the advancing civilization of the world. . . . It alone of all the religions of mankind has been capable of accompanying man in his progress from evil to good, from good to better."

The heathen religions being ethnical or national, were not missionary. Nor was the Jewish religion missionary. In the fifteen hundred years of its history we do not find that the Jews converted to their religion a village, town, or city, much less a nation. It is true they made some proselytes, but the Jewish system of religion was restricted to Israel as a nation. They were nowhere commanded to become a missionary people or to convert other nations to their religion. The Jewish religion was added to the former covenant and was designed at its consummation to bring the Messiah to the world. Its prophecies foretold and its prophets pointed out the coming One. It was said, speaking of certain kings: "And in the days of those kings shall the God of heaven set up a kingdom, which shall never be destroyed."[1] Isaiah, in speaking of the Messiah to come, said: "The government shall be upon his shoulder, and his name shall be called Wonderful, Counsellor, the Mighty God, the Everlasting Father, the Prince of Peace."[2] In fulfilment of these and many other prophecies, Christ came in the fulness of time and established a reign of universal love, of mercy and forgiveness, which has been in the world and swayed its destiny for nineteen hundred years, blessing and cheering the living, comforting the dying, and giving the hope of eternal life beyond the grave.

[1]Dan. ii. 44. [2]Isa. ix. 6.

CHAPTER II

THE KINGDOM OF HEAVEN

The Desire of Life and Happiness Deeply Implanted in the Human Heart. Jesus Came According to Prophecy to Establish a Kingdom. Introduced by John the Baptist. First Case of Gentile Healing. Rejection of the Jews. First Record of Pardon. Apostles Sent Forth. Second Record of Pardon. Healing on the Sabbath. Prophecy Regarding the Gentiles. The Kingdom. Second Case of Gentile Healing.

THE most important subject for human consideration is existence, being, life, "For what shall a man be profited if he shall gain the whole world and forfeit his life? or what shall a man give in exchange for his life?"[1] All sane persons do their utmost to perpetuate their existence and to secure the greatest good attainable in this life. If there be life beyond —a life that shall not be measured by years but by an eternal future—the happiness or misery of which is governed by actions here, the subject demands our most profound attention.

The desire of life and happiness is deeply implanted in the human heart. The laws governing natural or temporal life are being studied more and more year by year. How shall life be preserved and happiness secured are questions of very great moment when connected with our present existence. To

[1]Mark viii. 36, 37.

secure man's life and liberty and give him the right to pursue happiness, governments are established and laws are enacted by men. When we look over the world and see the vast efforts being put forth in all the departments of human industry, science, and invention for the present good of the race, to sustain and make happy this transient life of less than a century, we are startled when we consider the infinite greatness of eternal life which lies just beyond. And how incomparably less is the exertion to secure that boon, to know "the law of the spirit of" that "life," that everlasting felicity may be secured! Spiritual or eternal life is greater than the present just in proportion to its duration and enjoyment. A wise man therefore can not doubt or disbelieve without diligently inquiring, Is there a life beyond?

Jesus proposes to purify this life in preparation for a life to come. He came, according to preceding prophecy, to establish a kingdom. This is called by Matthew "The Kingdom of Heaven"; by Mark and Luke, "The Kingdom of God." This kingdom was announced before Jesus commenced His mission. "In those days came John the Baptist, preaching in the wilderness of Judea and saying, Repent ye for the kingdom of heaven is at hand." He preached the baptism of repentance for the remission of sins. "Then went out to him Jerusalem and all Judea, and all the region round about the Jordan, and were baptized of him in Jordan confessing their sins."[1] "And it came to pass in those days that Jesus came from Nazareth

[1]Matt. iii. 5, 6; Mark i. 4; Luke iii. 3.

of Galilee and was baptized of John in Jordan. And straightway coming up out of the water, he saw the heavens opened and the Spirit like a dove descending upon him; and there came a voice from heaven saying, Thou art my beloved Son in whom I am well pleased."[1] Thus briefly does John prepare the way of the Lord and introduce to the world the long expected Messiah, who is here acknowledged by God and anointed by the Holy Spirit.

Passing over His wondrous temptation and the foiling of Satan by the sword of the Spirit, the word of God, and also His sermon on the Mount, which stands alone among all writings for its union of wisdom, mercy and love, reversing the past and laying the foundation for a glorious future, we come to speak of His first intimations that we, the Gentiles, are to share in the blessings of His heavenly kingdom, to have part in His coming reign. This is recorded in the eighth chapter of Matthew and is the story of the healing of the Roman centurion's servant. The centurion said unto him: "Lord, my servant lieth at home sick of the palsy, grievously tormented. And Jesus saith unto him, I will come and heal him. The centurion answered and said, Lord, I am not worthy that thou shouldst come under my roof; but speak the word only and my servant shall be healed. . . . When Jesus heard it he marveled and said unto them that followed, Verily, I say unto you I have not found so great faith, no not in Israel. And I say unto you, That many shall come from the east and west, and

[1]Mark i. 9–11.

shall sit down with Abraham, Isaac, and Jacob in the kingdom of heaven. But the children of the kingdom [the Jews] shall be cast out into outer darkness."[1] Here is indicated the rejection of the Jews and the final extension of His pure religion to the uttermost bounds of the earth.

The first case recorded where Jesus pardoned sin is found in the story of the man afflicted with the palsy. "And behold, they brought to him a man sick with the palsy, lying on a bed: and Jesus seeing their faith, said unto the sick of the palsy, Son, be of good cheer, thy sins be forgiven thee. And behold, certain of the scribes said within themselves, This man blasphemeth. And Jesus, knowing their thoughts, said . . . But that ye may know that the Son of man hath power on earth to forgive sins (then saith he to the sick of the palsy), Arise, take up thy bed, and go into thine house. And he arose and departed to his house."[2] This example will be used in connection with other cases of pardon hereafter.

Passing again over the declaration of His extreme poverty and the demonstration of His superhuman power in calming the sea, casting out demons, healing the sick, giving sight to the blind, causing the dumb to speak, and raising the dead, we call attention to the sending forth of the twelve apostles. He commanded them saying: "Go not into the way of the Gentiles, and into any city of the Samaritans enter ye not: but go rather to the lost sheep of the house of Israel, and

[1]Matt. viii. 6–12.
[2]Matt. ix. 2–7; Mark ii. 5; Luke v. 20.

as ye go preach, saying, The kingdom of heaven is at hand."[1] And here it will be observed that the burden of the apostles' preaching is that "The kingdom of heaven is at hand," *i.e.*, is approaching, and that their mission is still confined to the Jews. Not even is the mixed race of Jews and Gentiles inhabiting Samaria to be visited. We, therefore, search in vain for anything thus far in the synoptic gospels addressed to the Gentiles directly as a people. Following this are Christ's instructions to His apostles as they go on this important mission, foretelling their persecution, commanding them not to fear, and promising reward to those who would receive them. About this time John, being in prison, sent two of his disciples to Jesus, who said unto Him, "Art thou he that cometh or look we for another?"[2] Jesus gave them evidence in what He said and did that He was the Messiah, and crowned it by stating, "The poor have the gospel preached to them." And when they departed Jesus said unto the multitude: "Verily I say unto you, among them that are born of women there hath not risen a greater than John the Baptist; notwithstanding he that is least in the kingdom of heaven is greater than he."[3] He passed from this wonderful statement in regard to the kingdom to pronounce woes on Chorazin, Bethsaida, and Capernaum because they repented not when His mighty works were done in them. These cities have long since been utterly destroyed. Their locations are unknown. Immediately after this, according to Luke, we have the second case

[1]Matt. x. 5–7. [2]Matt. xi. 3–5. [3]Matt. xi. 11.

of pardon, which is that of a sinful woman[1] who anointed Jesus in Simon's house. Jesus said unto her: "Thy sins are forgiven. And they that sat at meat with him began to say, Who is this that forgiveth sins also? And he said to the woman, Thy faith hath saved thee, go in peace." This woman for her good works, penitential tears, and faith, is pardoned by His word. She will live forever in history, and as long as Christianity is preached on the earth her story will give hope to the sinful. This case will also be considered later in connection with others.

After this the Pharisees charged His disciples with doing that which is not lawful upon the Sabbath-day. When He had justified them by the law He stated that "In this place is one greater than the temple."[2] Also, He says that "the Son of man is Lord even of the Sabbath-day." And yet for healing a withered hand on the Sabbath the Pharisees "held a council against him, how they might destroy him." This called forth from Him a prophecy of Isaiah in regard to the Gentiles: "Behold my servant, whom I have chosen, my beloved, in whom my soul is well pleased, I will put my Spirit upon him and he shall show judgment to the Gentiles. . . . And in his name shall the Gentiles trust."[3] This is the first direct statement in regard to the Gentiles trusting in His name. In this same chapter, the Pharisees charged Him with casting out demons by Beelzebub,

[1]Luke vii. 36-50; Matt. xxvi. 6; Mark xiv. 3.
[2]Matt. xii. 6-8 and 14.
[3]Matt. xii. 17-21.

the prince of demons, which furnishes the reason for Jesus teaching them no more plainly, but in parables. These parables all represent various phases of the kingdom of heaven. Christ never speaks "of getting religion," but of His government as a kingdom; of seeking the kingdom, entering the kingdom, hearing the words of the kingdom. The "kingdom of heaven is like unto a city," "to a grain of mustard-seed," etc. Christ established a kingdom, a government, a church and called upon persons to obey Him. "Take my yoke upon you," is His language.

After He had finished His instruction in parables He heard of the beheading of John the Baptist and departed by ship into a desert place. Even here multitudes followed Him and He healed their sick and fed them by His creative power. He who spake as never man spake, did as man never did, now trod the sea with superhuman power and received for the first time worship as the Son of God. In eagerness they sought to touch the hem of His garment that they might be healed. "And as many as touched were made perfectly whole."[1] He here gave the Pharisees a lesson on defilement, and then departed unto the coasts of Tyre and Sidon, which brings us to consider the second case of Gentile healing. "And behold a woman of Canaan came out of the same coasts, and cried unto him, saying, Have mercy on me, O Lord, thou son of David, my daughter is grievously vexed with a demon. But he answered her not a word.

[1]Matt. xiv. 36.

And his disciples came and besought him saying, Send her away, for she crieth after us. But he answered and said, I am not sent but unto the lost sheep of the house of Israel. Then came she and worshiped him, saying, Lord, help me. But he answered and said, It is not meet to take the children's bread, and to cast it to dogs. And she said, Truth, Lord: yet the dogs eat of the crumbs which fall from their master's table. Then Jesus answered and said unto her, O woman, great is thy faith: be it unto thee even as thou wilt. And her daughter was made whole from that very hour."[1]

The reluctance shown here in healing this Gentile seems at first to be in strong contrast with the principles of the universal philanthrophy and love which Jesus taught. But in accordance with God's plan—and His ways are not our ways—the gospel was to be preached first to the Jews, and not until after the resurrection of Christ was His heavenly kingdom to be proclaimed to the Gentile world, to the nations sitting in the regions and shadow of death.

From the coasts of Tyre and Sidon Jesus departed "and came nigh unto the sea of Galilee." Multitudes brought here their afflicted and He healed them, and when they saw the lame walk, the blind see, and heard the dumb speak, they glorified the God of Israel.[2] He also had compassion on the multitude who had been with Him three days, and miraculously fed them. After sending them away He took ship and came to the coasts of Magdala, where the Phari-

[1]Matt. xv. 22–28. [2]Matt. xv. 29–31.

sees and Sadducees tempted Him, desiring to be shown "a sign from heaven." He calls them hypocrites and tells them they "can discern the face of the sky," but could not "the signs of the times,"[1] and charges His disciples to beware of the leaven, that is, "the doctrine of the Pharisees and Sadducees."[2]

[1]Matt. xvi. 3. [2]Matt. xvi. 6-12.

CHAPTER III

PREPARATORY TEACHING

The Confession of Peter and the Church of Christ. The Significance of the Transfiguration. Sending out of the Seventy. The Prodigal Son. Forgiveness in the Church. Jesus and the Little Children. First Inquiry after Eternal Life.

THIS brings us to the consideration of two important questions, Peter's confession of Christ and the Church of Christ, which will be discussed more at length in succeeding chapters. "When Jesus came into the coasts of Cæsarea Philippi he asked his disciples saying, Whom do men say that I, the Son of man, am? And they said, Some say that thou art John the Baptist, some Elias, and others Jeremiah or one of the prophets. He saith unto them, But whom say ye that I am? Simon Peter answered and said, Thou art the Christ, the Son of the living God. And Jesus answered and said unto him, Blessed art thou, Simon Barjona, for flesh and blood hath not revealed it unto thee but my Father who is in heaven. And I say unto thee, That thou art Peter, and upon this rock I will build my church, and the gates of Hades shall not prevail against it. And I will give unto thee the keys of the kingdom of heaven; and whatsoever thou shalt bind on earth shall be bound in heaven: and whatsoever thou shalt loose on earth shall be loosed in heaven."[1] Here for the first time is the word "church" used, and it occurs only twice more before the death of Jesus. While the word church occurs only three times in the gospels, the word "kingdom," as applied to the government of Christ, which He was about to establish, is used some eighty times. It is spoken of as the "kingdom of God," "kingdom of heaven," "his kingdom," "my kingdom," "Gospel of the kingdom," and "my Father's kingdom." In the Acts of the Apostles and in the Epistles the word "church" is more frequently used than the word "kingdom."

When Peter here confessed the messiahship, Jesus says, "Upon this rock"—this truth confessed, "I will build my church." Not have built, but will build. And we have seen before that the kingdom was at hand—approaching. So the Church is spoken of here as still in the future, not yet an established fact. After He had taught His disciples thus plainly in regard to the foundation of His church He charged them "That they should tell no man that he was Jesus the Christ." He then began to show them how He must go to Jerusalem, suffer many things, be killed and raised up again the third day. He then took Peter, James, and John up into a high mountain and was transfigured before them. "And his face did shine as the sun, and his raiment was white as the light," while they beheld the king in His glory. Moses, the great lawgiver, and Elias, the great prophet, came from the unseen world to lay down their

[1]Matt. xvi. 18–19.

commissions at His feet, and God recalled them with the solemn injunction, "This is my beloved Son, hear ye him." Moses said: "A prophet shall the Lord your God raise up unto you of your brethren, like unto me; him shall ye hear in all things."[1] This prophet is here. He came to fulfil the law and demonstrated His right to reign as Prophet, Priest, and King, and will reign until "the kingdom and dominion, and the greatness of the kingdom under the whole heaven, shall be given to the saints of the Most High."[2]

The next day, after Jesus had come down from the mount of transfiguration, His disciples having failed to cast out a demon, Jesus rebuked their want of faith and healed the demoniac, and when He had come to Capernaum He paid tribute. "At the same time came the disciples unto Jesus saying, Who is the greatest in the kingdom of heaven?" He placed a little child in their midst as the model of His greatest subject, and was the first on earth who taught humility as the true road to greatness. According to Luke: "After these things the Lord appointed other seventy also, and sent them two and two before his face into every city and place, whither he himself would come."[3] Having instructed them how to treat those who would not receive them He then said: "And into whatsoever city ye enter, and they receive you, eat such things as are set before you: and heal the sick that are therein, and say unto them, The kingdom of God is come nigh unto you."[4] As John the Baptist had preached that

[1]Acts iii. 22. [2]Dan. vii. 27. [3]Luke x. 1. [4]Luke x. 8–9.

the kingdom of heaven was at hand, and as the twelve apostles had preached the same truth, so the seventy now proclaimed its near approach—"The kingdom of God is come nigh unto you." When the seventy had fulfilled their mission, had proclaimed the approach of the long-expected kingdom to the Jews, they returned "again with joy, saying, Lord, even the demons are subject unto us through thy name. And he said unto them, I beheld Satan as lightning fall from heaven,"[1] indicating the breaking of the power of him who had so long held unbounded sway over the vast dominions of death. But He told them to "rejoice not that the spirits are subject unto you, but rather rejoice because your names are written in heaven."

Shortly after this the Pharisees and Scribes murmured, saying, "This man receiveth sinners and eateth with them,"[2] which calls forth the ever memorable parable of the lost sheep, and shows that the great Shepherd follows with yearnings of tenderness those who stray from the fold, and that there is more joy in heaven over one sinner that repenteth than over ninety and nine just persons who need no repentance. This principle of the Father's love is still further unfolded by the touching story of the prodigal son. A son who had gone far from his parental home, wasted all the substance bestowed upon him by a kind father in riotous living and in the most debasing habits, and finally in poverty and distress hired himself to feed swine, yet when he came to himself, as he was about

[1]Luke x. 17–18. [2]Luke xv. 2.

to perish with hunger, he said, "I will arise and go to my father and will say unto him, Father, I have sinned against heaven and before thee and am no more worthy to be called thy son, make me as one of thy hired servants. And he arose and came to his father, but when he was yet a great way off his father saw him, and had compassion, and ran and fell on his neck and kissed him," and received him to his home with joy and gladness, saying, "This my son was dead and is alive again; he was lost and is found."[1] Thus it is shown how willing the Father is to forgive the returning penitent. This story will be told wherever the gospel is preached until the latest ages of time to show His deep, tender, and abiding forgiveness and love.

Not only did Jesus here teach how willing God is to forgive, but following this He taught His disciples how to forgive each other in His kingdom or church. "If thy brother shall trespass against thee, go and tell him his fault between thee and him alone: if he shall hear thee, thou hast gained thy brother. But if he will not hear thee, then take with thee one or two more, that in the mouth of two or three witnesses every word may be established. And if he shall neglect to hear them, tell it unto the church: but if he neglect to hear the church, let him be unto thee as a heathen man and a publican."[2] This is the second and last use of the word "church" by Jesus during His personal ministry, and shows the principle of forgiveness that was to predominate in it in succeeding

[1]Luke xv. 18–20, 24. [2]Matt. xviii. 15–17.

ages. "Father, forgive us our debts as we forgive our debtors," is the prayer He taught His disciples.[1] "Then came Peter to him, and said, Lord, how oft shall my brother sin against me, and I forgive him, till seven times? Jesus saith unto him, I say not unto thee, Until seven times but, Until seventy times seven."[2] Even this would not be as frequent as God forgives many who trespass against Him.

"When Jesus had finished these sayings He departed from Galilee, and came unto the coast of Judea beyond Jordan." Here, after giving the brethren a lesson on divorcement, "Then were there brought unto him little children, that he should put his hands on them, and pray: and the disciples rebuked them. But Jesus said, Suffer little children, and forbid them not, to come unto me; for of such is the kingdom of heaven. And he laid his hands on them and departed."[3] Jesus was the first on earth who gave such eminence to the innocence and purity of children. Earth's great teachers selected their models from the great, the strong, the wise, the mighty; He from the innocent and pure. He is preeminently the children's friend. He took them in His arms and blessed them and said: "Of such is the kingdom of heaven."

This brings us to consider the first sincere inquiry in regard to eternal life. One came and said unto Him: "Good master, what shall I do to inherit eternal life?"[4] Prior to this, it is recorded that, "a certain lawyer stood up and tempted him, saying, Mas-

[1]Matt. vi. 12. [2]Matt. xviii. 21, 22.
[3]Matt. xix. 13–15. [4]Luke xviii. 8–25.

ter, what shall I do to inherit eternal life?"[1] The answer was: "Thou shalt love the Lord thy God with all thy heart . . . and thy neighbor as thyself, . . . this do and thou shalt live."[2] Here is embraced the whole duty of man in every age, for it is recorded, "This is the love of God that we keep his commandments," and His commandments embrace the whole range of human obligation. This sincere person, who inquires in regard to the same great subject, is a most interesting character. We are told by Matthew that he was a young man; by Luke, that he was a ruler; by Mark, that Jesus loved him; and by all that he was very rich. When Jesus had commanded him to observe the principles of the decalogue which He mentioned, adding, "Thou shalt love thy neighbor as thyself," he said, "All these things have I kept from my youth up: what lack I yet?" "Jesus said unto him, If thou wilt be perfect, go and sell that thou hast, and give to the poor, and thou shalt have treasure in heaven: and come and follow me. But when the young man heard that saying, he went away sorrowful: for he had great possessions,"[3] preferring his present wealth to the heavenly treasure offered. Jesus used this example to show how difficult it is for a rich man to enter the kingdom of heaven, and succeeding ages have demonstrated its truth.

[1]Luke x. 25. [2]Luke x. 27, 28. [3]Matt. xix. 21, 22.

CHAPTER IV

CHRIST AS A TEACHER

Greatness and Humility. Christ Teaching in the Temple. Authority of the Scribes and Their Denunciation. Lament over Jerusalem. Answer to Three Questions.

AFTER this use of the expression "eternal life" for the second time, and its sorrowful rejection by the young man, Jesus said unto His disciples: "Every one that hath forsaken houses, or brethren or sisters, or father or mother, or wife or children, or lands for my name's sake, shall receive an hundredfold, and shall inherit everlasting life." In both these cases it will be observed that the stated or implied conditions are following Christ, doing His will, "I am the way, the truth and the life."

Again, He illustrates the kingdom of heaven by the laborers in a vineyard. Those who came at the eleventh hour received the same wages as those who came at an earlier hour, but it will be remembered that each came when bidden. After this: "Jesus going up to Jerusalem took the twelve disciples apart in the way, and said unto them, Behold, we go up to Jerusalem; and the Son of man shall be betrayed unto the chief priests and unto the scribes, and they shall condemn him to death, and shall deliver him to the Gentiles to mock, and to scourge, and to crucify him: and the third day he shall rise again."[1] "Then came to him the mother of Zebedee's children with her sons, worshiping him, and desiring a certain thing of him. . . . She saith unto him, Grant that these my two sons may sit, the one on thy right hand, and the other on thy left, in thy kingdom."[2] Jesus here gave them a lesson in regard to the great suffering which He and they were to endure; informed them that the request they made was not His to grant, but would be given to those for whom it was prepared by His Father. "And when the ten heard it, they were moved with indignation against the two brethren. But Jesus called them unto him, and said, Ye know that the princes of the Gentiles exercise dominion over them, and they that are great exercise authority upon them. But it shall not be so among you: but whosoever will be great among you, let him be your minister; and whosoever will be chief among you, let him be your servant. Even as the Son of man came not to be ministered unto, but to minister, and to give his life a ransom for many."[3] If this teaching had been observed in past ages persecution and suffering would not so darken the pages of history.

After this instruction Jesus left Jericho, healed two blind men on the way, and made His triumphal entry into Jerusalem. While a very great multitude spread their garments and strewed branches of trees in the way, and the multitude that went before and that followed after cried, saying, "Hosanna to the Son of

[1]Matt. xx. 17–19. [2]Matt. xx. 20, 21. [3]Matt. xx. 24–28.

David: Blessed is he that cometh in the name of the Lord; Hosanna in the highest."[1] "And Jesus went into the temple of God, and cast out all them that sold and bought in the temple, and overthrew the tables of the money-changers, and the seats of them that sold doves, and said unto them, It is written, My house shall be called the house of prayer; but ye have made it a den of thieves."[2]

After Jesus had prayed in the Temple, healed the blind and lame therein and received Hosannas to the Son of David from the children, He went out to Bethany. When He returned to the Temple the next day: "The chief priests and elders of the people came unto him as he was teaching, and said, By what authority doest thou these things? and who gave thee this authority?"[3] He answered them by asking whether the Baptism of John was from heaven or of men? To answer this question implied either their self-condemnation or the condemnation of the people. Therefore they said: "We can not tell. And he said unto them, Neither tell I you by what authority I do these things."[4] But He gave them a parable of a man who had two sons, illustrating how the publicans and harlots would precede them in entering the kingdom. And He goes still further and teaches them by the parable of the householder, who had planted a vineyard and had let it out to unfaithful husbandmen, who had repeatedly abused and slain his servants and finally his son, that they would be

[1]Matt. xxi. 9. [2]Matt. xxi. 12, 13.
[3]Matt. xxi. 23. [4]Matt. xxi. 27.

destroyed and the kingdom given to a more worthy people. "The kingdom of God shall be taken from you, and given to a nation bringing forth the fruits thereof."[1] This parable and the succeeding one in regard to "a certain king who made a marriage for his son,"[2] show conclusively the rejection of the Jews and the reception of the Gentiles. Not only did they refuse the invitation of the king, but they slew the servants sent to invite them. "But when the king heard thereof, he was wroth: and he sent forth his armies, and destroyed those murderers, and burned up their city. Then saith he to his servants, The wedding is ready, but they which were bidden were not worthy. Go ye therefore into the highways, and as many as ye shall find, bid to the marriage."[3] When Jesus had finished these parables the Pharisees and Sadducees each in succession tried to "entangle him" first in regard to paying tribute, second in regard to the resurrection, third in regard to the great commandment, in all of which they were foiled. In concluding He asked the Pharisees: "What think ye of Christ? whose son is he? They say unto him, The son of David. He saith unto them, How then doth David in spirit call him Lord, . . . If David then call him Lord, how is he his son? And no man was able to answer him a word, neither durst any man from that day forth ask him any more questions."[4]

The next discourse of Jesus is marvelous, in that it enjoins obedience to the Scribes and Pharisees and

[1]Matt. xxi. 43. [2]Matt. xxii. 2.
[3]Matt. xxii. 7. [4]Matt. xxii. 42–46.

yet denounces them as hypocrites, as proud, as blind guides, as fools, as whited sepulchers, full of dead men's bones, and of all uncleanness. "Fill up then the measure of your fathers. Ye serpents, ye generation of vipers, how can ye escape the damnation of hell?" Notwithstanding their character is thus described here and elsewhere, we are told that "Jesus spake to the multitude, and to his disciples, saying, The scribes and the Pharisees sit in Moses' seat: all therefore whatsoever they bid you observe, that observe and do; but do not ye after their works: for they say, and do not."[1] This very clearly teaches that the law of Moses was still binding. "They sit in Moses' seat." The binding authority of the law of Moses during Christ's personal ministry on the earth is recognized by Him and its sacrificial system enforced. In His sermon on the mount He says: "Therefore if thou bring thy gift to the altar, and there rememberest that thy brother hath aught against thee; . . . first be reconciled to thy brother, and then come and offer thy gift."[2] He also commanded a leper whom he cleansed: "Go thy way, show thyself to the priest, and offer the gift that Moses commanded, for a testimony unto them."[3] On His entry into the Temple He recognized its sacredness and at once began to reform its abuses. The sacrificial system did not cease until the great sacrifice was offered. Not until Jesus put away sin by the sacrifice of Himself and dying, exclaimed, "It is finished," "and the vail of the temple was rent in twain." Henceforth and forever there is no more holy or most holy

[1]Matt. xxiii. 1–3. [2]Matt. v. 23, 24. [3]Matt. viii. 4.

place on earth for His people "are a temple of the living God."[1] Ascending Jesus entered the Holy of Holies, into heaven, once for all, and all His followers are now kings and priests unto God and offer sacrifice of prayer and praise and reign with Him forever.

When Jesus was about leaving the Temple for the last time He exclaimed: "O Jerusalem, Jerusalem, thou that killest the prophets, and stonest them which are sent unto thee, how often would I have gathered thy children together, even as a hen gathereth her chickens under her wings, and ye would not. Behold, your house is left unto you desolate."[2] But still He had not yet taken "away the first that he may establish the second."[3] When He went out from the Temple and viewed the Temple buildings He said to His disciples: "There shall not be left here one stone upon another that shall not be thrown down."[4] His disciples then asked Him: "When shall these things be? and what shall be the sign of thy coming, and of the end of the world?"[5] The twenty-fourth chapter of Matthew is given to the answer of these three important questions in which He describes the great events, both physical and moral, which should take place in the world, until the winding up of Time's great drama. He begins by saying: "Many shall come in my name, saying, I am Christ; and shall deceive many. And ye shall hear of wars and rumors of wars: nation shall rise against nation, and kingdom against kingdom: there shall be famines, and pestilences, and earth-

[1]2 Cor. vi. 16; 1 Pet. ii. 5. [2]Matt. xxiii. 37, 38.
[3]Heb. x. 9. [4]Matt. xxiv. 2. [5]Matt. xxiv. 3.

quakes, in divers places. They shall deliver you up to be afflicted and shall kill you. Many false prophets shall rise, and shall deceive many, and this gospel of the kingdom shall be preached in all the world for a witness unto all nations. The sun shall be darkened and the moon shall not give her light, and the stars shall fall from heaven, and the powers of the heaven shall be shaken. And they shall see the Son of man coming in the clouds of heaven with power and great glory. And he shall send his angels with a great sound of a trumpet, and they shall gather his elect from the four winds from one end of heaven to the other. Be ye also ready, for in such an hour as ye think not the Son of man cometh." He continues further to illustrate His kingdom and coming by the parable of the wise and foolish virgins, and also of the talents, concluding His discourse by a description of the final judgment, in which He shows that we can minister to Him by ministering to His suffering children.

This brings us to the conspiracy against Christ. Having in the preceding pages called attention to all cases of pardon, except the thief on the cross, and all reference to the Gentiles found in the synoptical gospels of Matthew, Mark, and Luke, and about in their chronological order, as well as some other important matters connected with the life of Christ and recorded by the same authors, we will now, before speaking of the fulfilment of Christ's great mission by His death and resurrection, call attention to the teaching of John's gospel on the same subject.

CHAPTER V

CHRIST AS THE WORD OF GOD

The Gospel of John. The Preexistence of Christ as the Word of God. Nicodemus and the New Birth. Importance of Faith. Jesus Teaching the Samaritans. Jesus Reveals the Father. The Gentiles.

JOHN begins his gospel by stating the preexistence of Christ as the Word of God, attributing creative power to Him. "All things were made by him; and without him was not any thing made that was made. In him was life; and the life was the light of men." Thus the same divine being who created the world came also to redeem it; the same power manifest in creation came also to the rescue of the human race, bringing an everlasting redemption for the children of men. The author of life became the light and life of men. "He came unto his own, and his own received him not. But as many as received him, to them gave he power to become the sons of God, even to them that believe on his name: which were born, not of blood, nor of the will of the flesh, nor of the will of man, but of God."[1]

The first person to whom Jesus imparted instruction in regard to entering the kingdom of God, as

[1]John i. 11–13.

recorded by John, was Nicodemus, a ruler of the Jews. After he had recognized Jesus' divine mission, Jesus answered and said unto him: "Verily, verily, I say unto thee, Except a man be born again, he can not see the kingdom of God. Nicodemus saith unto him, How can a man be born when he is old? Can he enter a second time into his mother's womb, and be born? Jesus answered, Verily, verily, I say unto thee, Except a man be born of water and of the Spirit, he can not enter into the kingdom of God."[1] It must be remembered that the facts upon which His kingdom was to be established, and the Gospel based, had not yet taken place.[2] This passage shows clearly that there is a marked distinction between Judaism and Christianity, that a Jew and a ruler of the Jews, a member even of the Sanhedrin, had to be born again to enter Christ's kingdom. But what is meant by being born again? "Born of water and the spirit." This will be ascertained most clearly by examining the terms of induction into Christ's kingdom when it becomes established. The history of how persons were delivered "from the power of darkness and translated into the kingdom of God's dear Son," as given in many examples after its establishment, shows beyond a doubt the meaning or purport of being born again. And when all these cases have been passed in review there need be no doubt in regard to the new birth, or how it is accomplished. In concluding His conversation with Nicodemus He said: "And as Moses lifted up the serpent in the

[1]John iii. 3–5. [2]Matt. xvi. 18; 1 Cor. xv. 1–4.

wilderness, even so must the Son of man be lifted up: that whosoever believeth in him should not perish, but have eternal life. For God so loved the world, that he gave his only begotten Son, that whosoever believeth in him should not perish, but have everlasting life."[1] Here is set forth the death of Jesus for sin and God's great love for the world, which was to ultimate in salvation through faith in Jesus. John dwells much on faith in Jesus as the principle through which salvation may be attained. In fact, so much so, that some have been led to believe it the only condition of pardon—that persons are saved by faith alone. Faith is the great fundamental principle underlying the whole remedial system. We see a recognition of its great importance in the opening chapters of the Bible. There are only eleven chapters giving a history of creation in all its departments: the origin of man, the history of his fall, the destruction of the world, its repeopling by various nations, occupying a period of two thousand years, pausing at the birth of Abraham, the father of the faithful, while we have some thirteen chapters giving an account of his eventful life. Why should such a vast period of time, laden with matters of such deep interest to the human race, be passed with such brief notice, and a single life occupy so much space? Why should Adam, Noah, the preceding nations of the earth and the creation, with its vastness, occupy less space in God's revelation than the life of Abraham, which closed one hundred and seventy-five years from his birth? The answer is

[1] John iii. 14–16.

obvious, for in the life of this one man we have a type of faith, an example for all succeeding ages. By faith we understand that the world was formed by the word of God; through it is revealed all the coming glories of the future.

The chief object in the divine revelation was to save man from sin, from death and the grave, and not to teach him history. Hence, God developed early the principle of faith upon which His moral government should rest. It is the fundamental principle in the government of Christ. So much stress is placed upon it, that sometimes it is put for the whole remedial system—as where the apostle exhorts Christians to contend earnestly for the faith once delivered to the saints. Yet, strictly speaking, it does not embrace repentance or the godly life, but it leads to the one and sustains the other. "Without faith it is impossible to please him, for he that cometh to God must believe."

After Jesus taught Nicodemus in regard to the new birth, the wondrous love of God, the life-giving power of faith, He and His disciples came 'into the land of Judea; and there he tarried with them, and baptized. And John also was baptizing in Enon, near to Salim, because there was much water there: and they came, and were baptized. For John was not yet cast into prison. Then there arose a question between some of John's disciples and the Jews about purifying. And they came unto John and said unto him, Rabbi, he that was with thee beyond Jordan, to whom thou bearest witness, behold, the same baptizeth, and all men come to him."[1] Again, we are told, "That Jesus made and baptized more disciples than John, though Jesus himself baptized not, but his disciples." John alone mentions the fact that Jesus baptized, and the passages quoted give all the information we have in regard to the place where, and the considerable number that He baptized.

Leaving Judea, Christ, in passing through Samaria, stops at Jacob's well, and holds that ever-memorable conversation with the woman of Samaria. Notwithstanding the apostles, when sent on their mission to preach the approach of the kingdom, were commanded not to enter any city of the Samaritans, yet Jesus Himself stops to teach a poor woman in regard to the spiritual nature of the worship which He was establishing, which would not require a sacred mountain or a holy temple, but would be acceptable to God if offered "in spirit and in truth." Here is one of the first intimations given of the universal character of the Christian religion, a religion in which the Samaritans and the Gentiles might rejoice. And now, although the altar-fires have been extinguished on Mount Gerizim and Mount Zion for nineteen hundred years, and God has no one sacred place on earth, yet, from the continents of the earth and the islands of the sea, the prayers from millions of Christians—kings and priests to God go up unto Him like incense from His ancient altar. After this conversation we are informed that many of the Samaritans believed on Him. "For the saying of the woman,"[2] and

[1]John iii. 22–26. [2]John iv. 39.

"many more believed because of his own word; . . . saying, For we have heard him ourselves, and know that this is indeed the Christ, the Savior of the world."[1] After this He heals a nobleman's son at Capernaum. He attends a feast of the Jews at Jerusalem, and cures at the pool of Bethesda a man who had had an infirmity thirty-eight years. The Jews sought to kill Him, because He did this on the Sabbath day, but "Jesus answered them, My Father worketh hitherto, and I work. Therefore the Jews sought the more to kill him, because he not only had broken the sabbath, but said also that God was his Father, making himself equal with God."[2] Upon this Jesus claims to do all the works which His Father did. "For what things soever he doeth, these also doeth the Son likewise."[3] If the "Father raiseth up the dead, and quickeneth them, even so the Son quickeneth whom he will."[4] "All men should honor the Son, even as they honor the Father. He that honoreth not the Son honoreth not the Father that sent him."[5] And "he that heareth my word, and believeth on him that sent me, hath everlasting life."[6] "Verily, verily, I say unto you, The hour is coming, and now is, when the dead shall hear the voice of the Son of God: and they that hear shall live. For as the Father hath life in himself; so hath he given to the Son to have life in himself; And hath given him authority to execute judgment also, because he is the Son of man. Marvel not at this: for the hour is coming, in the which all that are in the

[1]John iv. 41, 42. [2]John v. 17, 18. [3]John v. 19.
[4]John v. 21. [5]John v. 23. [6]John v. 24.

graves shall hear his voice, and shall come forth; they that have done good, unto the resurrection of life; and they that have done evil, unto the resurrection of damnation."[1] Before concluding this discourse He said, "Ye will not come to me, that ye might have life."[2] The claims of Jesus as set forth here and in subsequent discourses, and, in fact, throughout the gospels, are such as were never made by any being on earth. He is represented as existing in the beginning. "Before Abraham was I am," as He is before all things and "by him all things consist." The fiat of creation, "the word of God," as the revealer of the fatherhood of God; "Neither knoweth any man the Father save the Son and he to whom soever the Son will reveal him." As, "the Son of God," "the bread of life," and "the light of the world," as "bringing life and immortality to light by the gospel," "prophet, priest and king," "the resurrection and the life," "the way, the truth and the life." Truly, never man spake as He spake, lived as He lived, or died as He died. After His conversation with Nicodemus there are no special terms of pardon given in John's gospel to any individual, but Jesus presents himself as the great object of faith, as "the Bread of Life," "the Door," "the Shepherd," "the Vine"; in fact, the Son of God and Savior, saying, "If I be lifted up from the earth I will draw all men unto me." Before leaving His disciples He said, "A new commandment I give unto you, That ye love one another as I have loved you."

[1]John v. 25–29. [2]John v. 40.

His discourse and prayer for His disciples before leaving them were new to earth and for the union of beauty, tenderness, and love have no parallel in human language.

In concluding our remarks on John's gospel we would observe that the Gentiles are not directly addressed in it. In fact, the word is not used by Jesus in John's record. It occurs only twice and is used by the Jews, as follows, when Jesus said: "Yet a little while am I with you, and then I go unto him that sent me. Ye shall seek me, and shall not find me: and where I am, thither ye can not come. Then said the Jews among themselves, Whither shall he go, that we shall not find him? Will he go unto the dispersed among the Gentiles, and teach the Gentiles?"[1]

The word Gentiles is used twenty-one times in the Old Testament. It occurs but sixteen times in the four gospels and seventy-one times in the other books of the New Testament. The chief reason for the infrequency of its use in the Old Testament no doubt may be found in the fact that the Jews were not a missionary people. Their religion was national, or ethnic. It was not given to the entire human race; Christ's personal ministry, and that of His apostles during His life, being confined to the Jews is the reason, no doubt, for the few references to the Gentiles during this period. Out of the sixteen times in which it is used in the gospels there are only two instances in which it is used to show that the Gentiles may have part or lot in the blessings of the gospel.

[1]John vii. 33–35.

This is the passage already quoted from Matthew which had been spoken by Isaiah when he said, "I will put my Spirit upon him, and he shall show judgment to the Gentiles . . . and in his name shall the Gentiles trust."[1] The frequent occurrence of the word in the other books of the New Testament may be accounted for from the fact that they narrate what occurred after the gospel was commanded to be preached to the Gentiles. Those who are not Jews might do well, therefore, to pay direct attention to the first enunciation of the gospel to them if they would know its requirements and enjoy its blessings.

[1]Matt. xii. 18–21.

CHAPTER VI

THE PASSION OF CHRIST

The Thief on the Cross. The Lord's Supper a Monument. The Betrayal and Crucifixion. The Resurrection and Commission. Terms of Pardon.

WE come now to the promise of Christ to the thief on the cross, mentioned only by Luke, as follows: "And one of the malefactors which were hanged railed on him, saying, If thou be Christ, save thyself and us. But the other answering rebuked him, saying, Dost not thou fear God, seeing thou art in the same condemnation? And we indeed justly; for we receive the due reward of our deeds; but this man hath done nothing amiss. And he said unto Jesus, Lord, remember me when thou comest into thy kingdom. And Jesus said unto him, Verily I say unto thee, To-day shalt thou be with me in paradise."[1] If it be granted here that the statement of Jesus "To-day shalt thou be with me in paradise," implied that the malefactor was pardoned, which we presume will not be denied, it is the last recorded case of pardon by Jesus during His life-mission on earth. It will be observed that the only evidence, so far as the record goes, that the thief had of being pardoned, or of being in paradise immediately after death, was the word of Jesus. Nor has the world had any additional

[1]Luke xxiii. 39–43.

evidence since. This case then forms no exception to the cases heretofore considered, for they were all pardoned by the word of Jesus.[1]

The last act in the great drama of human redemption is about closing, and Jesus instituted the Supper to be observed in memory of His death. While the Lord's Day is a perpetual monument, showing His resurrection, the Lord's Supper perpetuates the memory of His death. It has been observed from the night of His betrayal all down the ages; it testifies all over the world. As a monument it marks alike the place of His death and keeps in everlasting memory the fact. "As often as you eat this bread and drink this cup ye do show the Lord's death till He come."[2]

Having instituted this ordinance He was betrayed by Judas; arrested by a mob; condemned by the high priest on a confession of His own divinity; sentenced to death on the cross by Pilate; buried in the tomb of Joseph, and arose the third day, bringing life and immortality to light. The closing scenes in the life of Jesus will be new while time shall last. His last hours of sadness and grief will ever stir the deepest emotions of the human heart, and His death will call forth tears without end. The great heroes of earth conquered by their life; He by His death. They built empires by the shedding of the blood of others, but He, by His own blood shed for others, is conquering the world.

After Jesus rose from the dead He was manifested

[1]This case has been noted out of the order of the narrative to complete the cases of pardon during Christ's personal ministry.

[2]1 Cor. xi. 26.

to the apostles "By many infallible proofs, being seen of them forty days, and speaking of the things pertaining to the kingdom of God."[1] They asked Him saying "Lord, wilt thou at this time restore again the kingdom to Israel? And he said unto them, It is not for you to know the times or the seasons, which the Father hath put in His own power. But ye shall receive power, after that the Holy Spirit is come upon you; and ye shall be witnesses unto me both in Jerusalem and in all Judea, and in Samaria, and unto the uttermost part of the earth."[2] Before Jesus ascended He gave the great commission to the apostles to go into all the world and preach the gospel to every creature. This is variously recorded in the four gospels. Matthew records it thus: "And Jesus came and spake unto them, saying: All power is given unto me in heaven and in earth. Go ye therefore, and teach all nations, baptizing them in the name of the Father, and of the Son, and of the Holy Spirit: Teaching them to observe all things whatsoever I have commanded you: and, lo, I am with you alway, even unto the end of the world."[3] Mark's record is as follows: "And he said unto them, Go ye into all the world and preach the gospel to every creature. He that believeth and is baptized shall be saved; but he that believeth not shall be damned."[4] Luke, in giving the same commission, says: "Then opened he their understanding, that they might understand the Scriptures, and said unto them, Thus it is written, and thus it

[1]Acts i. 3. [2]Acts i. 6–8.
[3]Matt. xxviii. 18–20. [4]Mark xvi. 15, 16.

behooved Christ to suffer, and to rise from the dead the third day: And that repentance and remission of sins should be preached in his name among all nations, beginning at Jerusalem. And ye are witnesses of these things."[1] John, in his record, says: "Then said Jesus to them again, Peace be unto you: as my Father hath sent me, even so I send you. And when he had said this, he breathed on them, and saith unto them, Receive ye the Holy Spirit: Whosesoever sins ye remit, they are remitted unto them; and whosesoever sins ye retain, they are retained."[2]

In this commission, as given by these various writers, we have all that is required of an unpardoned person in order to pardon and acceptance with God. The order of these requirements is fully established, as is abundantly proven in the history of many cases of pardon, subsequently given. This order is as follows:

Matthew says: "Go teach all nations." Teaching therefore is the first essential. No requirement could be made of persons without teaching them. Paul confirms this when he says: "Faith comes by hearing." "How shall they believe in him of whom they have not heard?" After being taught or having learned the truth in regard to Jesus, faith is next required. Hence we read in Mark: "He that believeth and is baptized." After hearing, faith is the very first essential. When evidence is presented the first act of the mind is to believe, to doubt or reject it. If to believe, the only rational way is to act in harmony

[1]Luke xxiv. 45–48. [2]John xx. 21–23.

with the belief. "He that cometh to God must believe." Following this we have "coming to God," "turning to God," or repentance. Luke says that "Repentance and remission of sins should be preached in his name." It will be seen at once that it would be impossible to repent before having knowledge of sin or belief in a sinful state. Hence, faith always precedes and never succeeds repentance. Repentance implies having heard—having believed; it implies a reformation of life; it implies a ceasing to do evil and learning to do well. It implies sorrow for the past and turning to God with a full purpose of heart to love and serve Him. When persons have heard, when they have believed, when they have repented, then and not until then are they commanded to be baptized. Mark says, "He that believeth and is baptized shall be saved." Here faith and baptism are connected in order to salvation or pardon, the one being required as definite and specific as the other. God has been pleased to give prominence to positive law in all the institutions He has given to man. In the Patriarchal Jewish and Christian institutions it occupies an important place. Some are disposed to undervalue baptism, while they are perfectly willing to give prominence to other positive ordinances. But it should be remembered that baptism not only stands at the door into the church but is the only institution representing the burial of Christ. The Lord's Supper commemorates the death of Jesus, the Lord's Day His resurrection, and baptism both His burial and resurrection. Paul says: "Therefore we are buried with him by baptism into death, that like as Christ was raised up from the dead by the glory of the Father, even so we also should walk in newness of life."[1]

Whatever our education may have been in regard to the subject of baptism we must remember that baptism occupies a prominent place in the New Testament. The burden of John's preaching was that of "baptism of repentance for the remission of sins." Jesus, our great exemplar, was baptized. It was preached and practised during the life of Jesus, and after His death it is either stated or implied in every case of pardon. To the baptized, remission of sins was promised. Luke says: "Repentance and remission of sins should be preached in his name among all nations." And John says: "Whosesoever sins ye remit, they are remitted unto them; and whosesoever sins ye retain, they are retained." Remission of sins in Luke and John's record is undoubtedly the same as the salvation which is promised in Mark's gospel. "He that believeth and is baptized shall be saved." Saved from past sins—pardoned. "Their sins and their iniquities will I remember no more."[2] The various requirements of the great commission are, then, first, the preaching of the gospel; second, faith in the Lord Jesus Christ; third, repentance toward God; fourth, baptism "into the name of the Father, the Son, and the Holy Spirit"; fifth, remission of sins. The subsequent promise by the apostles, who acted as embassadors under this commission, is the gift of the Holy Spirit, and by continuing faithful unto death,

[1]Rom. vi. 4. [2]Heb. viii. 12.

eternal life. Those who thus heard, believed, and obeyed, were addressed by the apostles as saved, pardoned, justified, sanctified, adopted, redeemed, as saints, brethren, disciples of Christ, and Christians. And no others were so addressed.

CHAPTER VII

THE THREE REVELATIONS

Three Revealed Religions. Patriarchal not Abolished or Superseded by the Jewish. Christian Religion New and Universal.

THERE are three revealed religions recorded in the sacred Scriptures: the Patriarchal, the Jewish, and the Christian. The first and the last were general or universal; the Jewish was local or national. The first, given to the human family in its infancy, embraced the race and was designed to be obligatory until repealed or superseded by another. This religion belonged to the race—it spread over all the world, and in a pure or corrupted form has been observed by all nations. Even to-day, where Christianity is unknown, we find nations and peoples offering sacrifices and propitiating deity. Corrupted, debased, and idolatrous as this religion has become, we still find the great marks of its divine origin. When we look over the history of the world and find that sacrifice has been offered in nearly every nation under heaven, we feel assured that the altar and victim were not an invention of man, but had a divine origin. Various nations and countless peoples would not have invented a similar mode of worship, but must have drawn from a common source, which, no doubt, was the Patriarchal religion given in the first ages of recorded time and to all people.

We next observe that this religion was not abolished or superseded when the Jewish religion was given, at least only so far as the Jewish people were concerned, and much of it was incorporated in the Jewish system. Any law given by any authority is obligatory until it is repealed, and if it be repealed it must be repealed by the same authority which gave it, and to the same extent to which it was given. The Patriarchal religion was given by divine authority; it was given to the whole world, and never by divine authority repealed or superseded until Jesus said, "Go ye into all the world and preach the gospel to every creature." The fact of God having given a divine system of religion to one nation would not and could not repeal the religion of all nations. We have no divine warrant for assuming that this religion was abolished, but, on the contrary, there is much to show that it was still binding on other people, while the Jewish religion was in force. For God had regard for nations and peoples, for prophets, priests, and kings who were not His chosen people, Israel. Jethro, a priest of Midian, gave Moses instructions in regard to the government of the Jews.[1] Balaam, who had pronounced blessings on the children of Israel, was a prophet of God,[2] yet not an Israelite. God sent Jonah to preach to the people of Nineveh and received their repentance in sackcloth and ashes.[3] Wise men from the East came to worship Jesus at His birth and were "warned of

[1]Ex. xviii. [2]Num. xxii. 12–23, xi. 12.
[3]Book of Jonah.

God to depart another way."[1] The prayers and alms of Cornelius, a Roman centurion, "Came up for a memorial before God." And when Peter preached to him and those assembled with him, he said, "Of a truth I perceive that God is no respecter of persons; but in every nation he that feareth him, and worketh righteousness, is accepted with him."[2]

Not only did God accept those who worked righteousness but He punished those who did wickedly. He destroyed the seven nations of Canaan when they had filled up the measure of their iniquity.[3] He rained fire and brimstone on Sodom and Gomorrah, and drove Nebuchadnezzar from his throne to live as a beast until seven years passed over him, until he was willing to bless the Most High, saying, "I praised and honored him that liveth forever, whose dominion is an everlasting dominion; and his kingdom is from generation to generation; and all the inhabitants of the earth are reputed as nothing, and he doeth according to his will in the army of heaven and among the inhabitants of the earth; and none can stay his hand, or say unto him, What doest thou?"[4] The Patriarchal religion then was given to the human family in its infancy, and no doubt embraced the race and pointed forward dimly to the Coming One. The Jewish religion was national. "It was added because of transgressions, till the seed should come to whom the promise was made,"[5] which is Christ. The Jews had no command to preach their religion to the various nations or races of the earth. In this regard it was

[1]Matt. ii. 1–12. [2]Acts x. 34, 35. [3]Gen. xv. 15–21. [4]Dan. iv. 34, 35. [5]Gal. iii. 16–19.

like many pagan religions, it was confined to the nation. They despised the Gentiles, and were permitted to buy the heathen round about them and enslave them. Yet in them we have displayed, in a most wonderful manner, the justice of God. To them were committed the oracles of God, and through them the Messiah came teaching the brotherhood of man and the fatherhood of God.

We now remark that the last great religion was not only designed to be universal and supersede all other religions, but it was new. It was original in all its great features. It differed widely not only from the Patriarchal and Jewish but from all the religions known to earth. The religion of Jesus was not compiled from other systems; it was not borrowed from tradition, nor was it the deduction of philosophy. It was original; it was called, by the Jew and the Pagan, a new religion, a new doctrine. Looking forward, the prophets of old spake of the reign of Christ as a new covenant. John the Baptist, Jesus and His apostles, spoke of "its near approach," as the "kingdom of heaven," "the kingdom of God." The book which contains this religion is called the New Testament. It presents a new and living way under a new Prophet, Priest, and King. The facts upon which it rests are new, being nothing less than the death, burial, and resurrection of its great Author. The commands which it enjoins are new. Faith in the Lord Jesus and obedience to Him were never enjoined before. All other governments and religions recognize justice, but the Christian abounds in mercy. Humility here, as nowhere else, is taught as the road to greatness, and love for our enemies is not only commanded, but it is exemplified in the death of its Founder and His last prayer for His foes. In the New Testament we have revealed a new organization, with new officers, new laws, new ordinances and new worship. "If any man be in Christ, he is a new creature. Old things are passed away; behold, all things are become new."[1] By virtue of this relationship Christians are called the temple of God, and His Holy Spirit is said to dwell in them. They are called sons and daughters of the Lord Almighty, heirs of God and joint heirs with Christ, with whom they are to reign forever and ever. This new religion, with all that it implies of dignity, honor, and glory, was untaught before Jesus.

The promises of this religion are also new. It promises the forgiveness of sins, gives the guilty conscience the peace of God. There is no longer a remembrance of sin year by year, but a full and free pardon. "Their sins and iniquities I will remember no more, saith the Lord." Not only does it promise the forgiveness of sins, the gift of the Holy Spirit, but in the end everlasting life. No other religion ever promised such an immortality—a distinct, separate existence of a spirit clothed with a glorified and celestial body. It is new in being adapted to all nations, races, and conditions of men in all time. It is the light of the world, and grows brighter as the ages advance. It spans time with a triumphal arch, and throws upon the curtain of death the rainbow of

[1]2 Cor. v. 17.

hope. It is new because it has painted immortal beauties across the valley and beyond the shadow of death. Reveals the gates standing ajar through which its subjects may enter the everlasting kingdom and enjoy the fadeless splendor of the new heaven and the new earth, where sin and suffering, disease and death, shall never come; where the good and the holy shall meet the God they have loved and the friends they have lost; where they shall live and reign with Christ and run the high race of immortality with increasing delight, forever happy and forever young.

CHAPTER VIII

THE CHURCH

The Church of Christ Established. The Law and the Gospel Contrasted.

WE come now to the direct question, When and where was the institution called the "kingdom of heaven," the "kingdom of God," the "Church of Christ," established? If the precise date of its proclamation can be fixed, and this should be found subsequent to the death of Christ, it will be perceived that an important step has been gained, and that the field of inquiry in regard to pardon, under Christ, has been much reduced. In establishing this date we will call attention to some facts which seem conclusive to show that this new religion was not established before the death of Christ. First, as a new covenant, it was ratified by the blood of Christ; as a testament, it was not of binding force while the testator lived; as a kingdom, it was not established until the King ascended and was crowned; as a church, its history shows that it was not organized while Jesus lived on earth; as the great salvation, it only "began to be spoken by the Lord, and was confirmed unto us by them that heard him."[1] Finally, as the gospel it was founded

[1] Heb. ii. 3.

on the death, burial, and resurrection of Christ, and was not preached until these facts had transpired.[1] John the Baptist, Jesus and His apostles in the gospels, speak of the kingdom of heaven as "at hand"—"as approaching," but not as an established fact. But Paul says that God, "hath delivered us from the power of darkness, and hath translated us into the kingdom of his dear Son, in whom we have redemption through his blood, even the forgiveness of sins."[2] The kingdom was established then between these two periods of time. Again, the church was spoken of as still in the future, by Matthew, where Christ, in answer to Peter, said: "Upon this rock I will build my church; and the gates of Hades shall not prevail against it."[3] In the second chapter of Acts, last verse, we are informed that "The Lord added to the church daily those that were being saved." This still narrows its establishment to the time between these two periods. The word "church" occurs but three times in the gospels, and it is not spoken of as an established fact until the statement just quoted; after this it is used some ninety-five times in the singular and plural, and is always spoken of as an existing organization. Besides the apostles, the first officers of the church mentioned are the seven deacons, spoken of in the sixth chapter of Acts. In the succeeding history we have an organization given complete, with its elders, deacons, and evangelists.

When was the gospel of Christ first proclaimed?

[1] 1 Cor. xv. [2] Col. i. 13. [3] Matt. xvi. 18.

Christ did not claim all authority in heaven and on earth until after He had conquered death. Prior to this His mission was to the Jews and to developing principles which were to predominate in His coming reign. He now made use of the ever-memorable words first heard on earth: "Go ye into all the world and preach the gospel to every creature." He says: "Thus it is written, and thus it behooved Christ to suffer, and to rise from the dead the third day, and that repentance and remission of sins should be preached in his name among all nations, beginning at Jerusalem. And ye are witnesses of these things. And, behold, I send the promise of my Father upon you; but tarry ye in the city of Jerusalem, until ye be endued with power from on high."[1]

Upon this we would remark, first, that it was necessary for Christ to suffer and rise from the dead before remission of sins could be preached in His name among all nations. Second, that the proclamation was to begin at Jerusalem. And, third, that the apostles were not to begin to preach until they were endued with power from on high. In regard to this enduement for which they were to tarry, Jesus had previously spoken to His eleven apostles, after Judas had gone out to betray Him. In this last discourse, so full of deep sympathy, beauty and love, He says: "But the Comforter, which is the Holy Spirit, whom the Father will send in my name, he shall teach you all things, and bring all things to your remembrance, whatsoever I have said unto you."[2] "But when the Comforter is

[1]Luke xxiv. 46–49. [2]John xiv. 26.

come, whom I will send unto you from the Father, even the Spirit of truth, which proceedeth from the Father, he shall testify of me: And ye also shall bear witness, because ye have been with me from the beginning."[1] "It is expedient for you that I go away, for if I go not away, the Comforter will not come unto you; but if I depart, I will send him unto you. And, when he is come, he will reprove [or convict] the world of sin, and of righteousness, and of judgment."[2] From these passages we learn that the Comforter (the Advocate), the Holy Spirit, would not come until Jesus went away, and that when He was come He would teach the apostles all things and bring all things to their remembrance, and convict the world of sin and of righteousness and of judgment. How important then for us to know the precise time when this Advocate came to teach these wonderful things, clothed with authority from Jesus and the Father. Isaiah evidently spoke of this time over seven hundred years before, when he says: "And it shall come to pass in the last days, that the mountain of the Lord's house shall be established in the top of the mountains, and shall be exalted above the hills; and all nations shall flow unto it. And many people shall go and say, Come ye, and let us go up to the mountain of the Lord, to the house of the God of Jacob; and he will teach us of his ways, and we will walk in his paths; for out of Zion shall go forth the law, and the word of the Lord from Jerusalem. And he shall judge among the nations, and shall rebuke many people: and they

[1] John xv. 26, 27. [2] John xvi. 7, 8.

shall beat their swords into plowshares, and their spears into pruning-hooks: nation shall not lift up sword against nation, neither shall they learn war any more."[1] This prophecy not only shows that the word of the Lord was to go forth from Jerusalem, but that it was to go forth in the last days—that is, in the last days of the Jewish nation or institution, as will be shown hereafter.

Not only did the prophets point out the time and place of the gospel proclamation, but it was typified in the giving of the law to Moses. It was fifty days from the slaying of the paschal lamb in Egypt until the giving of the law on Mount Sinai. At the giving of the law, there were three thousand slain. "And there fell of the people that day about three thousand men."[2] Paul says: "Christ our passover is sacrificed for us."[3] It was just fifty days from the slaying or sacrifice of the lamb of God that taketh away the sin of the world, until the Apostles were endued with the Holy Spirit, according to the preceding promise, and Peter holding the keys of the kingdom opened that day its everlasting doors and three thousand entering were made alive. Well might Paul call the former law "The law of sin and death," and contrast it with "The law of the Spirit of life in Christ Jesus."[4]

This brings us to the time when the gospel was first proclaimed, and nowhere do we meet with such great contrasts as we do between the law and the gospel. The one was narrow, local, limited to the Jew and the

[1]Isaiah ii. 2–4. [2]Ex. xxxii. 28.
[3]1 Cor. v. 7. [4]Rom. viii. 2.

land of Palestine, the other embraced all mankind. The one taught hatred to our enemies, the other love for our foes. The one said, "An eye for an eye and a tooth for a tooth," the other, "Blessed are the merciful, for they shall obtain mercy." The first great king of the one when dying remembered his enemies and said to Solomon, "But his hoar head bring thou down to the grave with blood."[1] When in dying, David's greater Son and Lord remembered his enemies and betrayers and said, "Father, forgive them, for they know not what they do."[2]

The law treated its subjects as slaves, the gospel as freemen. Peter, who had suffered the galling servitude of the former, said it was "a yoke upon the neck of the disciples, which neither our fathers nor we were able to bear."[3] "Stand fast therefore in the liberty wherewith Christ hath made us free, and be not entangled again with the yoke of bondage,"[4] was the exhortation of the great apostle Paul who had been enslaved by the one and freed by the other. The first revealed God as Creator, the last as Father. The first was carnal, the last was spiritual; the first was earthly, the other heavenly. The law was silent in regard to life after death. All its rewards and punishments were earthly and temporal.[5] The gospel glows with immortality; it buds, blossoms, blooms, and is laden with the fruitage of eternal life. The law was given from Sinai amid scenes of indescribable terror, which caused even Moses to ex-

[1] 1 Kings ii. 9. [2] Matt. xxiii. 24. [3] Acts xv. 10.
[4] Gal. v. 1. [5] See Deut. xxviii.

claim, "I exceedingly fear and quake."[1] But fifty days after the death of Jesus, "when the day of Pentecost was fully come," we have the message of peace from the King of Peace. The Messiah has ascended to heaven, been crowned Lord of all and entered upon His mediatorial reign. The scenes that clustered around this sacred spot are hallowed scenes. They will live in the memory of man forever.

If upon giving the law not so much as even a beast should touch the mountain, the place whereon we now stand is holy ground. "If the ministration of death, written and engraven in stones, was glorious, so that the children of Israel could not steadfastly behold the face of Moses for the glory of his countenance; which glory was to be done away; how shall not the ministration of the spirit be rather glorious? For if the ministration of condemnation be glory, much more doth the ministration of righteousness exceed in glory. For even that which was made glorious had no glory in this respect, by reason of the glory that excelleth."[2] We stand then not where Moses stood, but upon ground hallowed by the bringing in of a better hope. The apostles have tarried in Jerusalem, as commanded, the Holy Spirit has fallen upon them as promised. Prophecy, promise and type are now fulfilled. Let us then approach with clean hands and pure hearts and unprejudiced minds and hear the first proclamation that ever reached the Gentile world —including all mankind—the story of remission of sins to be preached among all nations, beginning at

[1]Heb. xii. 21. [2]2 Cor. iii. 7–10.

Jerusalem. The story of love and suffering, of death and triumph, of the cross and the crown, which has cheered millions of the living and dying of earth, and will be sung as a new song by the redeemed in heaven.

CHAPTER IX

THE DAY OF PENTECOST

Peter's Sermon on the Day of Pentecost and the Pardon of the Three Thousand.

"AND when the day of Pentecost was fully come, they were all with one accord in one place. And suddenly there came a sound from heaven as of a rushing mighty wind, and it filled all the house where they were sitting. And there appeared unto them cloven tongues like as of fire, and it sat upon each of them. And they were all filled with the Holy Spirit, and began to speak with other tongues, as the Spirit gave them utterance. And there were dwelling at Jerusalem Jews, devout men, out of every nation under heaven. Now when this was noised abroad, the multitude came together, and were confounded, because that every man heard them speak in his own language. And they were all amazed and marveled, saying one to another, Behold, are not all these which speak Galileans? And how hear we every man in our own tongue, wherein we were born?"[1]

No wonder that these people who spoke seventeen languages or dialects were amazed when each heard them speak in his own language, "the wonderful

[1]Acts ii. 1–8.

works of God."[1] While some were in doubt, saying, one to another, "What meaneth this? Others mocking, said, These men are full of new wine." But Peter, to whom Jesus had given the keys of the kingdom and imparted the authority to open the kingdom of heaven on earth, "standing up with the eleven, lifted up his voice, and said unto them, Ye men of Judea, and all ye that dwell at Jerusalem, be this known unto you, and hearken to my words: For these are not drunken, as ye suppose, seeing it is but the third hour of the day. But this is that which was spoken by the prophet Joel: And it shall come to pass in the last days, saith God, I will pour out of my Spirit upon all flesh: and your sons and your daughters shall prophesy. . . . And it shall come to pass, that whosoever shall call on the name of the Lord shall be saved."[2] The last days spoken of here are the same as the last days spoken of by Isaiah and refer to the close of the Jewish dispensation or age. Jesus, while He lived, kept the Jewish law perfectly. He is the only one on record who met all its requirements; and when the Jews were challenged no one convicted Him of sin. He kept the law, and not "one jot or tittle" passed until all was fulfilled and was "abolished."[3] "He took it out of the way, nailing it to his cross," and dying exclaimed, "It is finished," and the "vail of the temple was rent." Now, all may approach "by a new and living way, which he hath consecrated for us, through the vail."[4]

[1]Acts ii. 11. [2]Acts ii. 14–21.
[3]See 2 Cor. iii. 7–18. [4]Heb. x. 20.

The last days have truly come. The starlight age has passed, the moonlight age is now closed. The law has waned to wax no more, "the sun of righteousness has arisen with healing in his wings," the everlasting gospel is being proclaimed for the first time on earth. "Ye men of Israel, hear these words: Jesus of Nazareth, a man approved of God among you by miracles and wonders and signs, which God did by him in the midst of you, as ye yourselves also know: Him, being delivered by the determinate counsel and foreknowledge of God, ye have taken, and by wicked hands have crucified and slain: Whom God hath raised up, having loosed the pains of death: because it was not possible that he should be holden of it."[1] Peter then goes on to apply a prophecy of David to Christ, which says: "Thou wilt not leave my soul in Hades, neither wilt thou suffer thine Holy One to see corruption."[2]

He speaks of His ascension and concludes this wonderful discourse by saying in the most direct manner, "Therefore let all the house of Israel know assuredly, that God hath made that same Jesus, whom ye have crucified, both Lord and Christ. Now when they heard this, they were pricked in their heart, and said unto Peter and to the rest of the apostles, Men and brethren, what shall we do?"[3] Never was there proclaimed to men greater facts, nor were they ever charged with greater crime. Nor from the depths of human conviction and anguish ever came a more direct, earnest and important inquiry, "What shall

[1]Acts ii. 22–24. [2]Acts ii. 27. [3]Acts ii. 36, 37.

we do?" This question demands and receives an answer about which there can be no mistake. Human language is incapable of making either the question or the answer plainer. "Then Peter said unto them, Repent, and be baptized every one of you in the name of Jesus Christ for the remission of sins, and ye shall receive the gift of the Holy Spirit. For the promise is unto you, and to your children, and to all that are afar off, even as many as the Lord our God shall call."[1] "Then they that gladly received his word were baptized; and the same day there were added unto them about three thousand souls. And they continued steadfastly in the apostles' doctrine and fellowship, and in breaking of bread, and in prayers."[2]

Here and now is opened before us the Christian age. Here we have the first gospel sermon preached by Peter under the ascended, ruling, reigning Christ. The gospel is now before us for the first time in its fulness. We have heard the first discourse based upon its great facts, listened to the first inquiry, "What shall we do?" heard the first command given by the authority of Christ, and witnessed the conversion of three thousand persons, and their baptism into the name of the Father, Son, and Holy Spirit. It is evident from the preeeding narrative, first, that these persons heard; second, that they believed; third, that they repented; fourth, that they were baptized; fifth, that they received the remission of sins and the gift of the Holy Spirit. Upon these conditions they became

[1]Acts ii. 38, 39. [2]Acts ii. 41, 42.

subjects of Christ's kingdom. They entered His Church and are the first recorded who "continued steadfastly in the apostles' doctrine and fellowship, and in breaking of bread, and in prayers."[1]*

We come now to a most important inquiry: Were the conditions here imposed applicable to that particular time and occasion only, or were they enjoined by divine authority upon all who subsequently entered the Church, and were they thus designed to be required of all persons alike in all succeeding ages of time? Is there uniformity or diversity in the system of pardon? Does the amnesty proclamation of Jesus

*It will be observed that this sermon of Peter at the opening of the kingdom was addressed to all "ye that dwell at Jerusalem," and "there were dwelling at Jerusalem Jews, devout men, from every nation under heaven." The Gospel was preached beginning at Jerusalem as commanded, and then in Judea and in Samaria and unto the uttermost part of the earth. Paul said, about one generation after the Gospel was first proclaimed, that it "was preached in all creation under heaven."[2]

This shows the very rapid advance of the kingdom after Pentecost. The apostles no longer preached the kingdom of heaven is at hand. Christ had ascended, and "for the suffering of death was crowned." "Being by the right hand of God exalted." The kingdom is now an established fact "and the gates of hades shall not prevail against it." Daniel speaks of this time, saying: "And in the days of those kings shall the God of heaven set up a kingdom, which shall never be destroyed, nor shall the sovereignty thereof be left to another people; but it shall break in pieces and consume all these kingdoms, and it shall stand forever."[3]

Christ "must reign, till he hath put all his enemies under

[1]Acts. ii. 42. [2]Col. i. 23; Rom. i. 5, xvi. 26. [3]Dan. ii. 44.

to the world enjoin the same terms upon all? Is there order and harmony in heaven's last great system of redemption, or is it chaos and confusion? If we know that our Redeemer liveth, may we not know how He redeems from sin and be fully assured of pardon? "What must I do to be saved?" will be asked as long as there is sin and a Savior. Reason, justice, mercy, and love require that this question, springing from the deepest wants of the human soul, should meet with an answer which can be understood and obeyed by all who sincerely ask it. Not only so, but we may expect uniformity in what is required both of saint and sinner. If there is any one thing better established than another it is the uniformity of God's laws both in nature and revelation. Under the former dispensations He required the same initiation of one as of another. He required the same sacrifice for the same sin, and imposed the same punishment for the same crime. We may expect, then, under this last and most perfect development of God's wisdom, mercy, and love, to find uniformity, order, and harmony. But before calling attention to the uniformity of the law of pardon by considering each individual case, we will first notice the order of God's revelation.

---

his feet," or God's "will be done on earth as in heaven." Now that the kingdom of heaven is established, there is no record or example of anyone anywhere under the guidance of inspiration, praying "Thy kingdom come," or preaching an approaching kingdom, even in the sense of "Thy will be done"; as an established kingdom may be extended but cannot come again in any sense.

[1]1 Cor. xv. 25.

CHAPTER X

THE NEW TESTAMENT SCRIPTURES

The Significance of the Gospels, the Acts, the Epistles, and The Book of the Revelation, and Their Place in the History of Pardon.

WE have called attention to the three religions recorded in the Bible, the Patriarchal, the Jewish, and the Christian. There are properly four great divisions in the Old Testament—history, law, prophecy, and poetry. Passing on to the New Testament, there are also four great divisions: The four gospels, the Acts of Apostles, the twenty-one epistles, and the book of Revelation. The four gospels contain the most wonderful history known to earth. There is nothing preceding or succeeding like them in the history of the world. They stand alone among all writings. The age of law, of prophecy, of wisdom, and of national power had long since passed from the Jewish people. The age of servitude, of sect, of party, and of tradition had come. Hypocrisy, bigotry, intolerance, and self-righteousness were ruling characteristics. While they boasted of Abraham as their father, Moses as their law-giver, and the prophets as their teachers, the Jews disregarded the faith of the one, the instructions of the other, and had gone about to establish their own righteousness, "teaching for doctrines the commandments of men."[1]

In this age and surrounded with such circumstances Jesus appeared. The gospel records of His life have no parallel in human history. Born as a Jew, and surrounded with the bigotry of His people and His times, He taught a philanthropy, mercy, and love unknown, unequaled, and which can never be surpassed. The four gospels give the birth, life, mission, death, resurrection, and ascension of the Being who has wrought the greatest changes in human society of all time. One of the most remarkable things about those who wrote the gospels is that they give a record of all Jesus did, taught, and suffered without a single note or comment of their own. No note of criticism, no word of praise or blame is given. Nothing to bias the mind or prejudice the judgment of others. True, we have expressions of their own deep love, and abiding affection for the Master, but from them the character of Jesus received no eulogium, no praise. John, alone, ventured so far as to tell us what his gospel was written for: Many other signs therefore did Jesus . . . but "these are written, that ye might believe that Jesus is the Christ, the Son of God; and that believing ye might have life through his name."[2] This may be stated, in a general way, to be the meaning or purport of all the gospels. In order to produce this faith and give this life they give us a record of the sayings and doings of Jesus, the wonderful events attending His birth and death, and crown all by the testi-

[1]Matt. xv. 9. [2]John xx. 30, 31.

mony of God, angels, and men. Even demons and Satan bear testimony to His superhuman power. We have, therefore, the Messiahship of Jesus and His divine mission confirmed, not only by miracles, signs, and wonders which God did by Him, and by His own declarations, but by every variety of evidence known to man. "These are written, that ye might believe that Jesus is the Christ, the Son of God." The testimony is ample. The Messiah of prophecy is the Christ of history.

The chief object of the first great division of the New Testament—the gospels—then is to produce faith. They did not give a record of the Church complete, nor the history of the admission of any one to its blessings and privileges. It is only in concluding that the terms are given upon which persons may enter the kingdom of the risen Lord. His ambassadors, however, were restricted from promulgating them until He ascended and they were endued with power from on high.

In the study of the New Testament it is very important to keep in mind the proper divisions of the book. Without doing this it will be impossible to gain an accurate knowledge of its system of pardon or salvation. The gospels were written giving the history of Jesus as an example; His teaching, as instructions, and His death as an atonement; and all this for the purpose of producing faith and obedience.

The Acts of the Apostles gives the history of the organization of the Church, the preaching of the apostles under the commission of Christ, beginning at Jerusalem, and continuing to preach in various parts of the world. It gives the missionary labors of the apostles and evangelists, gives the minute and detailed account of the pardon of masses of people and of many individuals. And here alone can we find a full account of how the gospel was preached, received, and obeyed. Here alone, of all the books of the New Testament, are we told how persons come into the Church of Christ. This, then, is the book to which the believing penitent will go and ask, as thousands heretofore have asked, "Lord, what wilt thou have me to do?" and receiving the same answer will do the same things and rejoice in the same hope.

The twenty-one epistles were written to organized churches and individuals—to Christians, giving instruction to officers, to members, in regard to all things pertaining to life and godliness. Here is set before the Christian his warfare, his race, his crown. Here are given in full the conditions upon which the Christian may enter the everlasting kingdom.

Fourteen of the twenty-one epistles were written by Paul. Paul was the great apostle to the Gentiles. He preached chiefly to them, and in his epistles is developed, as nowhere else, the true idea of the law and the gospel.

In no other epistles can we learn the distinction between the two. It is only by noting the fact that some of the other epistles seem to be general that we may infer that the Gentiles are addressed at all. In none of these epistles are the Gentiles alluded to favorably. Peter, addressing the strangers scattered abroad, commands them to have their "conversation honest among the Gentiles; that, whereas they speak against you as evil doers."[1] Again, he says: "For the time past of our life may suffice us to have wrought the will of the Gentiles, when we walked in lasciviousness, lusts, excess of wine, revelings, banquetings, and abominable idolatries: wherein they think it strange that ye run not with them to the same excess of riot, speaking evil of you."[2] John speaks of certain persons who went "forth, taking nothing of the Gentiles."[3] In the Book of Revelation the outer court is spoken of "as given to the Gentiles." Thus the word "Gentile" occurs but four times in these seven epistles and in the book of Revelation, while it occurs some forty-four times in Paul's epistles alone. In the epistles of Paul the Gentiles are treated on terms of equality.

Here there is neither Greek nor Jew, barbarian nor Scythian, bond nor free. But all are one in Christ. If Gentiles would know God's will, both as converted and unconverted, they must search the Scriptures from the giving of the great Commission by Christ until the close of the epistles by Paul. Here all barriers and race distinctions are broken down, and the Fatherhood of God and the brotherhood of man is developed and God's great love for the entire world is exemplified. Here for the first time the Jew and the Gentile meet in one family and rejoice together in the hope of the glory of God. The epistles then,

[1] 1 Pet. ii. 12. [2] 1 Pet. iv. 3, 4. [3] 3 John 7.

as a whole, were written to persons whose former sins had been forgiven, who had been adopted into the family of God; they were written to give instructions in regard to their walk and conversation; to teach them what they were to do, to suffer and finally to enjoy. The book of Revelation gives a prophetic history of the future of the Church, foretelling great calamities which were to come upon the earth, the sufferings and struggles of the saints of the Most High, and their final and glorious victory.

Of the gospels it may be said, "These are written that you might believe." The Acts of the Apostles gives a history of pardon and examples of conversion; the epistles direct Christians how to live; and the book of Revelation gives a prophecy of the future.

CHAPTER XI

THE GREAT SALVATION

A Review of the Three Cases of Pardon in the Gospels. The Significance of the Cross. The Great Salvation which Began to be Spoken by Christ.

HAVING called attention to the four divisions of the New Testament and the design of them, we will now, before proceeding with the history of each case of pardon recorded in Acts, refer again to the cases of pardon given in the gospels. There are only three instances of forgiveness recorded during Christ's personal ministry. The first one is the man afflicted with the palsy, and recorded by Matthew, Mark, and Luke. Jesus first forgave him, and then to demonstrate that the Son of Man had power on earth to forgive sins, He said to the sick of the palsy, "Arise, take up thy bed, and go unto thine house."[1] The next case given is a woman, who was a sinner, but who washed Jesus' feet with tears and wiped them with the hairs of her head. "And he said unto her, Thy sins are forgiven."[2] The last case is the thief on the cross. Jesus said unto him, "To-day shalt thou be with me in paradise."[3] These comprise all the cases of for-

[1]Matt. ix. 6; Mark ii. 11; Luke v. 20.
[2]Luke vii. 37–48. [3]Luke xxiii. 43.

giveness of sins, unless we consider the casting out of demons as equivalent to pardon.

Upon these we would remark, that in the first case Jesus demonstrated His power to forgive by working a miracle. In the second case, we have an example for all time of the pure and sinless One forgiving a sinful woman, and in the last case the depth of His mercy reaching to a man who was a self-condemned criminal. Thus we learn that even the lowest, the fallen, and most depraved of earth may hope in Jesus. But, says one, may I now be pardoned as the man afflicted with the palsy, the woman at Jesus' feet, or the thief on the cross? If all the circumstances were the same, no doubt that the same results would follow. We have no promise, however, that Jesus will ever tabernacle in the flesh again as He did in Palestine. Never again will a palsied man be let down through the roof of a house to be healed by the Lord. Never again will a sinful, sorrowing woman bedew His feet with tears, nor will His feet and hands be pierced with nails while a suffering, dying thief by His side asks to be remembered when He comes into His kingdom. It must never be forgotten therefore that these acts of pardon were performed while Jesus was personally on the earth, and that, too, before His death, and before He had given commandment to both saint and sinner. Before the death of Jesus His approaching reign was preached. After His death remission of sins was preached in His name among all nations, beginning at Jerusalem. While Jesus was personally on the earth He sowed broadcast His blessings and none could stay His hands or say "What doest thou?" But when He died and left His will to His executors, the blessings henceforth have been bestowed in accordance with His will. The New Testament was not of binding force while the testator lived. As well might we expect Him now to address the multitude as He did then, to heal the sick, cure the blind, raise the dead, as to pardon now, as He did then. He could not do this without violating His last will and testament, in which the terms of pardon are fully set forth. When He appeared to Paul, after His ascension, to make him an apostle, He did not state the terms of pardon, but sent him to one of His disciples to learn what to do. All blessings, after the death of Jesus, flowed in the broad, deep channel of the gospel, and all persons thereafter addressed supernaturally by Jesus, by angels, by visions, or by the Holy Spirit, were not pardoned by direct supernatural power, but were sent to ministers of the gospel to learn what they should do to be saved. It is important to note that in these three cases of pardon given in the gospels they were pardoned by the word of the Lord, but that there were no terms required in order to pardon. In all cases subsequent to the death of Jesus there are terms of pardon required, but the evidence of pardon is the same, being the word of the Lord spoken by divine authority.

Having briefly called attention to the three cases of forgiveness mentioned in the gospels, we now note the fact that there is only one case given in which

Jesus made known, in a figurative way, the terms of admission into the kingdom of God. This was in the case of Nicodemus. As admission into the kingdom was the subject of conversation here, this case, unlike the other three, agrees with the terms as declared when the kingdom became established, and the figurative language in regard to being born again, "born of water and of the Spirit,"[1] becomes intelligible when viewed in the light of the terms of pardon as announced on the day of Pentecost, and in all subsequent cases of admission into the Church of Christ or kingdom of God.

It should be borne in mind by every student of the Bible, that from the giving of the law on Sinai until the death of Jesus on Calvary, there is not a single command given to the Gentile world. There are some individual cases of Gentiles becoming Jews, but the Jews had no command to evangelize, none to preach their religion to the world; but their prophets were directed to predict the coming One and the universal reign of the Prince of Peace. John the Baptist's mission was to the Jews only. Christ's personal ministry, and that of His apostles during His life, was "to the lost sheep of the house of Israel"—to the Jews, and to develop principles which were to predominate in His coming reign. His kingdom was not established until He had conquered death: "For the suffering of death he was crowned."[2] His Church did not exist before He arose from the ruins of the grave, and it was built on the great facts con-

[1]John iii. 5. [2]Heb. ii. 9.

nected with the subversion of the empire of death, "and the gates of Hades shall not prevail against it." "That through death he might destroy him that had the power of death, that is, the devil; and deliver them, who through fear of death were all their lifetime subject to bondage."[1] He died that remission of sins might be preached in His name among all nations. He died for our sins. He died, and since His death the redeemed in heaven sing a new song. "For thou wast slain, and hast redeemed us to God by thy blood out of every kindred, and tongue, and people, and nation."[2] He died, and it is His dying love that is preached. He rose, and it is His risen power that makes Him almighty to save. He rose, and because He rose the gates of death are broken and liberty to the captive is proclaimed. He ascended, and "When he ascended up on high, he led captivity captive, and gave gifts unto men."[3] Then, and not until then, was wrought out and brought in an everlasting redemption for all the children of men.

We live on this side of the cross and should be determined not to know anything but "Jesus Christ and him crucified."[4] The banner of the cross is the banner of victory. The preaching of Christ crucified is "the power of God and the wisdom of God," altho it was to "the Jews a stumbling-block, and unto the Greeks foolishness."[5] "Though he were a Son, yet learned he obedience by the things which he suffered; and being made perfect, he became the author of

[1]Heb. ii. 14, 15. [2]Rev. v. 9. [3]Eph. iv. 8.
[4]1 Cor. ii. 2. [5]1 Cor. i. 23.

eternal salvation unto all them that obey him."[1] Paul says: "He is the head of the body, the church: who is the beginning, the firstborn from the dead; that in all things he might have the preeminence. For it pleased the Father that in him should all fulness dwell; and, having made peace through the blood of his cross, by him to reconcile all things unto himself; by him, I say, whether they be things in earth, or things in heaven."[2]

Again we remark before resuming the history that as a salvation the gospel only "began to be spoken by the Lord." "How shall we escape, if we neglect so great salvation; which at the first began to be spoken by the Lord, and was confirmed unto us by them that heard him; God also bearing them witness, both with signs and wonders, and with divers miracles, and gifts of the Holy Spirit, according to his own will?"[3] Jude called this salvation "the common salvation."[4] There are many special salvations spoken of in the Bible, but this common salvation, this great salvation, stands alone in its greatness and is complete in its blessings. Noah and his family were saved from the flood, the children of Israel were saved from Egyptian bondage; they were saved from their enemies and from the fiery serpents in the wilderness. They were saved over and over again from invading armies, from disease and pestilence, but all their salvations were temporal—earthly. All their blessings were in basket and in store—all belonged to time and sense. There was no promised salvation even for the pious Jews

[1]Heb. v. 8, 9. [2]Col. i. 18–20. [3]Heb. ii. 3, 4. [4]Jude 3.

covering time and eternity. No salvation from the grave, no eternal life, no heaven is promised, only prosperity, greatness, and dominion in this life. The law of Moses did not propose or answer the question, Does death end all? The five books of Moses, the religious system of the Jews, do not contain the words immortality, eternal life, nor do they promise heaven as the future abode of man. They are barren of all words containing the idea of future being, blessedness, or salvation. But the great salvation which at the first began to be spoken by the Lord proposed to save not only from the effects of sin and from the bondage of sin, but from the wages of sin. It saves from past transgressions, gives strength for present duty, and promises a future salvation from the grave and a glorious immortality. This great salvation "began to be spoken by the Lord." No government, no system of philanthropy, no religion ever proposed such a salvation—a salvation for Jew and Gentile, for bond and free, a salvation for all nations, for all races, and for all time.

It was not until after Jesus arose from the dead that He declared that all authority in heaven and earth was given to Him. "Go ye therefore into all the world and preach the gospel to every creature." At first it began to be spoken by the Lord, but it only began to be spoken by Him and was confirmed unto us by them that heard Him. God also bearing them witness both with signs and wonders and divers miracles and gifts of the Holy Spirit. It began to be spoken by the Lord but we must come to those who confirmed it unto us to know its history,—to the apostles, His ambassadors; to those commissioned to open the kingdom, to learn how to enter and enjoy the marvelous blessing of this complete salvation from sin, death and the grave.

A perfect salvation—perfect in its precepts, perfect in its promises. Nothing can be added to the depth of love contained in its facts, nothing to the purity of its commands, nothing to the fulness of its rewards. It embraces all of mercy, all of love, all of tenderness known in earth or heaven. It covers the whole range of human obligations, forbids all that is wrong, enjoins all that is right, and rewards all that is good. It explains all that is dark and mysterious in the hitherto unsolved problems of life and death. It cleanses the sinful, makes holy the vile, lifts up the fallen, comforts the lowly, cheers the sorrowing, relieves the suffering, and takes away the sting of death. Millions of its subjects now live in the hope of dying, and millions more have died in the hope of living. It is a great salvation, worthy of God to devise, Jesus to execute, and the Holy Spirit to consummate. It is a salvation into which "the angels desired to look," and they wondered at the depths of the mercy of God. It is the last great offer of heaven to earth, and is full, free, and everlasting.

CHAPTER XII

THE APOSTLES' PREACHING

Preaching of Peter and John. Imprisoned by Jews and Released by the Power of God. The Community of Interest.

WE now resume the consideration of the terms of pardon as developed in this great salvation, and the terms of admission into the kingdom of the ruling reigning sovereign, and the requirements made of persons on entering the Church, to the history of the forgiveness of sins as taught by Christ's own ambassadors, who were endued by the Holy Spirit.

We have called attention to the first gospel sermon preached after Jesus had finished the work given Him to do, and to the fact that three thousand gladly received the word. The terms of pardon required of this multitude were so plain that a wayfaring man or the most simple-minded need not err therein. At the conclusion of this discourse we are informed that "the Lord added to the church daily those that were being saved."[1] After this, when Peter and John were about going into the temple at the hour of prayer, Peter healed in the name of Jesus a man who was "above forty years old," and had been laid at the Beautiful Gate, being lame from his birth. When

[1]Acts ii. 47.

the people saw that the lame was healed, they ran together unto Solomon's Porch, looking earnestly on Peter and John as if by their own power or holiness they had made this man to walk. Peter charged them with having denied the Son of God, "in the presence of Pilate, when he was determined to let him go. But ye denied the Holy One and the Just, and desired a murderer to be granted unto you; and killed the Prince of life, whom God hath raised from the dead; whereof we are witnesses. And his name, through faith in his name, hath made this man strong . . . . given him this perfect soundness in the presence of you all. And now, brethren, I know that through ignorance ye did it, as did also your rulers . . . Repent ye therefore, and turn again, that your sins may be blotted out, when the times of refreshing shall come from the presence of the Lord."[1] This is the second time Peter addresses the betrayers of Christ in regard to their duty. The command here given does not differ from the commission given by Christ nor from the previous direction of Peter—hearing and believing are here both implied. Then they were commanded to repent and turn—to obey—that their sins might be blotted out, and they would receive "the gift of the Holy Spirit," or, that "times of refreshing may come from the presence of the Lord." Peter, continuing his discourse, says: "For Moses truly said unto the fathers, A Prophet shall the Lord your God raise up unto you of your brethren, like unto me; him shall ye hear in all things whatsoever he shall say unto you.

[1]Acts iii. 13–19.

. . . Yea, and all the prophets from Samuel and those that follow after, as many as have spoken, have likewise foretold of these days."[1] This is a wonderful statement. Moses' authority had passed away, a greater than Moses is here. He it is of whom Moses and the prophets wrote. Samuel, the head of the long line of Jewish prophets, and all his successors, have foretold these days—marvelous days—the last days of Judaism, the first days of Christianity. They marked the fading away of the old, the coming in of the new. If the prophets looked forward to these days, may we not look back to them, laden, as they are, with glad tidings for all people? Precious days, days hallowed by the greatest events that ever occurred on earth; days which gave man new faith, new hope, and started the world on a new career of glory. Days in which were wedded heaven and earth in Jesus and His Church, in bonds of love which are not broken in life nor parted in death. We should consider well the events of these days which marked the beginning of the Christian age, an age which on all succeeding ages has been telling with irresistible power.

The result of this discourse was that "the people, the priests, and the captain of the temple, and the Sadducees, came upon them, being grieved that they taught the people, and preached through Jesus the resurrection from the dead. And they laid hands on them, and put them in ward unto the morrow: for it was now evening. But many of those who heard the word believed; and the number of the men was about

[1]Acts. iii. 22–24.

five thousand."[1] Here it is simply stated that they believed, and that "the number of men was about five thousand." We have no warrant, however, for the conclusion that those who were added to the Church daily, or those who were numbered, had not complied with the same terms required on the day of Pentecost. That the terms are not stated in full in every case is not a proof that they were not enforced. No one will argue, because it is only stated that they were "added to the church," that they were added without faith or repentance. Neither can it be argued, because belief only is stated here, that they were not required to repent and to be baptized. Because all the terms of pardon are not stated in each individual case, it does not follow that they did not comply with all the terms. We must then look to the cases of pardon given in full if we would know what was done by each individual who is said to be "added to the Church," who "believed," or who became "obedient unto the faith." This is an important consideration. We should never recognize the obedience to one command, given either to saint or sinner, as covering the whole range of human obligation. If the system of redemption is perfect as a whole, it is perfect in all its parts, and each part must be complied with in order to perfect obedience. It would therefore follow, as a matter of justice and common right, that no more and no less should be required of one than of another under the same circumstances. If, therefore, it be shown that many persons at different places and various

[1]Acts. iv. 1-4.

times heard, believed, repented, and were baptized in order to receive pardon, it follows that this is the law of pardon, even if all these terms are not fully stated in each individual case, as they are not excluded.

When Peter and John were released from prison on the next day they were summoned by the "rulers and elders and scribes," and "the high priest" and others in regard to healing the lame man. They were asked, "By what power, or by what name, have ye done this? Then Peter, filled with the Holy Spirit, said unto them. . . . Be it known unto you all, and to all the people of Israel, that by the name of Jesus Christ of Nazareth, whom ye crucified, whom God raised from the dead, even by him doth this man stand here before you whole. . . . Neither is there salvation in any other: for there is none other name under heaven given among men, whereby we must be saved."[1] Abraham, Moses, David, and all the prophets were powerless to save. Jesus alone is vested with power to save; none ever preceded Him, none have succeeded Him with such power. Of all the mighty of earth none have demonstrated power to save. Jesus alone is able to save and strong to deliver. No other name given whereby we must be saved. This was true then, is true to-day, true to-morrow, and will be true until sin shall cease, until the grave gives back its dead, and time shall be no more.

"Now when they saw the boldness of Peter and John, and perceived that they were unlearned and ignorant men, they marveled; and they took knowl-

[1]Acts iv. 7–12.

edge of them, that they had been with Jesus. And beholding the man who was healed standing with them, they could say nothing against it. . . . And they called them, and commanded them not to speak at all nor teach in the name of Jesus. But Peter and John answered and said unto them, Whether it be right in the sight of God to hearken unto you more than unto God, judge ye. For we can not but speak the things which we have seen and heard. So when they had further threatened them, they let them go. . . . And being let go, they went to their own company, and reported all that the chief priests and elders had said unto them."[1] Having prayed to God, who hath made heaven and earth, the sea and all things, the place where they were assembled was shaken, "And they were all filled with the Holy Spirit, and they spake the word of God with boldness. And the multitude of them that believed were of one heart and of one soul."[2]

Then follows an account of the community of interest and the death of Ananias and Sapphira on account of "having lied to the Holy Spirit." This common interest—this community, which was confined to the Jerusalem church, so far as history informs us, was made necessary by the common need of the "multitude of them that believed," as no doubt there would be great difficulty in obtaining employment when they were despised and persecuted; and also on account of the sick that were healed. It was not compulsory but voluntary.

[1]Acts iv. 13–23. [2]Acts iv. 31, 32.

We observe, in regard to this distribution, that notwithstanding the fact that the apostles were given the power to work miracles, yet in this case of great necessity they did not feed the "multitude of them that believed," as Jesus fed the five thousand. But this community of interest was formed to care for the needy.

Jesus gave instructions to the twelve apostles and the seventy on their first mission, saying, "Take nothing for your journey, neither staff, nor wallet nor bread, nor money; neither have two coats"[1] but when this mission "to the lost sheep of the house of Israel" was finished and He was preparing them to "go into all the world," just before His betrayal He said: "When I sent you forth without purse, and wallet, and shoes, lacked ye anything?" and they said, "Nothing," and He said unto them, "But now, he that hath a purse, let him take it, and likewise a wallet,"[2] thus annulling His first instructions.

If the apostles or ministers after this went out as on the first mission, we have no record of it; but in contrast we learn from Paul, "Even so did the Lord ordain that they that preach the Gospel should live of the Gospel."[3] He says also to Christians, "Study to be quiet and to do your own business and to work with your own hands even as we charged you."[4] Again, "If any man provideth not for his own household he hath denied the faith and is worse than an unbeliever."[5] And again, "If any man will not

[1]Luke ix. 3. [2]Luke xxii. 35, 36. [3]1 Cor. ix. 14.
[4]1 Thess. iv. 11. [5]1 Tim. v. 8.

work neither let him eat."[1] After Christ's personal ministry ended the natural order seems to have been resumed, and men earned their living by the sweat of their brow. That it would be proper and right for persons who have no bread to pray for it there can be no doubt. The question may be asked, Should we pray for that which we already possess? "Your Father knoweth what things ye have need of, before ye ask him."[2] It would, therefore, be more appropriate for children of God who are abundantly blessed with temporal good to thank Him day by day for His goodness in having supplied their wants, and ask His direction in giving to the needy and for the advancement of His kingdom rather than vainly pray for their daily bread.

There is no further mention of the community of interest, but about ten years later Paul was sent from Antioch with a contribution for the church at Jerusalem,[3] and again after another period of about seventeen years he took offerings from the churches of Achaia and Macedonia for the poor saints in Jerusalem.[4]

Continuing the narrative we learn that "believers were the more added to the Lord, multitudes both of men and women."[5] They also healed a multitude of sick and afflicted in Jerusalem and of those brought to them "from the cities round about." "Then the high priest rose up, and all they that were with him, (which is the sect of the Sadducees,) and were filled

[1] 2 Thess. iii. 10. [2] Matt. vi. 8. [3] Acts xi. 27–29.
[4] Rom. xv. 26. [5] Acts v. 14.

with indignation. And laid their hands on the apostles, and put them in the common prison. But the angel of the Lord by night opened the prison doors, and brought them forth, and said: Go, stand and speak in the temple to the people all the words of this life."[1] Upon this it may be remarked, first, that the angel of the Lord did not speak to the people, but commanded the apostles to go and speak. And, second, that they were to speak "the words of this life." The life of which the apostles were to speak was couched in words—it was based on facts. The next day the apostles were not found in the prison, but in the temple teaching the people. They were brought without violence and set before the council, "And the high priest asked them, saying, Did not we straitly command you that ye should not teach in this name? and, behold, ye have filled Jerusalem with your doctrine, and intend to bring this man's blood upon us. Then Peter and the other apostles answered and said, We ought to obey God rather than men. The God of our fathers raised up Jesus, whom ye slew and hanged on a tree. Him hath God exalted with his right hand to be a Prince and a Savior, for to give repentance to Israel, and forgiveness of sins. And we are his witnesses of these things; and so is also the Holy Spirit, whom God hath given to them that obey him."[2] Here it will be observed first that Jesus after His death was exalted to be a Prince and a Savior. Second, that the apostles and the Holy Spirit bore witness to this fact. "When they heard

[1]Acts v. 17–20. [2]Acts v. 27–32.

this they were cut to the heart, and took counsel to slay them." But Gamaliel, a learned Pharisee, at whose feet Paul had been brought up, made a speech against this counsel. "And to him they agreed: and when they had called the apostles, and beaten them, they commanded that they should not speak in the name of Jesus, and let them go. And they departed from the presence of the council, rejoicing that they were counted worthy to suffer dishonor for His name. And daily in the temple, and in every house, they ceased not to teach and preach Jesus Christ."[1]

[1]Acts v. 40–42.

CHAPTER XIII

THE SEVEN CHOSEN

Seven Deacons Appointed. Stephen's Defense and Martyrdom. Philip Preaching in Samaria.

"In these days, when the number of the disciples was multiplied, there arose a murmuring of the Grecians against the Hebrews, because their widows were neglected in the daily ministration. Then the twelve called the multitude of the disciples unto them, and said, It is not reason that we should leave the word of God, and serve tables. Wherefore, brethren, look ye out among you seven men of good report, full of the Holy Spirit and of wisdom, whom we may appoint over this business. But we will give ourselves continually to prayer, and to the ministry of the word. And the saying pleased the whole multitude: and they chose Stephen, a man full of faith and of the Holy Spirit."[1] And six others, "whom they set before the apostles; and when they had prayed, they laid their hands on them," thus setting them apart for this work. The most noted of these were Stephen and Philip. After this we are informed the "word of God increased, and the number of the disciples multiplied in Jerusalem greatly; and a great company of the

[1]Acts vi. 1-5.

priests were obedient to the faith." The historian keeps constantly before us the rapid growth of the infant Church at Jerusalem. In the first place, he gives us an account of the conversion of about three thousand in a single day, and then we are informed "The Lord added to the church daily those that were being saved." Again, "That the number of them was about five thousand." Again, that the "believers were the more added to the Lord, multitudes both of men and women," and finally, that "the number of the disciples multiplied in Jerusalem greatly, and a great company of priests were obedient to the faith."

The historian now proceeds to give an account of "the great wonders and miracles," which Stephen did among the people, and his disputations with certain foreign Jews who had a synagogue in Jerusalem, but could not "resist the wisdom and the spirit by which he spake," and caused his arrest and "set up false witnesses which said, This man ceaseth not to speak blasphemous words against this holy place, and the law: for we have heard him say, that this Jesus of Nazareth shall destroy this place, and shall change the customs which Moses delivered us. And all that sat in the council, looking steadfastly on him, saw his face as it had been the face of an angel."[1] Then said the Hebrews, "Are these things so?" Stephen here proceeds to make his memorable defense from their own scriptures, beginning with Abraham and closing with the coming and betrayal of Jesus, and concludes

[1]Acts vi. 9–15.

his defense with this terrible rebuke: "Ye stiffnecked and uncircumcised in heart and ears, ye do always resist the Holy Spirit; as your fathers did, so do ye. Which of the prophets have not your fathers persecuted? and they have slain them which showed before of the coming of the Just One; of whom ye have been now the betrayers and murderers. Who have received the law as it was ordained by angels and kept it not. When they heard these things, they were cut to the heart, and they gnashed on him with their teeth. But he, being full of the Holy Spirit, looked up steadfastly into heaven, and saw the glory of God, and Jesus standing on the right hand of God. And he said, Behold, I see the heavens opened, and the Son of man standing on the right hand of God. Then they cried out with a loud voice, and stopped their ears, and ran upon him with one accord, and they cast him out of the city, and stoned him; and the witnesses laid down their clothes at a young man's feet, whose name was Saul. And they stoned Stephen, calling upon God, and saying, Lord Jesus, receive my spirit. And he kneeled down, and cried with a loud voice, Lord, lay not this sin to their charge. And when he had said this, he fell asleep."[1]

Thus died Stephen, looking into heaven and seeing the glory of God and Jesus not "seated"[2] but "standing" in token of deep sympathy for His suffering saint. Thus died Stephen like his Lord, praying for his enemies. Thus he died, the first Christian martyr. He headed the long list of martyrs whose suffering

[1]Acts vii. 51–60.
[2]Luke xxii. 69; Matt. xxvi. 64; Heb. x. 12.

constitutes the darkest page of human history, but whose crowns are the brightest jewels of heaven. He fell asleep in Jesus, the first representative of the martyred millions now under the throne of God who died in living faith and rejoice in ruling glory.

The story of the death of Stephen brings before us for the first time Saul, who was afterward called Paul, and who became the great apostle to the Gentiles, and who is the author of more than one-third of the New Testament. The sacred record says: "And Saul was consenting unto his death. And on that day there arose a great persecution against the church which was at Jerusalem; and they were all scattered abroad throughout the regions of Judea and Samaria, except the apostles. . . . As for Saul, he made havoc of the church, entering house after house, and haling men and women, committed them to prison. They therefore that were scattered abroad went everywhere preaching the word.

Then Philip went down to the city of Samaria and preached Christ unto them. And the people with one accord gave heed unto those things which Philip spake, hearing and seeing the miracles which he did. . . . And there was great joy in that city."[1] It will be remembered that Jesus, when He sent out the twelve apostles, said: "Go not into the way of the Gentiles, and into any city of the Samaritans enter ye not: but go rather to the lost sheep of the house of Israel."[2] But now Philip preached at Samaria. This accords with the Savior's command

[1]Acts viii. 1–8. [2]Matt. x. 5, 6.

after He rose, as recorded in Acts, "But ye shall receive power when the Holy Spirit is come upon you: and ye shall be my witnesses both in Jerusalem, and in all Judea, and in Samaria, and unto the uttermost part of the earth."[1] This was the order in which the gospel was to be preached, but had not yet been preached, to the Gentiles. Returning to the narrative, the historian says: But "a certain man, named Simon, was in the city before, using sorcery and bewitching the people of Samaria, saying that he was some great one. To whom they all gave heed from the least to the greatest, saying, This man is the great power of God. . . . But when they believed Philip preaching the things concerning the kingdom of God, and the name of Jesus Christ, they were baptized, both men and women."[2] Here we have the first use of the word "kingdom" after it was opened on the day of Pentecost. The word kingdom is sometimes used in reference to Christ's present reign on earth, sometimes in reference to His future reign in heaven; persons are spoken of as "translated into the kingdom of his dear Son."[3] Christ is also spoken of as the Judge of the "living and dead at his appearing and kingdom."[4] The kingdom is never spoken of hereafter as it was in the gospels as "approaching," as "at hand." It may now be divided into two great apartments: the present and the future kingdom, the kingdom of grace, and the kingdom of glory. To the faithful subjects of the present "An entrance

[1]Acts i. 8. [2]Acts viii. 9–12.
[3]Col. i. 18. [4]2 Tim. iv. 1.

shall be administered unto you abundantly into the everlasting kingdom of our Lord and Savior Jesus Christ."[1]

When the people of Samaria believed Philip's preaching, "They were baptized, both men and women." Because there is nothing said here in regard to their repentance it is not, therefore, to be presumed that they were impenitent when they were baptized, but we may assume that they turned to God with full purpose of heart.

[1] 2 Pet. i. 11.

CHAPTER XIV

MIRACLES

The Province of Miracles. Necessary to Establish the Gospel. Necessary Only in Age in Which They Occurred. They Have Ceased. Did Not Convey Pardon.

THE genuineness of the conversion of Simon, which immediately follows this, has been disputed and requires careful consideration, but before doing this we call attention to the province of miracles. "Then Simon himself believed also, and when he was baptized he continued with Philip, and wondered, beholding the miracles and signs which were done. Now when the apostles which were at Jerusalem heard that Samaria had received the word of God, they sent unto them Peter and John; who, when they were come down, prayed for them, that they might receive the Holy Spirit: (For as yet he was fallen upon none of them: only they were baptized in the name of the Lord Jesus.) Then laid they their hands on them, and they received the Holy Spirit."[1]

This gift of the Holy Spirit, conferred by prayer and the laying on of the apostles' hands, was a miraculous endowment, as is plainly evident, and it was confined to the apostolic age. The apostles had the power to

[1]Acts viii. 13–17.

work miracles; they conferred that power upon others, but there is no record that those thus endowed could confer it upon a third class. Philip wrought miracles, but not being an apostle, it seems he could not confer this power upon his converts. The church at Rome did not seem to have this power before Paul visited it. This is quite evident and is one of the strongest proofs that it was not established by Peter or any of the apostles. Paul, in writing to the Romans, says: "For I long to see you that I may impart unto you some spiritual gift, to the end ye may be established."[1] If the church at Rome had been founded by Peter, or if it had been founded by any of the apostles, its members would have been endowed with all the spiritual gifts belonging to the Church at that time. The strong presumption is, therefore, that the spiritual gift to which Paul refers is the same that was conferred by Peter and John on the people who "received the word of God" at Samaria, and which could only be conferred by an apostle.

So far as the history shows, miracles were confined to the apostolic age and were designed to cease. If this were not so, people in all ages would have a right to ask, nay, to demand, that the Church continue the working of miracles to prove her divine origin and mission. Miracles were for a confirmation of the testimony, and any proposition once proved is forever proved. The creation, according to the Bible, and so far as science has proven, began in miracle and ends in natural order—in a system of laws. Christianity

[1]Rom. i. 11.

began in miracle, and ends in the harmonious system of the gospel. Paul shows conclusively, in the twelfth and thirteenth chapters of First Corinthians, that miracles were to cease, after summing up all spiritual gifts, diversities of tongues, gifts of healing, miracles, supernatural knowledge, wisdom, and power. He says: "And yet show I unto you a more excellent way. Though I speak with the tongues of men and angels and have not love, I am become as sounding brass or a tinkling cymbal. And though I have the gift of prophecy and understand all mysteries and all knowledge, and though I have all faith so that I could remove mountains, and have not love, I am nothing. . . . Love never faileth: but whether there be prophecies they shall fail; whether there be tongues they shall cease; whether there be knowledge it shall be done away. For we know in part and we prophesy in part, but when that which is perfect is come then that which is in part shall be done away. . . . Now abideth faith, hope, love—these three, but the greatest of these is love."[1] Thus, after the testimony was confirmed, and the great propositions of the gospel were abundantly proved by the miracles, signs, and wonders, they ceased, and "the more excellent way" of faith, hope, and love continued and has been before the world for about nineteen hundred years.

While miracles have ceased, "Faith, Hope, and Love" abide. The Fatherhood of God, the brotherhood of man, the kinship of Jesus, His atonement, intercession, prayer and Providence and not miracles,

[1] 1 Cor. xiii. 1–13.

are the great factors to-day in blessing society and lifting up the race. The Providence of God is general, not special. Not only the facts warrant, but it seems reasonable that special miracles should have been confined to the Apostolic Age, and were for the confirmation of the facts of the gospel. If miracles were to become universal, then the Church of Christ everywhere would have power to heal the sick, cleanse the leper, give sight to the blind, and raise the dead. If no limit were placed upon miracles, especially the resurrection of the dead, would they not have power to prolong life and perpetuate it, and destroy God's natural order and man's volition? But affliction, persecution, suffering, and death were predicted. "It is appointed unto men once to die, and after this cometh the judgment."

That miracles should cease after the establishment of the system of redemption is in accordance with reason as well as revelation. This also harmonizes with God's mode in creation, which began in miracle, but is continued in all departments by natural order or law.

In the first place, the gospel could not have been established without miracles, for a supernatural proposition requires supernatural proof. In the second place, the facts proved were of such a nature that they could not occur over and over again, and the proof was required at the place and in the age in which they occurred. It would be impossible for people in all ages to see Jesus, be with Him in His personal ministry, hear Him talk, witness His death, and attest His burial and resurrection. These facts once proven and recorded were proved and established for all ages and all time. Miracles worked in one age would not be satisfactory proof of facts which occurred in another age. Would miracles worked to-day be satisfactory proof of the resurrection of Jesus which occurred nineteen hundred years ago?

In the third place, if miracles have ceased in the Church, are not worked by its members, if they do not form one department of the gospel, we have no right to expect them in another department. If they can not now be worked to confirm the faith of believers, as they were in the apostolic age, we have no right to infer that they can now be wrought to produce faith, or to convert unbelievers.

Again, we could not expect one of the various religious bodies to-day to possess the power to work miracles. If miracles were an evidence of the Messiahship of Jesus and were confined to the Apostolic Age, it is plainly evident that it would be absurd to expect them to be performed now, or by one of the existing religious bodies and not by the others. If one alone could perform miracles, as they were performed in the primitive Church, it would give it divine sanction, as they would be performed by the authority of Christ, or in His name. Again, if they could be performed by the multitude of religious bodies as they now exist, while they are teaching opposing and contradictory doctrine, it would make God the author of division, contradiction, and confusion, and would prove them all divinely appointed. Nicodemus said, "No man can do these miracles that thou doest, except God be with him."[1]

Again, there is a class of pretended miracles, which are claimed to be performed to-day through the influence of shrines, bones, relics, and things blessed, which is most unreasonable and absurd. If miracles were to follow the Church they would be universal and not local, and only the credulous or ignorant could believe that miracles would be performed in one locality and not in another, on a certain few who alone could reach a sacred spot and be healed by assumed merit in a relic or a shrine, or receive a specific blessing in one temple and not another. "God is no respecter of persons." The gospel promises no blessing on conditions that can be fulfilled by one and not by another, in one place and not in another. Such pretensions are contrary to the whole spirit and genius of Christ's religion.

In the fourth place, after the establishment of the gospel we have no warrant for assuming that God would grant the working of miracles for the conversion of some and not for conversion of others. The great majority of believers in all ages have been converted by hearing the word and testimony concerning Jesus, and did not hear or see anything supernatural to convince them of the truth of Jesus or assure them of pardon. Shall we then believe the testimony of the favored few in regard to their supernatural conversion, and that, too, when they can not confirm it with a single proof? "God is no

[1]John iii. 2.

respecter of persons." When the testimony is presented all may hear, believe, and obey on terms of perfect equality. There is no case of conversion given in any land or any age where the gospel has not been heard. "Faith comes by hearing."

In the fifth place, no one was ever pardoned by a miracle. Miracles were performed by apostles, evangelists, and others to convince persons of the truth of their mission and the facts of the gospel, and to produce obedience, but never to convey pardon. No vision, no angel, no miracle of any kind anywhere ever communicated pardon directly to any one. It is not the province of miracle to pardon, but to direct to the means of pardon.

After the day of Pentecost there are only two miracles recorded which were performed directly or without any human intervention to convince persons who were not believers. These are both connected with the introduction of the gospel to the Gentile world. The first one is where the Lord spoke to Paul, and the other is where the angel spoke to Cornelius. But the Lord did not pardon Paul when He appeared to him on the way, nor did the angel pardon Cornelius. The Lord told Paul to "Arise and go into Damascus, and there it shall be told thee of all things which are appointed for thee to do."[1] The angel said to Cornelius: "Send men to Joppa and call for Simon, whose surname is Peter, who shall tell thee words whereby thou and all thy house shall be saved."[2] Remarkable as the fact may seem to some, after the death of Christ,

[1]Acts xxii. 10. [2]Acts xi. 13, 14.

in the age of miracles (which ceased with the apostles), there is no divine record that there was ever given directly by Jesus, God, angel, or the Holy Spirit, the blessing of pardon to any son or daughter of Adam's race, but all had to comply with the established terms of pardon in order to receive the blessing. This is the truth of history.

Finally, the conclusion to be drawn from all this is that those who look to dreams, visions, or even angels as speaking peace and pardon to their souls, have no divine warrant that pardon ever was or ever will be conveyed in such a manner. If an angel of light should approach and preach or speak pardon to a sinner, his evidence of sins forgiven would be infinitely below the evidence of those who have obeyed the requirements of the gospel, for such rest their faith on a sure foundation, not on dreams, visions, nor even the voice of an angel, but the word of God which liveth and abideth forever—on words which shall finally judge them. Jesus says, "The word that I have spoken, the same shall judge him in the last day." There can be no stronger evidence of pardon given than to be declared pardoned by the King and the Judge. These conclusions turn our attention back from the modern abuses and wonder-workers "to the law and to the testimony. If they speak not according to this word, it is because there is no light in them."[1] Paul says: "Though we or an angel from heaven preached any other gospel unto you than that which we have preached unto you, let him be accursed."[2]

[1]Isa. viii. 20. [2]Gal. i. 8.

CHAPTER XV

CONVERSIONS

Simon the Sorcerer. The Conversion of the Ethiopian. The Place of Baptism. The Divine Confession.

HAVING called attention to the subject of miracles as connected both with the Church and conversion, we now return to the case of Simon. "And when Simon saw that through the laying on of the apostles' hands the Holy Spirit was given, he offered them money, saying, Give me also this power, that on whomsoever I lay hands he may receive the Holy Spirit. But Peter said unto him, Thy money perish with thee, because thou hast thought that the gift of God may be purchased with money: Thou hast neither part nor lot in this matter, for thy heart is not right in the sight of God. Repent, therefore, of this thy wickedness and pray God if perhaps the thought of thine heart may be forgiven thee. For I perceive that thou art in the gall of bitterness and in the bond of iniquity. Then answered Simon and said, Pray ye to the Lord for me that none of these things which ye have spoken come upon me."[1] This case has sometimes been cited as showing that baptism is not connected with the forgiveness of sins.

[1]Acts viii. 18-24.

But this proves too much, for it lies with equal force against faith, as we are informed that "Simon himself also believed, and when he was baptized he continued with Philip and wondered, beholding the miracles and signs which were done." If he was a true believing penitent when he was baptized, there can be no doubt in regard to his pardon. It will be borne in mind that Peter only charges him with the one sin, and enjoins upon him repentance and prayer, which is the law of pardon for erring Christians. He says: "Repent, therefore, of this thy wickedness, and pray God if perhaps the thought"—not the thoughts, but the thought—"of thy heart may be forgiven thee. For I perceive that thou art in the gall"—not yet in, but —"in the gall of bitterness and the bond of iniquity." While the prevailing opinion is that Simon was a hypocrite and had not been pardoned or converted, yet the history as here given does not prove that such was the fact. The subsequent history of Simon, as given by early writers, in regard to his great wickedness, his following and encountering Peter, and his violent death, is involved in difficulty, contradiction, and must be considered unreliable.

We are next informed, that "They, when they had testified and preached the word of the Lord, returned to Jerusalem, and preached the gospel in many villages of the Samaritans."[1] Here follows the story of Philip's preaching to "a man of Ethiopia," which we will transcribe in full as showing the use of miracles, as well as how the gospel was preached, believed, and

[1]Acts viii. 25.

obeyed. "And the angel of the Lord spake unto Philip, saying, Arise, and go toward the south unto the way that goeth down from Jerusalem unto Gaza. which is desert. And he arose and went: and, behold, a man of Ethiopia, an eunuch of great authority under Candace, queen of the Ethiopians, who had the charge of all her treasure, and had come to Jerusalem for to worship, was returning, and sitting in his chariot read Esaias the prophet. Then the Spirit said unto Philip, Go near, and join thyself to this chariot. And Philip ran thither to him, and heard him read the prophet Esaias and said, Understandest thou what thou readest? And he said, How can I, except some man should guide me? And he entreated Philip to come up and sit with him. And the place of the Scripture which he was reading was this: He was led as a sheep to the slaughter; and as a lamb dumb before his shearer, so he opened not his mouth. In his humiliation his judgment was taken away; and who shall declare his generation? for his life is taken from the earth. And the eunuch answered Philip and said, I pray thee of whom speaketh the prophet this? of himself or of some other man? Then Philip opened his mouth and began at the same scripture and preached unto him Jesus. And as they went on their way they came unto a certain water, and the eunuch said, See, here is water, what doth hinder me to be baptized? And Philip said, If thou believest with all thy heart thou mayest. And he answered and said, I believe that Jesus Christ is the Son of God. And he commanded the chariot to stand still: and they went down both into the water, both Philip and the eunuch, and he baptized him. And when they were come up out of the water, the spirit of the Lord caught away Philip, and the eunuch saw him no more: and he went on his way rejoicing. But Philip was found at Azotus: and passing through he preached in all the cities till he came to Cæsarea."[1]

The first thing to be noted in this case is that the angel of the Lord spake unto Philip directing him where to go; and when he had come to the place the Spirit said, "join thyself to this chariot." Thus we find that here the mission of the angel of the Lord and the Spirit was to bring the preacher to the hearer, and not to pardon the sinner. Again, it will be observed, that Philip began from the prophecies to preach Jesus. This rule was followed in the days of the apostles when preaching to the Jews or to the proselytes to the Jewish faith. The person here addressed was either a Jew or a proselyte to the Jewish faith. He preached Jesus. What are we to understand by this expression? We are informed "Moses of old time hath in every city those who preached him, being read in the synagogues every sabbath day."[2] Thus to preach Moses was to teach his law. To preach Jesus was to teach the requirements of His gospel. It was to tell the story of the cross, to present in full the terms of His amnesty proclamation; the requirements of Him who had a right to teach and direct and rule and reign as the Prophet, Priest, and King. Again, it is evident that in preaching Jesus he

[1]Acts viii. 26-40. [2]Acts xv. 21.

preached baptism. Nor can Jesus be preached without preaching baptism. Notwithstanding we may be disposed to deem it of light importance, or non-essential, yet it was taught by Christ, enjoined by Him in His great commission. It was required by Peter at the opening of the gospel age. After Pentecost it is either stated or implied in every case of pardon, and no unbaptized person is ever addressed as pardoned, sanctified, or saved. The epistles addressed to the Corinthians speak of them as having been baptized. And there is no record of any one anywhere having been admitted into the Church of Christ without baptism. While it is the only ordinance in the gospel uniting the sacred names of the Father, Son, and Holy Spirit, yet being only a part of a perfect system it may not be deemed more important than hearing, believing, or repenting, but is as universally enjoined and implied as any of these terms of pardon. After hearing Philip preach, the eunuch evidently understood baptism to be the consummating act in receiving Christ; hence he asked to be baptized and immediately went on his way rejoicing.

It is important to note that here we have the first case of a responsive confession of faith in Jesus required immediately before baptism. Philip said unto him, "If thou believest with all thy heart thou mayest." And he answered and said, "I believe that Jesus Christ is the Son of God." While this confession of the eunuch is considered an interpolation, we have the following proof that such was the practise. Christ says, "Every one therefore who shall confess me before men, him will I also confess before my Father who is in heaven."[1] Paul, in speaking of the righteousness of faith in contrast with the righteousness of the law, says: "If thou shalt confess with thy mouth the Lord Jesus, and shalt believe in thy heart that God hath raised him from the dead, thou shalt be saved. For with the heart man believeth unto righteousness, and with the mouth confession is made unto salvation."[2] Again he says to Timothy: "Thou hast professed a good profession before many witnesses." "I charge thee in the sight of God . . . and of Jesus Christ, who before Pontius Pilate witnessed the good profession" or confession.[3] Again, when Christ asked Peter, "Who say ye that I am?" he answering said, "Thou art the Christ, the Son of the living God." And Jesus said, "Upon this rock"—this truth confessed—"I will build my church."[4]

The confession that "Jesus is the Christ, the Son of the living God," is the great truth of the Christian religion. Around this, as the center, all things else in the system revolve. This embraces the whole system. The Son of God is as truly the Center of the Christian system as the physical sun is the center of our solar system. If a person were to confess that the sun is the center of the solar system, and the light and the heat of the system, it would then be folly to ask, "Do you believe that it lights all the planets of the solar system, together with all the great divisions of the

[1] Matt. x. 32. [2] Rom. x. 9, 10.
[3] 1 Tim. vi. 13. [4] Matt. xvi. 13–18.

earth, such as Europe, Asia, and America?" for the very plain reason that he confessed all in the first great proposition. So in confessing Christ the person confesses Him in His whole official character, as the Prophet, Priest, and King. As Prophet to teach, as Priest to atone, and as King to reign, as "There is no other name given under heaven or among men whereby we must be saved." There is no other confession required by Christ in order to participate in His great salvation. It is the good confession—the divine confession, and the only authorized confession. It is a confession that all will finally make either in hope or fear, "for we shall all stand before the judgment seat of Christ. For it is written, As I live, saith the Lord, every knee shall bow to me, and every tongue shall confess to God."[1] Christ made it and died, His followers make it and live. It is the divine creed, the foundation of the Christian Church, and the only one which may rightfully be enjoined upon subjects entering Christ's Church in any age or any land or by any authority. No man, no church, has any divine warrant for demanding more of a penitent believer in order to be baptized or received into church membership, and no man or church has a right to require less.

[1]Rom. xiv. 10, 11.

CHAPTER XVI

SAUL AND HIS CONVERSION

Saul of Tarsus. Called to be an Apostle. Are People now Converted like Saul?

THE next case of pardon is that of Saul of Tarsus, afterward called Paul, the Apostle. This is the most important conversion recorded after the death of Jesus. It is important, not only on account of the greatness of the person, but as an example of pardon and as the beginning of the history of a person showing the most untiring zeal and devotion in the cause of the Master during a long life of the greatest labors and suffering every inscribed upon the rolls of time. He is emphatically our apostle—the apostle to the Gentiles. He not only labored more abundantly than all the apostles, but to him the Gentile world owes more than to all the rest.[1] No one man ever lived on earth having wrought such changes and having made such deep impression on succeeding ages. His conversion is recorded in the 9th chapter of Acts, and repeated in the 22d and 26th chapters and referred to in the Epistles. Taken altogether we have a complete history of this great man's change from Judaism to Christianity, and the marvelous events which called him to the apostleship and to the light and liberty of the gospel.

[1]Acts xxii. 21, xviii. 9, xxiii. 11, xvi. 6, xxvii. 23; 2 Tim. iv. 17.

If we except the dying vision of Stephen and the vision of Ananias and the vision of John on Patmos, Saul is the only one recorded to whom Jesus appeared after His ascension. He appeared to him four times. He called him personally to be an apostle and sent him far hence to the Gentiles. He spoke to him "in a vision by night," in Corinth. He stood by him when persecuted at Jerusalem and said, "Be of good cheer, Paul, for as thou hast testified of me in Jerusalem so must thou bear witness also at Rome." His divine mission or ambassadorship was recognized by the inspired apostles at Jerusalem. He was filled with and directed by the Holy Spirit. The angel of God stood by him on the tempest-tossed sea, and gave him the lives of all who sailed with him on its dark and troubled waters. And when at Rome at this first answer before Nero his friends forsook him, yet the Lord stood with him and strengthened him that he might continue to preach "that all the Gentiles might hear," and he was delivered "out of the mouth of the lion."

We come now to the record of his conversion. The sacred historian says: "And Saul, yet breathing out threatenings and slaughter against the disciples of the Lord, went unto the high priest, and desired of him letters to Damascus to the synagogues, that if he found any of this way, whether they were men or women, he might bring them bound unto Jerusalem. And as he journeyed he came near to Damascus, and suddenly there shined around about him a light from heaven."[1] Paul informs us that this light was at mid-

[1]Acts ix. 1–3.

day, and that it was "above the brightness of the sun, shining round about me and them that journeyed with me. And when we were all fallen to the earth I heard a voice speaking to me and saying in the Hebrew tongue, Saul, Saul, why persecutest thou me? . . . And I said, Who art thou, Lord? and He said, I am Jesus whom thou persecutest; but arise, stand upon thy feet, for I have appeared unto thee for this purpose, to make thee a minister and a witness both of things which thou hast seen and the things in which I will appear unto thee, delivering thee from the people and the Gentiles unto whom now I send thee, to open their eyes and to turn them from darkness to light, and from the power of Satan unto God, that they may receive forgiveness of sins and inheritance among them which are sanctified by faith that is in me."[1] "And I said, What shall I do, Lord? and the Lord said unto me, Arise and go into Damascus, and there it shall be told thee of all things which are appointed for thee to do. And one Ananias, a devout man, according the the law, having a good report of all the Jews which dwell there, came to me and said to me, Brother Saul, receive thy sight."[2] This Ananias was a disciple, and to him the Lord said in a vision, "Ananias. And he said, Behold I am here, Lord. And the Lord said unto him, Arise and go into the street which is called Straight, and inquire in the house of Judas for one called Saul of Tarsus, for behold he prayeth."[3] Paul now says he "came unto me and

[1]Acts xxvi. 13–18. [2]Acts xxii. 10–12. [3]Acts ix. 10, 11.

stood and said unto me, Brother Saul, receive thy sight. And the same hour I looked up upon him and he said, The God of our Fathers hath chosen thee that thou shouldst know his will and see that Just One, and shouldst hear the voice of his mouth. For thou shalt be his witness unto all men of what thou hast seen and heard. And now, why tarriest thou? arise, and be baptized and wash away thy sins, calling on the name of the Lord." [1]

These quotations give the leading facts in Paul's conversion. We will now call attention to them in their proper order. It is important to note these facts well, as many in modern times claim to have been pardoned as Saul was. The first fact of significance was the light which shone around him and those that journeyed with him. The remarkable feature in regard to this light is that it was seen at midday and that it was "above the brightness of the sun." Those who claim to have seen such a light, we believe, universally lay the scene in the darkness of the night, at which time persons are liable to see brilliant and unexpected lights which may result from natural causes. But not only was the light seen by Saul at midday, and above the brightness of the sun, but it was seen by those who journeyed with him, and they all fell to the earth and Saul arose from the ground a blind man. No man converted in modern times can relate such experience attested by witnesses. The next fact is that the Lord appeared to Saul. There is no other case recorded, after the ascen-

[1] Acts xxii. 13–16.

sion of Jesus, in which He appeared to an unpardoned person. This may be considered a remarkable fact when viewed in the light of modern teaching and practise. How many prayers have been offered appealing to Jesus to "come down now," and this, too, when Paul, the only one to whom the ascended Savior ever appeared before he was pardoned, speaking by apostolic authority on this subject, expressly forbids such petitions, and assigns the reason for this prohibition. He says: "Say not in thy heart who shall ascend into heaven (that is to bring Christ down), or who shall descend into the deep (that is to bring Christ up again from the dead). But what saith it. The word is nigh thee, even in thy mouth and in thy heart; that is, the word of faith which we preach. That if thou shalt confess with thy mouth the Lord Jesus, and shalt believe in thy heart that God hath raised him from the dead, thou shalt be saved. For with the heart man believeth unto righteousness and with the mouth confession is made unto salvation."[1] It would seem from this that Paul anticipated "that in the latter time some shall depart from the faith,"[2] and that they would even call upon Christ to leave His mediatorial throne. Hence he warns them not to conceive such an idea in their heart, but presents the all-sufficiency of "the word of faith, which we preach," and declares the divine confession of this faith—that is, the gospel—which he has delivered unto them to be "the power of God unto salvation."[3]

[1]Rom. x. 6–10. [2]1 Tim. iv. 1. [3]Rom. i. 16.

If we are forbidden the thought of calling "Christ down from above," why then did He appear to Saul? The reason is ample. The Lord said, "I have appeared unto thee for this purpose, to make thee a minister and a witness." He appeared for the purpose of making him an apostle. Not only so, but to make him an apostle to the Gentiles. He could not have been a witness nor have filled the apostolic office without the Lord appearing to him. That he understood it thus is evident from the fact that he referred to it as a proof of his apostleship when he says, "Am I not an apostle? Have I not seen Jesus Christ our Lord?"[1] The primary object of the appearance of Jesus to Saul was to make him an apostle, and not to convert him. No one therefore has a right to expect the Lord to appear unto him unless he expects to be made an apostle as Saul was. If Jesus had an apostle to call now, no doubt He would appear personally and call him. But as Paul completed the apostolic list no one has been called since. The record of nineteen hundred years may be searched in vain for a like example.

The next important consideration in this case is that the Lord did not pardon Saul as He had pardoned others before His death. Nor did He even tell him what he should do in order to be pardoned, but said to him to go into Damascus and "there it shall be told thee of all things which are appointed for thee to do." This gives us the important information that there were "things appointed for Saul to do." Now, were these things appointed especially for Saul, or

[1] 1 Cor. ix. 1.

were they things required alike of all who would obtain the forgiveness of sins? Was Saul, who was called to be an apostle, required to do more, or permitted to do less, than any other sinner who sought pardon through the crucified Savior? Let the sequel answer. After Saul had arrived in Damascus, we are next informed that the Lord appeared to Ananias in a vision and said: "Arise, and go into the street that is called Straight, and inquire in the house of Judas for one called Saul of Tarsus, for, behold, he prayeth." Visions and voices, angels and the Holy Spirit directed Peter, Philip and others, but the Lord Himself called Saul and directed Ananias to go to him. When Ananias came he said to Saul: "The Lord Jesus that appeared unto thee in the way as thou comest has sent me that thou mightest receive thy sight and be filled with the Holy Spirit." It will be observed here that the Holy Spirit was not imparted to Paul by Jesus, for after Ananias came to him and told him "thou shalt be his witness unto all men of what thou hast seen and heard," he had not yet received his sight nor the Holy Spirit, but was still unpardoned, and, like the "man of Ethiopia," he had to comply with the last act appointed for him to do before "he could go on his way rejoicing" or "receive meat and be strengthened." Hence, Ananias said to him, "Arise and be baptized and wash away thy sins, calling on the name of the Lord."[1]

[1]Acts xxii. 16.

CHAPTER XVII

WORK OF THE APOSTLE PAUL

Saul and His Pardon. An Estimate of His Wondrous Life.

THIS brings us to the final inquiry, Did Saul comply with the law of pardon heretofore established? Did he believe, repent, and be baptized before he was pardoned? That he believed is evident from the fact that he asked the Lord, "What wilt thou have me to do?" That he repented is evident from his submission to the voice of the Lord and his humble attitude in continuous prayer. Now, if faith, repentance, and prayer complete the terms of pardon, as preached and practised by many in modern times, why was not Saul pardoned on these terms? Had he not faith? Did he not repent and pray to God earnestly? Certainly. No one could give stronger evidence of true faith and sincere repentance than the believing, sorrowing, praying Saul. Why did not Ananias say to him, as many would now say, "Pray on, brother Saul; the Lord will hear and bless you." "Only believe on the Lord, give up thy sins." "Oh Lord, come and speak peace to his soul." "Come down, Lord, come just now"? Not a word do we hear of all this, but Ananias said to the believing, penitent, praying Saul, "Why tarriest thou? Arise and be baptized and wash away thy sins, calling on the name of the Lord." So far as the record shows Saul complied with the terms enjoined upon all; that is, with the law of pardon as given by Jesus just before He ascended, as enjoined by Peter on the day of Pentecost at the opening of the gospel age, and as preached by Philip at Samaria. This law, originated by Jesus and expressed by His ambassadors, was perfect, easily comprehended by the ignorant, and equally adapted to the wise. It was competent alike to forgive the murderers and betrayers of Christ, to pardon a persecutor like Saul, and to save a pious person like Cornelius.

Finally, in summing up the history of the pardon of Saul, we will observe that, before any one can justly claim to be pardoned as Saul was, it is essential for the Lord to appear to him; that he should see a light at midday above the brightness of the sun; that others should also see it and fall to the ground with him; that he should be stricken with blindness; that he should be directed by the Lord to go to a place where it should be told him things appointed for him to do; that in going he should be led by the hand of others; that after arriving the Lord should appear in a vision to a "disciple" giving directions where to find him; that he should have fasted three days and be praying; that the minister, on arriving, should work a miracle, restore his sight, and give him instructions about things appointed for him to do, and all this, too, before he is pardoned. And that, finally he should have to "arise and be baptized and wash away his sins, calling on the name of the Lord."

Having now given the history of the pardon of Paul, it may be well to pause for a moment and consider some facts connected with the life of this great man. He was born in Tarsus, a city of Cilicia, a city renowned as a place of education and commerce. He was brought up at the feet of Gamaliel, one of the most learned Jews of his age. He was of the tribe of Benjamin, a Pharisee, and a Hebrew of the Hebrews. As touching the law, he was blameless. While he was a Jew he was also a Roman citizen, and that, too, in an age when it was said that it was greater to be a citizen of Rome than to be a king. In an age when one before whom he was brought for trial said, "With a great sum obtained I this freedom," Paul said to him, "I was freeborn." Saul was present and consented unto the death of Stephen, who was the first Christian martyr. He was then a young man, for the rioters who stoned Stephen laid down their clothes at the feet of a young man named Saul. Little did he then anticipate thirty years of toil and labor and suffering in the same cause for which Stephen died, and that finally he should share a similar fate, cheered by the same glorious hope. After Saul was pardoned, he began to preach the faith which he had destroyed. It is a remarkable fact that Saul was the only person pardoned after the death of Jesus, the circumstances of whose pardon are given, of whom we have any subsequent history in the New Testament. It is true Paul mentions some in his epistles whom he had baptized, but all those, the history of whose pardon is given, do not appear again in the sacred story. Not a page of the New Testament was composed by any one nor a paragraph given of their history. But Paul, who was born out of due time (as an apostle), aside from Christ, is not only the author of more of the New Testament than any one, but the most important human character in sacred history. As the events connected with the conversion of Saul were more wonderful than those connected with the conversion of any one man, so was his subsequent history the most marked. In fact, the wonderful events connected with his call would lead us to anticipate the greatest results from his calling. As the birth of Jesus was supernatural, so was His life superhuman. The miracle of His birth would lead us to anticipate the greatness of His life, and the matchless events of His life confirmed the wonders of His birth, and the story of His birth and life are both confirmed to us by the still greater events connected with His death. And we are fully assured of all the facts connected with His existence from the manger to the cross, and from the cross to the crown, by the mighty influence which they have exerted upon the world for more than nineteen hundred years.

So with Paul. If the Lord called him and committed to him the greatest mission of the ages, giving him the world as his field, and the ingathering of the Gentiles as his harvest, we may expect his influence to be unequaled by man and only surpassed by the Lord Himself. In this we will not be disappointed. For as the events of his conversion were great, they were exceeded by the greater events of his life. We search history in vain for his superior. In fact, nowhere on its pages do we find his equal. The Gentile world owes to him, as to no other man, a debt of gratitude which increases as the ages advance. Paul was the greatest missionary preacher of all time. In his missionary journeys, extending over Asia and Europe, he planted most of the churches recorded in the New Testament. He opposed the binding of the old covenant on his new converts. He obtained a decree from the apostles and church at Jerusalem freeing the Gentiles from the Jewish law, carrying it with him when he revisited the churches. In accordance with this decree he taught that the Jewish law was "passing away" or "abolished,"[1] and gives us the broad distinction between it and the gospel, showing the incompleteness of the one and the completeness of the other. Yet after all his struggles in behalf of the liberty of the gospel, his life was harassed, his converts were troubled, and his labors were embarrassed by Judaizing teachers who sought to entangle his converts in the "yoke of bondage." But he proclaimed the oneness of the race, the equality of the Jews and Gentiles, male and female, bond and free, the unity of the Church and the oneness of its members.

Without the history of Paul's life and teaching the Church would be incomplete as an organization. While Peter speaks of elders among them commanding them to feed the flock, yet before this Paul ordained elders in a number of churches and instructed them in their duties, and later on he wrote to Titus to ap-

[1] 2 Cor. iii. 13.

point elders in every city and to both Timothy and Titus he gave their qualifications. He speaks of deacons and their duties, of ministers or evangelists and their work, thus giving a full list of the officers of Christ's Church.

He reasoned as a sage, taught more wisely than any philosopher, reproved like a prophet, and advised like a father. He denounced divisions, opposed heretics, warned his brethren, rebuked Peter, foretold the perilous times of the future, and revealed the rise, progress, and overthrow of the Man of Sin. In his life and teaching the whole range of Christian obligation for all classes, races, and people is presented more full, perfect, and complete than by any other apostle, evangelist, or teacher under Christ. His life is a model unequaled in the history of man. He trod in the footsteps of the Master, and devoted his body "a living sacrifice" for the good of the human race. He said, "I will most gladly spend and be spent for your souls."[1] He alone of all has said, "Be ye followers of me, even as I also am of Christ."[2]

One-third of the New Testament is given to his life and epistles. He was, indeed, the great apostle to the Gentiles and, truly, he "labored more abundantly than they all." Time will be found too short to tell the story or reveal the results of his life, but away out in the cycles of eternity they will be unfolded. As a man he is the greatest moral hero of earth. His labors and sufferings, his troubles and trials, his conflict and triumph are the greatest recorded in the annals of

[1] 2 Cor. xii. 15. [2] 1 Cor. xi. 1.

time. He is great whether preaching the gospel, scourged as a felon, stoned by a mob, or refusing worship as a god. He is great whether standing in the midst of Mars Hill proclaiming the unity of the human race, or in Corinth glorying in the Cross of Christ, whether in the hovels of the lowly he addresses the poor or in a kingly palace Felix trembles when he reasons of temperance, righteousness, and judgment to come. Great whether fighting wild beasts at Ephesus, defending himself before a Jewish council or a Roman court. He is great whether in perils on land or tempest-tossed on sea. He was great and mighty in labor, but greater still when we hear him for the last time in Rome making his final defense before Nero. At his first answer no man stood with him, but all forsook him, yet the Lord delivered him out of the mouth of the lion, and he prayed for his cowardly friends.

Solomon at the close of his life said, "How dieth the wise man? As a fool. . . . I hated all my labor . . . seeing I must leave it"[1] to another man; "and who knoweth whether he will be a wise man or a fool." But Paul's last words have come ringing down the ages, and will go on and on until they die away on the shores of eternity: "I have fought a good fight, . . . I have kept the faith, henceforth there is laid up for me a crown."[2] Rest, Paul, in peace in the stormless beyond—in the land of the fadeless and deathless—the wisest, greatest, and best of the race—the apostle, prophet, and martyr of God.

[1]Eccles. ii. 16–19. [2]2 Tim. iv. 7.

CHAPTER XVIII

CALL OF THE GENTILES

The First Case of Gentile Pardon. Cornelius and His Household. The Appearance of the Angel to Cornelius and the Vision of Peter. Peter's Sermon to the Gentiles.

AFTER Saul was pardoned he preached Christ at Damascus, but when the Jews took counsel "to kill him" he escaped from Damascus and went to Jerusalem, where he attempted "to join himself to the disciples, but they were all afraid of him and believed not that he was a disciple. But Barnabas took him and brought him to the apostles,"[1] relating the circumstance of his conversion, "and how he had preached boldly at Damascus in the name of Jesus." Here again "he spake boldly in the name of the Lord Jesus and disputed against the Grecians, but they went about to slay him, which, when the brethren knew, they brought him down to Cæsarea and sent him forth to Tarsus. Then had the churches rest throughout all Judea and Galilee and Samaria, and were edified; and walking in the fear of the Lord and in the comfort of the Holy Spirit were multiplied."[2]

Here for a time Saul disappears from view and Peter comes to the front. We are informed that when Peter had "passed throughout all quarters, he came

[1]Acts ix. 26, 27. [2]Acts ix. 29–31.

down also to the saints which dwelt at Lydda." Here he healed a man named Æneas who had been afflicted with the palsy eight years. "Peter said unto him, Æneas, Jesus Christ maketh thee whole, arise and make thy bed. And he arose immediately. And all that dwelt at Lydda and Saron saw him, and turned to the Lord." We need not here remark on what is meant by turning to the Lord, but will only observe that it was to receive Him, believe in and obey His requirements. "If ye love me ye will keep my commandments." While Peter was at Lydda there was a woman named Tabitha, a disciple, of Joppa, who being sick died, "whom when they had washed they laid in an upper chamber, and the disciples sent for Peter, who when he had come entered the upper chamber where the body was: and all the widows stood by him weeping, and showing the coats and garments which Dorcas made while she was with them. But Peter put them all forth and kneeled down and prayed; and turning to the body said, Tabitha, arise. And she opened her eyes, and when she saw Peter, she sat up and he gave her his hand and lifted her up, and when he had called the saints and widows presented her alive, and it was known throughout Joppa and many believed in the Lord."[1] In both these cases a miracle seems to be the occasion of the people "believing or turning to the Lord." But the miracles were not wrought upon the person converted, but upon others, and thus produced the faith or caused the turning. It is worthy of notice that only one

[1]Acts ix. 39–42.

person was restored to life by Peter, and one by Paul, so far as the inspired record shows, after the death of Christ.

While Peter tarried at Joppa he was called in a miraculous manner to open the door of the gospel of grace to the Gentiles. The gospel had now been preached, according to the command of Christ, "In Jerusalem, in all Judea, in Samaria," and now began, for the first, its proclamation to the people embraced in the expression, "unto the uttermost parts of the earth."

This brings us to the consideration of the gospel as preached to and received by Cornelius and those assembled with him. Peter, on the day of Pentecost, opened the kingdom to the Jews, and notwithstanding the commission given by Christ "Go ye into all the world and preach the gospel to every creature," and His final directions just before He ascended, yet a series of miracles seem still to be required to convince Peter that the Gentiles were not "common or unclean," but convinced, he, having the keys, opened the door of the kingdom to the Gentiles. It will be borne in mind that this was eight years after the gospel had been preached to the Jews, in Jerusalem, and it had spread throughout all Judea, and in Samaria, but was yet understood to be confined to the Jews, for when the apostles and brethren that were in Judea heard that the Gentiles had also received the word of God they "contended with him (Peter) saying, Thou wentest in to men uncircumcised, and didst eat with them." And Peter had to rehearse the whole matter, and "when they heard these things they held their peace and glorified God, saying, Then hath God also to the Gentiles granted repentance."[1]

The first great epoch of the gospel was its presentation to, and reception by, the Jews. The second was its proclamation to the Gentiles. The first case in the second epoch is one in which the Gentile world has been, and always will be, deeply interested. It is important and demands our most careful consideration. It is worthy of note that this case of Cornelius, like that of Saul, is first recorded by the historian and repeated twice thereafter by Peter.[2] So that these two important cases, both connected with the Gentiles, one giving an account of the calling of their apostle, and the other their first reception of the gospel, are each recorded three times. In contrast with this it may be stated that there is no other case of pardon given in the New Testament the circumstances of which are repeated. These examples showed to the Jews that the Gentiles were to be received into "the fulness of the blessing of the Gospel of Christ." And they furnish examples for all time showing how the first persons connected with the preaching of salvation to the Gentiles were pardoned. In regard to this last case, as already intimated, the record is not only interesting, but full. We will therefore quote freely: "There was a certain man in Cæsarea called Cornelius, a centurion, of the band called the Italian band, a devout man and one that feared God with all his house, which gave much alms to the people and

[1]Acts xi. 18. [2]Acts x., xi., xv.

prayed to God always. He saw in a vision, evidently about the ninth hour of the day, an angel of God coming in to him saying, unto him, Cornelius. When he looked on him he was afraid, and said, What is it, Lord? And he said unto him, Thy prayers and thine alms are come up for a memorial before God. And now send men to Joppa and call for Simon, whose surname is Peter. He lodgeth with one Simon, a tanner, whose house is by the seaside. He shall tell thee what thou oughtest to do." Or, as Peter says, "Words whereby thou and all thy house shall be saved."[1]

While these men were on their journey to Joppa, "Peter went up upon the housetop to pray about the sixth hour, and he became very hungry and would have eaten, but while they made ready he fell into a trance, and saw heaven opened, and a certain vessel descending unto him, as it had been a great sheet knit at the four corners and let down to the earth: wherein were all manner of four-footed beasts of the earth, and wild beasts, and creeping things, and fowls of the air. And there came a voice to him, saying, Arise, Peter, kill and eat. But Peter said, Not so, Lord, for I have never eaten anything that is common or unclean. And the voice spake unto him again the second time, What God hath cleansed, that call thou not common. This was done thrice, and the vessel was received up again unto heaven. . . . While Peter thought on the vision the Spirit said to him, Behold three men seek thee. Arise, therefore, and get thee down, and go with them,

[1]Acts xi. 14.

doubting nothing, for I have sent them."[1] After he went down and inquired the reason of their coming, they made known their mission by stating that "Cornelius, the centurion, a just man, and one that feareth God, and of good report among all the nations of the Jews, was warned from God by an holy angel to send for thee into his house, and to hear words of thee. Then called he them in and lodged them; and on the morrow Peter went forth with them and certain brethren from Joppa accompanied him. (Six brethren.) And on the morrow they entered into Cæsarea. And Cornelius waited for them, and had called together his kinsmen and near friends. And as Peter was coming in, Cornelius met him, and fell down at his feet, and worshiped him. But Peter took him up saying, Stand up; I myself am a man. And as he talked with him he went in and found many that were come together. And he said unto them, We know how that it is an unlawful thing for a man that is a Jew to keep company with or come unto one of another nation; but God hath showed me that I should not call any man common or unclean."[2] Cornelius now relates the marvelous manner in which he was led to call for Peter, and concludes by saying: "Now, therefore, we are all here present before God, to hear all things that are commanded thee of God. Then Peter opened his mouth and said, Of a truth I perceive that God is no respecter of persons. But in every nation he that feareth him and worketh righteousness is accepted with him."[3] Peter here preaches Jesus to these Gen-

[1]Acts x. 9–20. [2]Acts x. 22–28. [3]Acts x. 33–35.

tiles, giving the great events of His wonderful life from the baptism of John until His death on the cross, and His resurrection from the dead and appointment by God to be the "judge of the living and the dead," and concludes by saying: "To him give all the prophets witness, that through his name whosoever believeth in him shall receive remission of sins. While Peter was yet speaking these words the Holy Spirit fell on all who heard the word." Peter in rehearsing this, says: "The Holy Spirit fell on them as on us at the beginning. Then remembered I the Word of the Lord how that he said, John indeed baptized in water but ye shall be baptized in the Holy Spirit. If therefore God gave them the like gift as he did unto us, who believed on the Lord Jesus Christ, what was I that I could withstand God?"[1] Again, he says: "And God, who knoweth the hearts, bears them witness, giving them the Holy Spirit, even as he did unto us and put no difference between us and them, purifying their hearts by faith."[2] But we are informed that "those of the circumcision who believed" were astonished, as many as came with Peter, because that on the Gentiles also was poured out the gift of the Holy Spirit, for they heard them speak with tongues and magnify God. Then answered Peter, Can any man forbid water that these should not be baptized who have received the Holy Spirit, as well as we? And he commanded them to be baptized in the name of the Lord. Then prayed they him to tarry certain days."[3]

[1]Acts xi. 15–17. [2]Acts xv. 8, 9. [3]Acts x. 45–48.

CHAPTER XIX

WHAT SHALL I DO TO BE SAVED?

Morality and Devotion not Sufficient. Obedience to Christ's Authority Required. Baptism of the Holy Spirit—the Gentile and the Jew.

HAVING quoted thus fully from the sacred narrative of this important case, we will now call attention to the leading features in the record. Cornelius was a Roman centurion, a captain of one hundred men, and was stationed at Cæsarea. He was a devout man and feared God with all his house. He was a benevolent and a praying man. He seemed to be well acquainted with the Jewish religion and worshiped God according to its requirements and was "Of good report among all the nation of the Jews."[1] The vision he saw was in daytime, at three o'clock in the afternoon. In this vision he saw an angel who directed him to send for Peter, saying, "He shall tell thee what thou oughtest to do," or, as Peter puts it, "Shall tell thee words whereby thou and all thy house shall be saved." It will be observed that the angel did not preach the gospel to him, but told him that Peter would tell him words whereby he and all his house should be saved. Here again we find that salvation is couched in words. This is in harmony with

[1]Acts x. 22.

"The things appointed" for Saul to do, and is what he afterward called "The word of faith which we preach," and is in accordance with the teaching of Christ when He said, the "Words that I have spoken the same shall judge him in the last day." Here we learn the important lesson that there was something more required under Christ than devotion, benevolence, prayer, and good report—more than moral character. He had to be told words and obey words or submit to Christ's authority in order to be saved.

The next consideration is the vision of Peter which occurred at the sixth hour, or at midday. The great vessel seen by Peter, containing all manner of unclean animals, and birds and creeping things, and the voice commanding him to slay and eat such things as were considered unclean by the Jews, was understood by Peter to teach that he should not consider the Gentiles common or unclean. After this the Spirit directed Peter to go with the men sent by Cornelius, "doubting nothing, for I have sent them." We next observe that Peter, when he came to the house of Cornelius, unlike an impostor, refused to be worshiped, claiming to be only a man. It should always be borne in mind that there were considerable numbers present at the house of Cornelius, he having "called together his kinsmen and near friends." The discourse which Peter preached to them was a clear and strong presentation of the great facts connected with the life and mission of Christ.

But here we come to the most remarkable scene witnessed since the day of Pentecost, and in some respects even more wonderful than the occurrence on that day. For we are informed that "while Peter was yet speaking these words the Holy Spirit fell on all who heard the word." They also "spoke with tongues and magnified God." Peter says, "As I began to speak, the Holy Spirit fell on them as on us at the beginning." Now, there is a marked difference between the persons on whom the Holy Spirit fell on this occasion and those "at the beginning." On the day of Pentecost, so far as the record shows, there were none in the house but disciples when the Holy Spirit descended, and they began to speak with tongues. Being all Galileans, the multitude, when they came together, marveled because they each heard them speak in their own language. But here these Gentiles—the audience—these hearers, "spoke with tongues." Not only so, but Peter says, "As I began to speak the Holy Spirit fell on them."[1] Even before they were fully informed in regard to Christ, or had sufficient evidence to produce faith in Him, the Holy Spirit fell on them. Hence Peter says, "God gave them like gift as he did unto us who believed on the Lord Jesus Christ." This is a marvelous statement and is conclusive proof that they were not pardoned by the Holy Spirit, nor when they were baptized by the Holy Spirit, else they were pardoned without faith in the Lord Jesus and before they heard the word by which they were to be saved. The Holy Spirit fell on them as Peter began to speak, consequently before they heard the story of salvation. Peter states that this is a ful-

[1]Acts xi. 15.

filment of the preceding promise in regard to the baptism of the Holy Spirit. He says: "Then remembered I the word of the Lord, how that he said, John, indeed, baptized in water, but ye shall be baptized in the Holy Spirit." This undoubtedly refers to the promise of Christ to His apostles just before He ascended, after commanding them "that they should not depart from Jerusalem, but wait for the promise of the Father." He says, "For John indeed baptized in water, but ye shall be baptized in the Holy Spirit not many days hence."[1] From this we learn that the apostles were not baptized in or by the Holy Spirit before the ascension of Christ, nor were they endued with it prior to this. That the promise to the apostles, both of the baptism and enduement of the Holy Spirit, was fulfilled on the day of Pentecost will not be disputed.

There are only two cases given of the baptism of the Holy Spirit in the New Testament. The first occurred at the opening of the "kingdon of heaven" to the Jews, the second at its opening to the Gentiles. The one on the day of Pentecost, the other at the house of Cornelius. We will make the statement still more sweeping by observing that the history of the world for two thousand years furnishes no other example of the baptism of the Holy Spirit. We say this in full view of all the modern preaching about and praying to God for the baptism of the Holy Spirit.

In giving a history of pardon it is important to discuss fully the supernatural which was connected with

[1]Acts i. 5.

the various cases of pardon in the age of miracles. It is important to learn what was temporary and what was permanent, what was required to establish the new faith, and what was to continue or abide as the law of pardon. When we find men preaching and practising contrary to the facts of history, may we not demand the authority for such practise, or require them to give us a display of some kind of supernatural power and endowment now as was shown on the memorable occasions to which they refer as proof? If the baptism of the Holy Spirit is taught as existing now, we have a right to demand a divine promise that it was to continue and not be shorn of all its visible displays, or to be shown these matchless displays now.

We are informed that the Holy Spirit fell on the Gentiles as it did on the apostles "at the beginning." How, then, did it fall on the apostles at the beginning? We are informed that "They were all with one accord in one place, and suddenly there came a sound from heaven as of a rushing mighty wind and it filled all the house where they were sitting, and there appeared unto them cloven tongues like as of fire and it sat upon each of them. And they were all filled with the Holy Spirit and began to speak with other tongues as the Spirit gave them utterance."[1] This baptism of the Holy Spirit was something that could be seen and heard and enabled them to speak with tongues. It was a stupendous miracle—one of the greatest displays of the supernatural ever witnessed on

[1]Acts ii. 1–4.

earth. When the baptism of the Holy Spirit occurred on the day of Pentecost, three thousand Jews were convinced that Jesus was the Christ. The baptism of the Holy Spirit at Cæsarea convinced Peter and the Jews who were with him that the Gentiles were to share the blessings of the gospel of Christ. The apostles were baptized to convince the Jews of the Messiahship of Christ. The Gentiles were baptized to convince the apostles and Christian Jews that God had granted also to the Gentiles repentance unto life. If the first was important for the Jews, the last was equally important for the Gentiles. Without the one the Jews would not have believed. Without the other the Gentiles could not have heard, because the apostles and all the Christians yet considered it unlawful to preach to the Gentiles.

CHAPTER XX

OPERATIONS OF THE SPIRIT

Three Different Manifestations of the Holy Spirit. The Baptism. The Gift by Laying on of the Hands of the Apostles. The Promise to All upon Obedience. Two Improper Uses Noticed.

WE now remark that there are three manifestations, endowments, or gifts of the Holy Spirit spoken of or promised in the New Testament scriptures. We will call attention briefly to each. We have scriptural authority for calling them all gifts. Peter said of the baptism of the Holy Spirit, which occurred at the reception of the Gentiles, "God gave them the like gift as he did unto us who believed."[1] First, the baptism of the Holy Spirit was with an outward demonstration—something which could be seen and heard by others. "A sound from heaven as of a rushing mighty wind"; and "cloven tongues like as of fire, and it sat upon each of them." Not only had this baptism an outward manifestation, such as could be attested by those who were not subjects of it, but it was a direct gift from heaven, without conditions or any intervening person or agency.

Second, the gift of the Holy Spirit, which was conferred by the laying on of the apostles' hands, is never called a baptism. It was unlike the baptism, not be-

[1]Acts xi. 17, xv. 8.

ing connected with anything which could be seen or heard, but was like it in that it enabled the recipient to speak with tongues. This gift, as before shown, was only imparted by the apostles. We have but two examples of the baptism of the Holy Spirit, one at Jerusalem, the other at Cæsarea. There were two instances of the apostles conferring the gift by laying on of hands, one at Samaria, by Peter and John,[1] the other at Ephesus by Paul.[2] This gift was conferred after baptism and was conferred on Christians only.

Third, there is another gift of the Holy Spirit promised to all who obey the gospel. This is the more important, being promised to all as a blessing in connection with the remission of sins. Many scriptures refer to this great blessing. Peter promised it in the opening speech of the gospel age when he said, "Repent and be baptized every one of you in the name of Jesus Christ for the remission of sins, and ye shall receive the gift of the Holy Spirit." It will be observed that the baptism of the Holy Spirit in both instances was miraculous. In the one the disciples alone were the subjects, in the other the unbelieving Gentiles. In view of the modern teaching, too much stress can not be placed upon the fact that there is only this single instance given in which the persons receiving the baptism of the Holy Spirit were unbelievers. The use that was made of this was to convince the Jews of the reception of the Gentiles, and there is no reference made to the effect it had or was intended to have upon the Gentiles or those who were the subjects

[1] Acts viii, 17. [2] Acts xix. 6.

of it. Aside from this single instance there is no example—no promise that any other persons had received or would receive any gift of the Holy Spirit before obedience to the gospel. This then was a special case—a miracle performed on one class for a specific purpose, and witnessed by another class. It was of such a nature as to be both seen and heard. For Peter says, "It fell on them as it did on us at the beginning." And at the beginning, speaking of Jesus, he said, "He hath shed forth this which ye now see and hear." It is not reasonable, therefore, to expect another demonstration of the same kind, unless we find all the circumstances the same. If God had another Gentile world to be converted by the preaching of the gospel, and other apostles who did not yet understand that the gospel was to be preached to the Gentiles, but considered them "common and unclean," no doubt there would be given such a vision as Peter witnessed and such a baptism as overwhelmed Cornelius, "his kinsmen, and near friends."

It has been stated that miracles were confined to the first age of the Church and connected with its establishment, and were for the confirmation of the testimony, to prove the facts of the gospel and confirm its establishment for all time and then were to cease. They could not reasonably continue confirming facts which had transpired ages past and become history. We may therefore conclude, and correctly, too, that the baptism of the Holy Spirit and the gift of the Spirit conferred by the laying on of the apostles' hands, both being miraculous, ceased also. These gifts fulfilled their end and passed away. Now abideth the gift of the Holy Spirit promised by Peter on the day of Pentecost to those who witnessed the baptism of the Holy Spirit. These were commanded to repent and be baptized in order to receive remission of sins and the gift of the Holy Spirit. This gift was exclusively promised to the obedient as the Scriptures abundantly testify.

In closing this investigation we will direct attention to some of this testimony. Peter says: "We are his witnesses of these things, and so is also the Holy Spirit whom God hath given to them that obey him."[1] Paul, writing to Christians, says: "The love of God is shed abroad in our hearts by the Holy Spirit which is given unto us."[2] Again, speaking of God, "Who hath also given unto us his Holy Spirit."[3] Again, addressing the Corinthian Christians, he says: "Know ye not that your body is the temple of the Holy Spirit which is in you, which ye have of God?"[4] To Titus he says, speaking of the love of God, our Savior, "According to his mercy he saved us by the washing of regeneration and renewing of the Holy Spirit."[5] John, speaking of those who kept His commandments says, "We know that he abideth in us by the Spirit which he hath given us."[6] Again, Paul says to the Galatian Christians, "Because ye are sons God has sent forth the Spirit of his Son into your hearts, crying Abba, Father." This was not to make them sons, but because they were sons. How shall we know then that Christians have the Spirit? By their fruits ye

[1]Acts v. 32. [2]Rom. v. 5. [3]1 Thess. iv. 8.
[4]1 Cor. vi. 19. [5]Titus iii. 5. [6]1 John iii. 24.

shall know them. "Do men gather grapes of thorns or figs of thistles?" The fruits of the Spirit are fully described by Paul in Galatians. "But the fruit of the Spirit is love, joy, peace, long-suffering, gentleness, goodness, faith, meekness, temperance. Against such there is no law."[1] From these passages and many more we find that it was clearly taught that the Holy Spirit was given to those who obeyed; that it was given because they were saints, and that none but baptized persons are ever said to possess it—to be partakers of the Holy Spirit or addressed as being the temple of the Holy Spirit. How widely does this differ from much of the preaching heard to-day. In fact, many preach and pray more about the Holy Spirit than they do about Jesus Christ. They preach about and pray for the baptism of the Holy Spirit, through which they expect the pardoning mercy of God, and this, too, in the face of the scriptural facts which show that pardon never was conferred in this way. In fact, the whole order of the gospel is reversed. They preach the Holy Spirit and promise Christ, but the divine plan was to preach Jesus Christ and promise the Holy Spirit.

Having called attention thus fully to the various gifts of the Holy Spirit, endeavoring to confine our statement strictly to the historical view of this important subject as given in the Scriptures, and the abuse which is made of it in modern times, and the proper place it occupies in the system of pardon or forgiveness, we now return to the closing scene at the

[1]Gal. v. 22, 23.

house of Cornelius. We are told that the Jews who came with Peter were astonished "Because that on the Gentiles also was poured out the gift of the Holy Spirit, for they heard them speak with tongues and magnify God. Then answered Peter, Can any man forbid water that these should not be baptized, who have received the Holy Spirit as well as we? And he commanded them to be baptized in the name of the Lord. Then prayed they him to tarry certain days." Finally, we learn many important lessons from this case of Cornelius. First, that the angel appeared to him to direct him to send for Peter, and not to pardon him. That the vision was to show Peter that the Gentiles were not unclean, and that in addition to this the Holy Spirit directed him to go with the messengers, nothing doubting. That the baptism of the Holy Spirit convinced the Jewish witnesses, and doubly assured Peter that the Gentiles were accepted. That Peter preached in order to produce faith in Christ and lead them to repentance. That when they heard these words by which they were to be saved they were baptized. We may then conclude that this outpouring of the Holy Spirit was confined to this particular time and occasion, so far as the Gentiles were concerned, and for the specific purpose assigned by Peter, to show that God had accepted them. This is evident from the fact that hereafter in all the history of Gentile conversions we have no such wonderful miracle wrought, but "it pleased God by the foolishness of preaching to save them that believe."[1] The

[1] 1 Cor. i. 21.

lessons thus learned from the history of this case are all vitally important, establishing the unity of the gospel as preached both to Jew and Gentile. Yet the facts are too often improperly used, as the following:

First, the outpouring of the Spirit here described is improperly used as a proof that persons are pardoned by immediate, direct, supernatural influence of the Holy Spirit. There is no evidence that the Gentiles here, or any other persons anywhere, were ever pardoned in this way. In the second place, it is improperly used to prove that these persons were pardoned before baptism. This would prove too much, and, in fact, destroy the whole remedial system, for it would at the same time prove that they were pardoned before they had knowledge of Jesus or faith in Him as the Savior. It will be remembered that the Holy Spirit fell on them as Peter began to speak. And he says, that "God gave them the like gift as he did unto us who believed on the Lord Jesus Christ." We can not therefore conclude that they were pardoned by the Holy Spirit before they heard—before they believed. This case, then, so far as hearing, believing, and being baptized, forms no exception to those whose history we have considered. It may be that Cornelius, being a just man, needed no repentance, as repentance is toward God.[1] But faith being toward Christ, he needed knowledge of Jesus and faith and obedience to Him, hence he was commanded to be baptized. But it will be observed that it is only affirmed of Cornelius and his household that they feared God. The

[1]Acts xx. 21.

others assembled with them needed repentance as well as baptism. In harmony with the cases heretofore observed these people received and obeyed the gospel. Peter says that "God made choice among us that the Gentiles by my mouth should hear the word of the gospel and believe."[1] The angel says, Peter "shall tell thee words whereby thou and all thy house shall be saved."[2] And Peter, concluding his discourse on Jesus, says: "That through his name whosoever believeth in him shall receive remission of sins."[3] Again, he says, that God "put no difference between us and them, purifying their hearts by faith."[4] "And he commanded them to be baptized in the name of the Lord."[5]

The history of this case shows conclusively that these Gentiles complied with the established and universal law of pardon which was first given by Christ in the commission enjoined in the beginning at Jerusalem, at Samaria, on the desert road, and required of Paul in Damascus. However contrary it may be to our preconceived notions, or the modern preaching or practise, yet there is no record of any one being baptized before he had faith or after he was pardoned, and no unbaptized person is ever addressed as a Christian.

[1]Acts xv. 7. [2]Acts xi. 14.
[3]Acts x. 43. [4]Acts xv. 9.
[5]Acts x. 47.

CHAPTER XXI

MISSIONARY WORK OF THE CHURCH

Church of Christ a Divine Organization; Terms of Admission Uniform as in All Organizations. The Church at Antioch. Paul's First Missionary Journey. Christ's Church Established in Asia Minor.

AFTER the account of the first preaching of the gospel to the Gentiles, Peter relates its reception by them to the Jews at Jerusalem. We are then informed "That they who were scattered abroad upon the persecution that arose about Stephen traveled as far as Phœnicia and Cyprus and Antioch, speaking the word to none but unto the Jews only: and some of them were men of Cyprus and Cyrene, who when they were come to Antioch, spake unto the Grecians preaching the Lord Jesus." The result was that "a great number believed and turned to the Lord." It is supposed to be about one year after Peter opened the kingdom to the Gentiles before the gospel was preached to the Greeks at Antioch. All that is said in regard to the acceptance of these Gentiles is that "a great number believed and turned to the Lord." This "turning to the Lord," "added to the Lord," necessarily implies that they complied with the same terms enjoined by Him and His ambassadors upon others. If any historian would once give a full account of how persons became members of any society or institution, and the laws of initiation, and would thereafter continue the history of the growth or development of such an organization, we would not expect him to repeat and re-repeat the full requirements in each and all cases of initiation, but would expect only to be informed of the growth of the society or the number of members added, feeling assured that all complied with the same terms.

All human governments, societies, organizations have positive and definite laws which are imposed upon all who become members. All well-organized institutions have a uniform mode of admitting members. And when there are a number of terms required in order to admission, no one thinks of becoming a member in violation of the constitution and laws of such organization. If men would observe the same common-sense rule when seeking admission to the Church o Christ, superstition and error would vanish, and Christian people would soon be relieved from the absurd and humiliating position they now occupy before the world of having all sorts of men preaching all sorts of doctrine and imposing various terms of pardon not taught by Christ or enjoined by His apostles. Christianity is a divine system; it is order, harmony, law; "the law of the Spirit of life in Christ Jesus hath made us free from the law of sin and death." No person should ever make the mistake or commit the folly of selecting a case as a model of pardon where only one term of pardon is mentioned, such as faith, turning, baptism, for there is no case on record where there is any one of these terms required to the exclusion of the other. In addition to the commission given by Christ, it is remarkable how many cases of pardon we have recorded, and how plainly and fully the terms are stated. Even if we should find a single example of a person having been pardoned by hearing alone, by faith alone, by repentance alone, or baptism alone, we would not be justified in presenting such a case as an example of pardon. All informed persons would consider it an exception to the rule, unless it were stated by divine authority that henceforth the exception was to become the rule. But when we find no exception to the rule, no example of pardon by compliance with one condition alone, what right have persons to teach one of these terms alone as the condition, much less to substitute conditions never imposed in any case of alien pardon, such as baptism of the Holy Spirit or any direct supernatural agency?

In connection with the preaching of the gospel at Antioch we have the third mention of Barnabas, who became a traveling companion of Saul. We are informed that "Then tidings of these things came unto the ears of the church which was in Jerusalem, and they sent forth Barnabas that he should go as far as Antioch, who, when he came and had seen the grace of God, was glad and exhorted them all that with purpose of heart they would cleave unto the Lord: for he was a good man and full of the Holy Spirit, and of faith, and much people was added unto the Lord."[1] Then Barnabas departed to Tarsus to seek Saul, and

[1]Acts xi. 22–24.

when he found him he returned with him to Antioch, where they preached to great multitudes for a whole year. "And the disciples were called Christians first in Antioch."[1] The church at Antioch having been informed by the prophet Agabus of an impending famine, "determined to send relief to the brethren dwelling in Judea," which they did "by the hands of Barnabas and Saul."[2] Thus the Gentiles, having been made partakers of the spiritual blessings of the Jewish Christians, showed their gratitude by ministering unto them in "carnal things."[3] The historian now comes back to things which occurred in Jerusalem, giving an account of the slaying of James, the brother of John, by Herod, with the sword. And when he saw that this "pleased the Jews, he proceeded further to take Peter also." Here follows the history of Peter's imprisonment, the incessant prayer of the church to God for him, his deliverance at night by the angel of God, his reception at the house of Mary, the mother of Mark, "where many were gathered together praying,"[4] and the smiting of Herod and his violent death. After this we are informed that "the word of God grew and multiplied, and Barnabas and Saul returned from Jerusalem when they had fulfilled their ministry and took with them John whose surname was Mark."[5]

Here at Antioch began the real life-work of Saul. From this on we have to look to the record of Saul's travels and preaching for the history of all specific

[1]Acts xi. 26. [2]Acts xi. 30. [3]Rom. xv. 27.
[4]Acts xii. 12. [5]Acts xii. 24, 25.

cases of pardon. After the close of the 11th chapter of Acts we have no further record of the preaching of any apostle or the pardon of any sinner, except what we learn through Paul and his traveling companions. We are informed that "in the church at Antioch there were certain prophets and teachers" who, "as they ministered unto the Lord and fasted, the Holy Spirit said, Separate me Barnabas and Saul for the work whereunto I have called them. And when they had fasted and prayed and laid their hands on them they sent them away."[1] Here we have the church at Antioch with its large Gentile membership sending Saul with Barnabas on the first missionary journey. Paul made three missionary tours, the first through Asia Minor, the last two through Asia Minor and part of Europe. He began all three of these journeys from Antioch, and closed the last one at Jerusalem. The city of Antioch, aside from Jerusalem, was the most important place connected with the early spread of Christianity. So far as the record shows it was here that Christianity first took root among the Gentiles. This church was large, for we are informed that "a great number believed and turned unto the Lord"; and again, under the preaching of Barnabas, "a great multitude was added to the Lord." Here the disciples were first called "Christians," which has designated them both in suffering and triumph through all the ages since. During the first part of this missionary tour of Saul and Barnabas, Mark was with them. They sailed to Cyprus and

[1]Acts xiii. 2, 3.

preached in the synagogue of the Jews. But the first-mentioned convert is a Gentile, Sergius Paulus, the proconsul of the country, "Who called for Barnabas and Saul, and desired to hear the word of God." But "a certain sorcerer, a false prophet—a Jew—whose name was Bar-Jesus, . . . withstood them, seeking to turn away the proconsul from the faith."[1] He was smitten with blindness.

Saul is here for the first time called Paul. And from this on he is designated by the name of Paul. "And when the pro-consul saw what was done he believed, being astonished at the doctrine of the Lord."[2] Here it will be observed that only belief is stated, but it is not stated to the exclusion of any other requirements. After this "Paul and his company having set sail from Paphos came to Perga in Pamphylia; and John, departing from them, returned to Jerusalem. But when they departed from Perga they came to Antioch in Pisidia and went into the synagogue on the sabbath day and sat down. And after the reading of the law and the prophets the rulers of the synagogue sent unto them saying, Ye men, and brethren, if ye have any word of exhortation for the people, speak."[3] When this invitation was extended Paul arose and delivered a discourse covering the whole sweep of Jewish history from the time of the captivity in Egypt until the death of Jesus under Pilate. He appealed to the Law and the Prophets and the Psalms, the testimony of John the Baptist and the fulfilment of all that was written in regard to Jesus, to His death and to the

[1]Acts xiii. 6–8. [2]Acts xiii. 12. [3]Acts xiii. 13, 15.

ample testimony of many witnesses in regard to His resurrection, and concludes by saying: "Be it known unto you, therefore, men and brethren, that through this man is preached unto you the forgiveness of sins, and by him all that believe are justified from all things from which ye could not be justified by the law of Moses."[1] No wonder, after hearing such startling news, that "when the Jews were gone out of the synagogue the Gentiles besought that these words might be preached to them the next sabbath. . . . And the next sabbath day came almost the whole city together to hear the word of God. But when the Jews saw the multitude they were filled with envy and spake against those things which were spoken by Paul, contradicting and blaspheming. Then Paul and Barnabas spoke out boldly and said, It was necessary that the word of God should first be spoken to you, but seeing ye thrust it from you, and judge yourself unworthy of eternal life, lo, we turn to the Gentiles. For so hath the Lord commanded us saying, I have set thee for a light of the Gentiles, that thou shouldest be for salvation unto the ends of the earth. And the Gentiles hearing this rejoiced and glorified the word of the Lord. And as many as were disposed to eternal life believed. And the word of the Lord was spread abroad throughout all the region."[2] Here again we are informed that the Gentiles hearing believed. But the Jews raised "persecution against Paul and Barnabas, and expelled them out of their coasts, but they shook off the dust of their feet against them and came

[1]Acts ix. 13–32. [2]Acts xiii. 46–49.

unto Iconium. And the disciples were filled with joy and with the Holy Spirit."[1]

Being again driven through the influence of the Jews from Iconium, they went to Lystra and Derbe. Here they preached the gospel, and at Lystra Paul healed a man who had been lame from his birth, "which, when the people saw, they said, The gods are come down to us in the likeness of men. And they called Barnabas, Jupiter; and Paul, Mercurius, because he was the chief speaker." Then the priest brought oxen and garlands and would have offered sacrifice with the people. We will now quote in full the first recorded speech of Paul to the Gentiles: "Which when the apostles, Barnabas and Paul heard of, they rent their clothes, and ran in among the people, crying out, and saying, Sirs, why do ye these things? We also are men of like passions with you and preach unto you that ye should turn from these vanities unto the living God, which made heaven and earth, and the sea, and all things that are therein: who in times past suffered all nations to walk in their own ways. Nevertheless he left not himself without witness, in that he did good and gave us rain from heaven and fruitful seasons, filling our hearts with food and gladness. And with these sayings scarce restrained they the multitudes from doing sacrifice unto them."[2] We call attention to this argument in contrast with his preaching to the Jews, and that he made no reference to prophecy and the Jewish Scriptures. After all this, through the influence of

[1] Acts xiii. 50–52. [2] Acts xiv. 14–18.

some of the Jews who had come from Antioch and Iconium, Paul was stoned in this same city and left for dead, but reviving soon "the next day he departed, with Barnabas, to Derbe." "And when they had preached the gospel to that city and had made many disciples, they returned to Lystra, to Iconium, and to Antioch, confirming the souls of the disciples. . . . And when they had ordained them elders in every church, and had prayed with fasting, they commended them to the Lord on whom they believed."[1] Continuing their journey they passed through other districts and cities, and after an absence of some six years they sailed from Attalia to Antioch in Syria, whence they had been commended to the grace of God for the work which they had accomplished. "And when they were come and had gathered the church together they rehearsed all that God had done with them and how he had opened the door of faith unto the Gentiles. And there they abode a long time with the disciples."[2] Thus ended the first missionary journey, full of joy and sorrow, suffering and triumph.

[1]Acts xiv. 20–23. [2]Acts xiv. 27, 28.

CHAPTER XXII

THE FIRST COUNCIL

The Conference at Jerusalem. Judaism and Christianity. Corrupt Religions. The Decree and its Binding Force.

DURING the time that Paul remained at Antioch a question of vast importance to the Church of Christ in regard to the law of Moses was raised, discussed, and finally decided at Jerusalem. There were "certain men came down from Judea and taught the brethren, Except ye are circumcised after the custom of Moses ye can not be saved." Paul and Barnabas disputed this, having no little discussion with them. It was finally "determined that Paul and Barnabas and certain other of them should go up to Jerusalem unto the apostles and elders about this question."[1] "They therefore being brought on their way by the Church passed through both Phœnicia and Samaria, declaring the conversion of the Gentiles, and they caused great joy unto all the brethren, and when they were come to Jerusalem they were received of the church and of the apostles and elders, and they rehearsed all things that God had done with them." But, strange to relate, there were even in the church at Jerusalem members of the sect of the Pharisees who contended "that it was needful to circumcise

[1]Acts xv. 2.

them and to command them to keep the law of Moses."[1] This council is a very important one, consequently we will quote its proceedings in full.

"And when there had been much questioning, Peter rose up and said unto them, Brethren, ye know that a good while ago God made choice among you, that by my mouth the Gentiles should hear the word of the gospel and believe. And God who knoweth the heart bear them witness, giving them the Holy Spirit even as he did unto us; and he made no distinction between us and them, cleansing their hearts by faith. Now, therefore, why make ye trial of God that ye should put a yoke upon the neck of the disciples which neither our fathers nor we were able to bear? But we believe that we shall be saved through the grace of the Lord Jesus in like manner as they. And all the multitude kept silence, and hearkened unto Barnabas and Paul rehearsing what signs and wonders God had wrought among the Gentiles through them. And after they had held their peace James answered, saying, Brethren, hearken unto me: Symeon (Peter) hath rehearsed how first God visited the Gentiles, to take out of them a people for his name. And to this agree the words of the prophets; as it is written, After these things I will return, and I will build again the tabernacle of David which is fallen; and I will build again the ruins thereof, and will set it up; That the residue of men may seek after the Lord and all the Gentiles upon whom my name is called, saith the Lord who maketh these things known from of old.

[1]Acts xv. 3–5.

Wherefore my judgment is that we trouble not them that from the Gentiles turn to God; but we enjoin them that they abstain from pollutions of idols and from fornication and from what is strangled and from blood. For Moses from generations of old hath in every city them that preach him, being read in the synagogues every Sabbath. Then it seemed good to the apostles and the elders, with the whole church, to choose men out of their company and send them to Antioch with Paul and Barnabas, namely, Judas, called Barsabas, and Silas, chief men among the brethren, and they wrote thus by them. The apostles and the elders, brethren, unto the brethren who are of the Gentiles in Antioch and Syria and Cilicia, greeting: Forasmuch as we have heard that certain who went out from us have troubled you with words subverting your souls; to whom we gave no commandment; it seemed good unto us having come to one accord to choose out men and send them unto you with our beloved Barnabas and Paul, men that have hazarded their lives for the name of our Lord Jesus Christ. We have sent therefore Judas and Silas who themselves also shall tell you the same things by word of mouth. For it seemed good to the Holy Spirit and to us to lay upon you no greater burden than these necessary things: that ye abstain from things sacrificed to idols, and from blood, and from things strangled, and from fornication; from which if ye keep yourselves it shall be well with you. Fare ye well. So they when they were dismissed came down to Antioch; and having gathered the multitude together they delivered the epistle; and when they read it they rejoiced for the consolation."[1]

It is a remarkable fact that this is the only council of which we have any record in the New Testament as having been held to consider the binding obligations of any religious principle; it was held to consider a question which caused then, and still causes, much strife among the believers in Christ. There is this difference, however, between those engaged in this dispute then and now. Then it was the Jewish Christians endeavoring to bind Jewish law on Gentile Christians. Now, the dispute is wholly confined to the Gentiles, many of whom are not content with the self-imposed bondage of the Jewish law, but, while galling under the yoke, seek to impose many of its burdens on others. It will be observed this conference was convened because of a request from the church at Antioch, which sent a committee composed of Paul, Barnabas, and others, for an opinion upon a troublesome and disputed question raised among them by members of the church at Jerusalem. The committee was "received of the church and the apostles and the elders." As to the proceedings, first, Barnabas and Paul told their story. After much "questioning" (discussion) Peter spoke of his presentation of the gospel to the Gentiles and its reception by them. Then the multitude kept silence while Barnabas and Paul rehearsed the signs and wonders God wrought among the Gentiles by them. Then James spoke, referring to Peter's work and to prophecy in regard to the Gentiles, closing with a

[1]Acts xv. 7-31.

recommendation which was approved by "the apostles, and the elders with the whole Church." It is said they all with one accord indorsed the action. The recommendation or decree was given unanimously, the Holy Spirit approving. In the message from the conference they stated that it was from "the apostles and elders, brethren, to the brethren." It was not sent to the officers of the church, but to the brethren among the Gentiles. The significant thing is, that even here under the apostles and in Jerusalem is convened one of the most representative bodies of which we have any record—that the whole Church, together with the apostles and elders, took part, and all with one accord joined in the recommendation. The apostles themselves did not usurp or claim authority over the elders of the church or its members. Here is demonstrated the dignity and authority of the members of the church, that each citizen of the kingdom was sovereign and was so recognized by the apostles and elders. It was not a council as many in succeeding ages have been, composed of high church dignitaries alone, usurping authority and commanding obedience to their decrees, but it seemed good to the whole church to issue a decree enjoining only necessary things upon the brethren among the Gentiles. This is one of the best models for a deliberative body that is recorded anywhere in history, whether religious or political. The decree was not an edict or bull of a pope, but the recommendation of a deliberative body. It may be noticed that Peter was in this body, and spoke in very different language from his so-called successor at Rome. He issued no edicts such as emanate from that source to bishops and cardinals who command the churches to obey his authority, but only made a recommendation which was seconded by James and unanimously approved by the whole Church, the Holy Spirit concurring. Notwithstanding this full discussion and this important decision, some in modern times have become more like Jews, both in spirit and teaching, than Christians. They have formed organizations, fashioned their institutions with ritualistic service, with priests having robes, conducting ceremonies, and performing rites more like Moses than Christ. Many assemblies, councils, and ecclesiastical organizations to-day exercise more authority, issue more edicts, and impose more burdens on their subjects than did the Jewish council or sanhedrin at Jerusalem on the Jews. Persons who are conversant with history and informed in regard to the Christian religion of to-day, as preached and practised by many, will recognize at once that a large per cent of it is composed of about equal parts of Judaism, Heathenism, and Christianity. (See infra, Chapter XXXV, page 285.)

Protestantism is not free from this admixture. In many of the denominations it is not difficult to recognize Judaism in preaching and practise. "Even unto this day when Moses is read the vail is upon their heart."[1] Some forms of worship partake too much of the character of heathen worship. We should not approach God in the boisterous manner of the prophets of Baal, who were mocked by Elijah,[2] but should

[1] 2 Cor. iii. 15. [2] 1 Kings xviii. 26–28.

worship God as a Father, and be assured that a "meek and quiet spirit is in the sight of God of great price."[1]

We now remark that there is no intimation in this decree that the gospel was not complete in itself, enjoining all that is right and forbidding all that is wrong, without regard to the law of Moses. But the reason for sending this letter was evidently twofold. First, to settle the dispute in regard to binding the law of Moses on the Gentiles. And, second, to conciliate the Jewish Christian in the various cities. The reason assigned by James for this action was because "Moses was preached in every city, being read in the synagogue every sabbath day." The law of Moses was strict in regard to things mentioned in this decree. It will be observed that only one matter forbidden had strictly a moral bearing. This was practised to a great extent, and being common, it was difficult to prohibit this crime. They may have been required to abstain from the other matters simply because they were an abomination to the Jews. Paul did not thereafter seem to place much stress on eating meats offered to idols, but makes it a matter of conscience, and would not eat any meat if it would cause his brethren to stumble.[2] In regard to abstaining from things strangled and from blood, there is a difference of opinion whether this was meant to be observed by all people and through all time, or was intended only to conciliate the Jewish Christians in the various cities of that age. It is safest, however, to abstain from such food now. It is known that animals which are

[1] 1 Pet. iii. 4. [2] 1 Cor. viii. *passim.*

fed on blood become more savage, and its use may tend to brutalize man. When the epistle had been read to the multitude at Antioch "they rejoiced for the consolation." Paul on his next journey carried this decree with him. He went through the cities delivering it to be kept.[1] Upon this decree we note that the crime which is prohibited is also denounced in the New Testament Scriptures. We do not look to the decree alone for its prohibition. We have no right, therefore, to infer that it was prohibited simply because it was a part of the law of Moses. If this decree was enjoined because it contained things which were part and parcel of the Mosaic law, they are the only things enjoined after the death of Christ for a similar reason. The things enjoined under Christ are enjoined by virtue of His authority, and not by virtue of any authority inspired or uninspired before Him. He said, "All authority hath been given unto me in heaven and on earth."[2] He delegated authority to His ambassadors, saying, "as the Father hath sent me, even so send I you."[3] All preceding religions were abolished by Him. The Patriarchal religion, given to the whole world, was superseded by the Christian. The Jewish religion, given to that people alone for a specific purpose, was taken out of the way. All its ceremonies, all its ordinances, all its laws, even its very constitution written and engraven on stone, were abolished under Christ.[4] Moses, the great law-giver, Elijah,

[1]Acts xvi. 4. [2]Matt. xxviii. 18.
[3]John xx. 21. [4]2 Cor. iii. *passim.*

the great prophet, the representatives of all Jewish law and all prophecy given before Jesus, came back from the regions of the dead and amid scenes of indescribable glory on the Mount of Transfiguration laid down their commissions at His feet and talked with Him about His death for the redemption of the human race.[1] God recalled them and vested Jesus with all authority, saying, from a bright cloud above, "This is my beloved Son, hear ye him." The Christian world now is as free from the binding authority of all religion given before Christ as any nation is civilly free from another. The law which was added to the promise concerning Christ "on account of transgression"[2] until He should come, fulfilled its end and passed away, but from all this it does not follow that there is not much reenacted under Christ which was enjoined under Moses and the prophets. All that was moral and that was eternally right, both as regards man and God, embraced in the former, was reenacted under Christ. But it is therefore not to be observed now because Moses and the prophets enjoined it, but because it is right and Christ and His ambassadors commanded it. We as Americans do not now submit to any law because it was formerly enjoined upon the colonies by Great Britain, but because it is reenacted by the Constitution or laws of our government. After our forefathers had abolished the English law and rule in the colonies they, in forming a new nation, reenacted all such laws as were considered just and right and adapted to our form of government. Not only so,

[1]Matt. xvii. *passim.* [2]Gal. iii. 17–29.

but they added many others with the intention of promoting greater good and giving greater liberty. So Jesus, in establishing His Church or Kingdom, enacted all that was moral, just, and good. Not, however, because such principles were found in the Jewish law or religion, but because they were right in themselves. Not only so, but He went beyond all law and all religion which preceded Him, and enjoined a higher morality and purer devotion and deeper love than were known before on earth.

The importance of the decree and its bearing on the subject in hand will be seen when it is observed that many religious teachers even now refer inquiring sinners to the Old Testament Scriptures for terms of pardon, for instructions in regard to the forgiveness of sins, for the answer to the question, What must I do to be saved? But if language has meaning, and inspiration authority, then may we understand that this decree freed once and forever all Gentiles from the yoke of Jewish bondage, and since it was issued no man, no angel, has had any authority to bind any part of the Jewish religion on the Gentile world not re-enacted under Christ.

CHAPTER XXIII

PAUL'S SECOND MISSIONARY JOURNEY

The Decree Delivered to the Churches. Timothy and Luke. Paul in Europe. Conversion of Lydia.

AFTER the decree had been delivered to the church at Antioch and they had rejoiced for the "consolation," Judas and Silas remained for some time exhorting and confirming the brethren. When they had fulfilled their mission "it pleased Silas to abide there still." Paul and Barnabas also remained for a time in Antioch, "teaching and preaching the word of the Lord." Then Paul proposed to Barnabas to revisit with him the brethren in every city where they had preached. Barnabas was willing to do this, but determined to take with him his sister's son, Mark.[1] But Paul objected on account of Mark having left them while on a former journey, not going with them to the work, "and the contention was so sharp" that they parted, "and Barnabas took Mark and sailed unto Cyprus," his native country. "And Paul chose Silas and departed, being recommended by the brethren unto the grace of God." Paul, in commencing this second missionary journey, went first "through Syria and Cilicia confirming the churches,"[2]

[1]Col. iv. 10. [2]Acts xv. 32–41.

and then came to "Derbe and Lystra." There was here a certain disciple named Timotheus, whose mother was a Jewess, but whose father was a Greek. As Paul desired that he should go with him he "circumcised him, because of the Jews which were in those quarters; for they all knew that his father was a Greek. And as they went through the cities they delivered to them the decree to keep that was ordained by the apostles and elders who were in Jerusalem. The churches were established in the faith, and increased in numbers daily."[1]

It is a fact worthy of remark that while Paul was passing through the cities of Asia Minor, delivering the final decree of the apostles and elders freeing the Gentile world from Judaism and triumphing in the liberty of the gospel, he caused Timothy to be circumcised. But the reason for this is given. It was on account of the Jews who were in those parts. It was done that they might not be offended in having an uncircumcised person preach to them. It will be observed that Timothy had become a disciple before this—no doubt on Paul's former visit—but was not required to be circumcised until Paul desired him for the work of the ministry. He was in Christ before this, and Paul taught that "in Christ Jesus neither circumcision availeth anything nor uncircumcision."[2] It is here we have the first mention of Timothy, who afterward became so famous and so endeared to Paul.

When Paul and Silas had been joined by Timothy,

[1]Acts xvi. 1–5. [2]Gal. v. 6.

the historian only names the districts in Asia Minor through which they passed and their course directed by the Holy Spirit until they came down to Troas. At this place "a vision appeared to Paul in the night. There stood a man of Macedonia and prayed him, saying, Come over into Macedonia and help us."[1] Here the party was joined for the first time by Luke, the sacred historian who wrote the Acts. He now ceases to speak of them as "they" and substitutes the word "we."

This is the first ray of historical light we have in regard to Luke. He is mentioned only three times hereafter. There is nothing known with certainty in regard to his nationality, parentage, birthplace, or burial place. No herald has announced his birth, no biographer sketched his life, no monument marks his tomb. And yet he is one of the most important characters who ever lived or acted on the stage of human life. To him we owe a debt of gratitude for one of the most complete histories of the life of Jesus, for the only history of the organization of the Church, for the only record of any discourses delivered by any apostle or evangelist, for the only record of the great events and great men connected with the early spread of Christianity over the world, and for a history of the eventful life of Paul, closing with his imprisonment at Rome. No other historian of the New Testament has covered so many and so great events, laden with such deep interest to the human race. He is called by Paul "the beloved physician." He not only

[1]Acts xvi. 9.

traveled with Paul and journeyed with him to Rome, and was with him in his first imprisonment, but remained alone with him when, he said, "the time of my departure is come."

After Paul had seen the vision and been joined by Luke, they sailed from Troas for Europe. Landing on the continent at Neapolis, they journeyed to Philippi, which was the chief city in that part of Macedonia. Being a Roman colony, it had special privileges. Luke now says: "And we were in that city abiding certain days, and on the sabbath day we went forth out of the gate by a riverside where prayer was wont to be made. And we sat down and spake to the women who were come together. And a certain woman named Lydia, a seller of purple, of the city of Thyatira, who worshiped God, heard us: whose heart the Lord opened to give heed unto the things which were spoken by Paul. And when she was baptized, and her household, she besought us, saying, If ye have judged me to be faithful to the Lord, come into my house and abide there. And she constrained us."[1] Here we have given the first account of the preaching of the gospel in Europe, and the first convert was an Asiatic woman who, like Cornelius, was a worshiper of God. Here began the sowing of the seed on the continent of Europe, which soon became the great battle-field of the cross.

In regard to Paul's preaching at Philippi, we observe that he sought first to preach to the worshipers of the true God. Consequently he went to a

[1]Acts xvi. 12-15.

place where they were known to congregate on the Sabbath. The result of this speaking to the women who resorted there was that Lydia, "whose heart the Lord opened to attend to the things spoken by Paul," "heard." Then, it is stated, the Lord opened her heart. A very important question is raised here, and that is, How did the Lord open Lydia's heart? Did He open it by the preaching of His inspired apostle or by a direct miracle—by an abstract operation without visible means? It will be observed that her heart was not opened to hear, but simply to "attend to the things which were spoken by Paul." This brings us to consider another important question: Is the preaching of an inspired apostle sufficient to open the heart? If it is, then it is not reasonable to expect means to be employed beyond and above this, for if the Lord employed such means He employs means not necessary. If all the means required to open her heart were present, why expect other means?

The rule is that God does for us only such things as we can not do for ourselves. Could Lydia believe? Could she repent? Could she obey the inspired teaching of the apostle, or was an immediate, abstract operation required in her case? If so it will not be in harmony with the general scope and meaning of the Scriptures. It may be here stated as an absolute fact, that originating truth and presenting it properly attested belong to God, and that hearing, believing, repenting, and obeying belong to man. If the Lord opened the heart of Lydia abstractly, or independent of Paul's preaching, then this case forms an exception to all the cases thus far passed in review. Again, if the Lord opened her heart abstractly or miraculously, then persons can not be condemned for rejecting preaching, and all that large portion of Scripture reproving and condemning persons for rejecting offered salvation is worse than meaningless. Christ and His ambassadors universally turned from presenting the truth to persons who rejected it; when they closed their eyes and hardened their hearts; when they "judged themselves unworthy of eternal life."

Again, this abstract theory would clash with many other passages of Scripture, such as, "The gospel . . . is the power of God to salvation,"[1] it "pleased God by the foolishness of preaching to save them that believe."[2] And, finally, it would destroy man's responsibility and accountability. The infinitely wise Being certainly would not hold man responsible for an act which He alone could perform. The fact is that man went away from God by hearing a falsehood, believing a falsehood, and acting upon a falsehood. He comes back by hearing the truth, believing the truth, and obeying the truth. What are we then to understand by the expression, "whose heart the Lord opened that she attended to the things spoken by Paul"? Simply that she "became obedient to the faith"—the Lord opened her heart through the instrumentality of His inspired apostle. When it is stated that "the Lord added to the church daily," we do not understand that they were added without the instrumentality of the gospel. As the whole gospel

[1]Rom. i. 16. [2]1 Cor. i. 20.

is properly ascribed to the Lord, so any part, however minute, connected with pardon may be called His work. But in no part have we a right to expect Him to interfere in such a way as to mar the harmony of the whole. We need not, therefore, expect Him to open the heart of one by a miracle, and require others to believe and obey on the presentation of the truth. This case of Lydia forms no exception to those we have considered. "In attending to the things which were spoken by Paul," she no doubt complied with the terms of pardon, believing, repenting, and, we are informed, "she was baptized and all her household." Thus we find here, as in the preceding cases, that baptism was the consummating act in receiving Christ. After Lydia was baptized she invited Paul and his companions to abide with her at her house, which they did.

While Paul remained in the city he was annoyed by a bondmaid possessed with a spirit of divination, who, it is said, "brought her masters much gain by soothsaying: The same following after Paul and us, cried out, saying, These men are the servants of the Most High God, who proclaim unto you the way of salvation, and this she did for many days. But Paul, being grieved, turned and said to the spirit, I command thee in the name of Jesus Christ to come out of her. And he came out the same hour." This is the first case on record in which Paul is said to have cast out a spirit. When the masters of this bondmaid saw "that the hope of their gain was gone,"[1] they arrested Paul and Silas.

[1]Acts xvi. 19.

CHAPTER XXIV

PAUL AT PHILIPPI

The Conversion of the Jailer. He Preached the Word of the Lord. More than Faith Required.

THIS brings us to the conversion of the Philippian jailer. We are now informed that "the multitude rose up together against them; and the magistrates rent off their clothes and commanded to beat them with rods. And when they had laid many stripes upon them they cast them into prison, charging the jailer to keep them safely: who having received such a charge thrust them into the inner prison and made their feet fast in the stocks. And at midnight Paul and Silas prayed and sang praises unto God, and the prisoners were listening to them. And suddenly there was a great earthquake so that the foundations of the prison were shaken: and immediately all the doors were opened and every one's bands were loosed. And the jailer awaking out of sleep and seeing the prison doors open drew his sword and was about to kill himself, supposing that the prisoners had fled. But Paul cried with a loud voice, saying, Do thyself no harm: for we are all here. And he called for a light and he sprang in, and came trembling and fell down before Paul and Silas, and brought them out and said, Sirs, what must I do to be saved? And they said, Believe on the Lord Jesus Christ, and thou shalt be saved and thy house. And they spake to him the word of the Lord and to all that were in his house. And he took them the same hour of the night and washed their stripes and was baptized, he and all his, immediately. And he brought them into his house and set meat before them and rejoiced, believing in God with all his house."[1]

The conversion of the Philippian jailer has caused much discussion in the religious world, and therefore all the facts connected with it require careful consideration. It will be borne in mind that he was a Gentile, that before Paul and Silas were imprisoned, they had been in the city a number of days preaching; that during part of this time they were followed by a demoniac who "cried, saying, These men are the servants of the Most High God, who proclaim unto you the way of salvation."[2] That the jailer had learned something of the character of their mission from this circumstance or from them, or through common report, is manifest by the question he asked: "Sirs, what must I do to be saved?" This is the most important question ever asked by man. It is here put by the anxious jailer in its plainest and most concise form. The answer was, "Believe on the Lord Jesus Christ, and thou shalt be saved, and thy house."[3] This answer, though plain and direct, has caused much discussion. It is the favorite text with all those who teach faith alone or faith to the

[1]Acts xvi. 22–34. [2]Acts xvi. 16, 17. [3]Acts xvi. 31.

exclusion of other requirements of the gospel. Thousands of sermons have been preached from this text, without regard to the context, to prove that faith only is required in order to salvation. While faith stands first in order, after hearing, as we have seen, yet this is the only case of pardon after the giving of the commission by Christ in which it is commanded before hearing. In other cases, it will be remembered, it was stated "that hearing they believed," that "believers were added"; "If thou believest with all thy heart thou mayest." But in this case alone it was directly enjoined first.

We will now consider whether all the terms of pardon required in other cases were also enjoined in this one. When the jailer inquired what he should do, it is evident from the context that he had no definite knowledge of Jesus; hence, he was first commanded to "believe on the Lord Jesus Christ." But he could not believe in Him without knowledge of Him, for Paul himself says, "How can they believe in him of whom they have not heard?" Hence, "they spake to him the word of the Lord and to all that were in his house." This brings us to the important inquiry, What is meant by "speaking to him the word of the Lord"? What does "the word of the Lord" embrace? If this is taught fully in the Scriptures we may know definitely and precisely what was required of the jailer and his house in order to salvation. Isaiah and Micah both, in prophesying of "the last days" of the Jewish reign, say that "Out of Zion shall go forth the law, and the word of the Lord from Jerusalem."[1] These prophecies had reference to the proclamation of the gospel under Christ, and are referred properly to the same time spoken of by Christ when He said: "Thus it is written and thus it behooved Christ to suffer and to rise from the dead the third day, and that repentance and remission of sins should be preached in his name among all nations beginning at Jerusalem."[2] We now remark that the expressions "the word of the Lord," "the word," and "the word of God," all frequently refer to the whole system of gospel grace; a few examples will suffice. Paul, writing to the Thessalonians, says, "For from you hath sounded forth the word of the Lord, not only in Macedonia and Achaia, but also in every place."[3] Again, to the same people: "Finally, brethren, pray for us that the word of the Lord may run and be glorified."[4] "When the apostles that were at Jerusalem heard that Samaria had received the word of God they sent unto them Peter and John."[5] "And the apostles and brethren that were in Judea heard that the Gentiles also received the word of God."[6] "Who shall tell thee words whereby thou and all thy house shall be saved."[7] Sergius Paulus "called for Barnabas and Saul and sought to hear the word of God."[8] "God made choice among us that the Gentiles by my mouth should hear the word of the gospel and believe."[9] "Being born again not of corruptible seed but of incorruptible by the word of God which liveth and abideth

[1] Isa. ii. 3; Micah iv. 2. [2] Luke xxiv. 46, 47. [3] 1 Thess. i. 8.
[4] 2 Thess. iii. 1. [5] Acts viii. 14. [6] Acts xi. 1.
[7] Acts xi. 14. [8] Acts xiii. 7. [9] Acts xv. 7.

forever."[1] From these passages of Scripture, and many more to the same import which it is not necessary to quote, it is plainly evident that the word of the Lord spoken to the jailer and his house was the same as predicted by the prophets in these identical words when they said that "Out of Zion shall go forth the Law and the word of the Lord . . . from Jerusalem." They were the same words that were enjoined by Jesus in His commission and preached by all of His inspired apostles and ambassadors. If we should desire to know then what was required of the jailer in order to salvation, we have only to refer to the commission given by Christ and the preaching of the word of the Lord as predicted on the day of Pentecost, to the discourse of Philip at Samaria, to his instructions to the eunuch, to the conversion of Saul, to the discourse of Peter delivered at the house of Cornelius, to the preaching of Paul on any occasion where his discourses are reported, or to the proclamation of the word of the Lord to the unpardoned by any inspired ambassador of Jesus. From all these we learn that to preach the Word of the Lord to the unpardoned was to teach faith, repentance, and baptism in order to pardon. When the jailer asked, "What must I do to be saved?" he was commanded "to believe on the Lord Jesus Christ," because he did not have faith in Him. In order to present the gospel plan of salvation and produce this faith, "they spake unto him the word of the Lord and to all that were in his house." That he was repentant

[1]1 Pet. i. 23.

is shown by his washing their stripes and setting meat before them. In speaking the word of the Lord, repentance was preached as well as faith. When Peter preached the word of the Lord on the day of Pentecost, three thousand asked at the close of the discourse the same question asked here by the jailer, "What must we do?" The answer in their case was, "Repent and be baptized every one of you in the name of Jesus Christ for the remission of sins, and ye shall receive the gift of the Holy Spirit." In their case faith was not enjoined, but it will be observed that they asked the question in deep anguish, after being convicted and convinced by hearing the word of the Lord, while the jailer asked the question in deep anxiety before hearing the word. The people on the day of Pentecost believed before they inquired. The jailer inquired before he believed. The reason for not requiring faith in the one case was because they believed. The reason for enjoining it in the other was because it was not possessed. The first step had been taken in the one case and it was required to be taken in the other. In harmony with this we have the example of the conversion of Paul himself, who had taken the first two steps; therefore Ananias only commanded him "to arise and be baptized and wash away thy sins, calling on the name of the Lord." That he believed is evident from the fact that he asked, "Lord, what wilt thou have me do?" That he had repented was shown by the fact that he was praying, hence he was only commanded to be baptized. In these three cases we have all the requirements enjoined by Christ in His commission—directly and positively commanded. The jailer was first commanded to believe, when in speaking to him "the word of the Lord," repentance and baptism were enjoined as well as faith, because embraced in it. Hence, we are informed that "he was baptized and all his straightway and rejoiced, believing in God with all his house." As all his house believed with him, all were capable of believing as well as rejoicing. The people at the opening of the kingdom were not commanded to believe, because they had already believed, but were required to repent and be baptized. Paul was only commanded to be baptized because when addressed he was a believing penitent. These persons, then, were severally addressed in accordance with their condition or the state of their mind at the time. There can be no better reason given for commanding an essential thing than that it has not been done; there can be no better reason for omitting to enjoin it than that it has been done. The history of pardon, as given in the New Testament, furnishes no example of an inspired teacher committing the folly of commanding an unnecessary thing to be done, or of enjoining a duty already performed.

It is a remarkable fact that in all the cases of pardon thus far given there is only one in which faith is first commanded. How strangely does this contrast with many scenes of modern revival, where faith is enjoined without regard to the steps already taken. And it is enjoined day after day, often week after week, and that, too, upon the same believing, sorrowing, penitent person. How often have we heard it repeated and re-repeated on such occasions, "Believe on the Lord—only believe. Lord, give him faith," and from the person thus addressed the answer would come back in distress, "I do believe." Yet no Philip there to take the "good confession" and baptize him that he might "go on his way rejoicing." No Ananias to say, "Arise, and be baptized, and wash away thy sins, calling on the name of the Lord." No Paul there to baptize him the same hour of the night, that he might rejoice, believing in God. No, not even an "Aquila and Priscilla" there to "expound unto him the way of God more perfectly," but all persons are directed to toil on, sorrow on, and pray on, and expected to rejoice in the Lord before they obey Him. How different this from the expressed history of pardon. No one here is said to rejoice in the Lord before baptism. The Christian religion, as presented by inspiration, does no violence to the constitution of either body or mind, but violent forms of religion frequently injure both. It was after the Ethiopian was baptized that he "went on his way rejoicing." And it was after the jailer was baptized that he "rejoiced, believing in God with all his house."

Notwithstanding Paul and Silas had been liberated during the night, their stripes had been washed and they had preached the word of the Lord to the prison-keeper and his house, causing them to rejoice in the liberty wherewith Christ makes free, yet the morning found them still in prison. But a message was sent to the keeper of the prison to let them go. Paul here, for the first time, asserted his Roman citizenship and refused to go out privately, because they had been beaten openly, contrary to Roman law. When the magistrates heard "that they were Romans" they feared, "and they came and besought them, and brought them out and asked them to depart out of the city. And they went out of the prison, and entered into the house of Lydia; and when they had seen the brethren they comforted them, and departed."[1]

[1]Acts xvi. 39, 40.

CHAPTER XXV

THE THESSALONIANS

The City of Philippi. Paul Preaches to the Thessalonians. The Epistles to the Thessalonians.

WITH the history of the conversion of the Philippian jailer closes all minute detail of individual cases of pardon. While many individuals were converted and many churches were organized, in the subsequent travels of Paul and his companions, it is only stated that they "believed, and consorted with Paul and Silas."[1] "Believed on the Lord." That "hearing, they believed and were baptized."[2] It is not remarkable, however, that no more cases are minutely described, but rather that so many were given and the requirements so fully stated. The cases already given embrace Jew and Gentile, cover a variety of races, differing in education, in belief, in character, separated by distance, by time and by circumstances. Yet all were required to obey, whether the betrayers of Christ who were forgiven and rejoiced in the hope which their crime brought to the world, whether a pious Ethiopian from the dark continent, a devout Roman soldier of Cesarea, the persecuting Saul of Tarsus, whether Lydia of Thyatira or the keeper of

[1]Acts xvii. 4. [2]Acts xviii. 8.

the Roman jail at Philippi. These examples and more are not only sufficient to show the universal character of the Christian religion and its adaptation to all races, classes, and conditions of men, but to the universal law of pardon enjoined upon all. All examples of pardon harmonize and are sufficient for instruction for all people and in all time.

Philippi is the first city visited by Paul where converts are mentioned as a result of his preaching, and to whom he subsequently addressed an epistle. We have the simple statement of his passing through Galatia in Asia Minor before this, and of the Christians to whom he wrote the Galatian epistle. Only extensive ruins now mark the place where this important city once stood, yet time has not destroyed the record of Paul's labors and sufferings here. We still have the example of two important conversions, and the epistle addressed to the church ten years later. Paul was driven from its walls. Although the walls of the city have crumbled, the "word of life" preached by its river side, the story of the song of redemption sung in the deepest recesses of its prison, the word of the Lord spoken in the night-time, and the inspired epistle written to the church with its words of warning, its assurance of faith and comfort of love, all remain and will remain to instruct the sinner and cheer the saint until time shall cease to be.

From the style of the narrative being changed from the first to the third person, and Paul and Silas having left Philippi, it is evident that Luke remained. Timothy also remained, but joined Paul and Silas shortly thereafter at Berea. Luke does not appear again in Paul's company until, on the third missionary journey, he visits Macedonia the second time. On the second journey he sailed with Paul from Troas for Philippi. On the third journey he informs us that "we sailed away from Philippi . . . to Troas."[1] It is quite probable that he remained at Philippi during the seven years of Paul's absence. However this may be, he rejoined him here, and from this on we have reason to believe that he was with him to the close of his eventful career—journeying with him to Rome and being with him at his final trial. It is a remarkable fact, that Paul, in closing his own record, also closes that of Luke. Among his last and saddest words are, "only Luke is with me." Here the curtain drops and the records of the great apostle and great historian close together, leaving the pleasant reflection that Paul's faithful chronicler in life stood by him in death.

Paul and Silas, on leaving the city of Philippi, traveled over the great Roman road "which connected Rome with the whole region north of the Ægean Sea."[2] Passing through Amphipolis and Apollonia on this great highway, they came to the important city of Thessalonica, "where there was a synagogue of the Jews. And Paul, as his custom was, went in unto them, and for three sabbath days reasoned with them out of the Scriptures: Opening and alleging that Christ must needs have suffered and risen again from the dead; and that this Jesus whom I preach to

[1]Acts xx. 6. [2]Smith's Bible Dictionary, page 900.

you is the Christ."[1] The result of this preaching was that "some of them believed and consorted with Paul and Silas; and of the devout Greeks a great multitude, and of the chief women not a few." Here we find Paul pursuing his usual custom and preaching the gospel to the Jews first and proving its great facts by an appeal to their sacred Scriptures. Paul here preached Christ Jesus to the people. Now, to preach Christ Jesus was to preach Him in His whole official character, as Prophet, Priest, and King as Prophet to teach, as Priest to atone, and as King to reign. In preaching Christ he preached more than faith, for we are informed that they believed and joined themselves to Paul and Silas. When it is said that Moses is "preached, being read in the synagogues every sabbath day,"[2] we understand that the law of Moses or the Jewish religion was preached. When Christ was preached by His ambassadors the whole system of which He was the Author and Finisher was preached. There is therefore no implication here when it is said that those present "believed and consorted with or joined themselves," that they joined on different terms from others, or without becoming obedient to the faith. That we are correct in this conclusion is amply demonstrated by the much fuller information given by Paul himself in his two epistles to this church.

While the Galatians and the Philippians were the first peoples visited by Paul to whom he thereafter wrote, yet to the Thessalonians belongs the honor of

[1]Acts xvii. 2, 3. [2]Acts xv. 21.

receiving the first epistle written by the inspired apostle. The first and second epistles to the Thessalonians were written during the second missionary journey of Paul. These were written about the close of the year A.D. 52, or the beginning of A.D. 53, from Corinth. These are not only the first epistles of Paul, but if not the first, they are among the very earliest written records of Christianity. These epistles should be read in connection with the brief history here given by Luke. We will therefore call attention to the more ample testimony given in them in regard to the preaching and reception of the gospel at Thessalonica. In the opening of both these epistles those addressed are spoken of as "In God the Father and the Lord Jesus Christ."[1] Twice reference is made to their reception of the gospel, "Our gospel came not unto you in word only, but also in power, and in the Holy Spirit."[2] "He called you by our gospel to the obtaining of the glory of our Lord Jesus Christ."[3] Paul says, "Ye became followers of us and of the Lord."[4] They are said to have "received the word . . . and turned to God from idols."[5] That from them "sounded out the word of the Lord."[6] And Paul says, "Pray for us that the word of the Lord may have free course and be glorified even as it is with you."[7] Three times he tells them of having spoken the gospel of God to them. "We were bold in God to speak unto you the gospel of God."[8] "We were willing to have imparted unto

[1] 1 Thess. i. 1; 2 Thess. i. 1. [2] 1 Thess. i. 5. [3] 2 Thess. ii. 14. [4] 1 Thess. i. 6. [5] 1 Thess. i. 6, 9. [6] 1 Thess. i. 8. [7] 2 Thess. iii. 1. [8] 1 Thess. ii. 2.

you not the gospel of God only, but also our own souls."[1] 'We preach unto you the gospel of God."[2] They are addressed as being in the kingdom. "Walk worthy of God, who hath called you into his kingdom and glory."[3] Again, "that ye may be counted worthy of the kingdom of God for which you also suffer."[4] And, finally, they were said to have received the gift of the Holy Spirit. Therefore, he "that rejecteth, rejecteth not man but God who giveth his Holy Spirit unto you."[5]

These passages show most clearly that the Christians at Thessalonica complied with all the terms of pardon before appointed. They were said to have "turned to the Lord," "to be in Christ," and Paul teaches plainly how persons came into Christ. "Know ye not that all we who were baptized into Christ Jesus were baptized into his death."[6] We are told that they were "called by the gospel," and the gospel is declared to be "the power of God unto salvation." Again, that they became followers of Paul and the Lord. To follow the Lord was to follow Him in His appointed way. We have called attention to His appointments. Again, we are informed, "that they received the word." That, "the word of the Lord soundeth out from them." "That the gospel of God was preached to them." "The word of the Lord," and "the gospel of God" embraced the whole system of pardon of salvation through Christ as already shown. Again, from the

[1]1 Thess. ii. 8. [2]1 Thess. ii. 9. [3]1 Thess. ii. 12.
[4]2 Thess. i. 5. [5]1 Thess. iv. 8. [6]Rom. vi. 3.

statement of the Jews, as given by Luke, we learn that Paul, in preaching, preached the kingship of Jesus, for they charged him with saying, "There is another king, one Jesus."[1] This accords with Paul's own statement to the church when he exhorts them to "Walk worthy of God who hath called you into his kingdom and glory." Now, as these persons were in the kingdom they must have been baptized in order to obtain citizenship, or else they came in contrary to the expressed teaching of Christ, for He said, "Verily, verily, I say unto you, except a man be born of water, and of the Spirit he cannot enter into the kingdom of God."[2] Thus we find that the ordinance of baptism which Jesus submitted to and commanded to be obeyed in order to citizenship in the kingdom of God, was necessarily enjoined here. Finally, these persons were said to have received the gift of the Holy Spirit.

It would not be important to dwell on these plain matters of fact were it not also a plain matter of fact that the positive commands of God, the teaching of His inspired apostles, and the example of all the cases of pardon thus far given are either designedly or ignorantly disregarded, in most cases of modern conversion. But few preachers anywhere give the Scriptural answer to the question, "What must I do to be saved?" or even refer inquirers for information to the history of the many specific cases of pardon given under Christ.

[1]Acts xvii. 7. [2]John iii. 5.

CHAPTER XXVI

OPPOSITION TO PAUL

Paul Opposed by Both Jews and Judaizers. The Gospel and the Bereans. Paul Arrives at Athens. Preaches in the Synagogue.

FROM the history of the Thessalonians, as given by Luke and Paul, we have the following facts: That Paul preached Jesus to them, that some of the Jews believed and a great multitude of devout Greeks, that they turned to God or repented. These facts are positively stated. And that they were baptized is just as evident, because they were addressed as being "in Christ," and "in the kingdom of God," and baptism is required before entering either. It is also stated that they had received the gift of the Holy Spirit. Thus, having submitted to the law of pardon required of all, they were addressed as brethren and exhorted to "rejoice evermore" and "pray without ceasing." Only two members of this flourishing church are spoken of by name: these are Aristarchus and Secundus—they evidently became traveling companions of Paul. The last named is only mentioned once by Luke. Aristarchus was arrested by a mob in Ephesus. He journeyed with Paul to Rome and Paul spoke of him while there as a fellow laborer and "fellow prisoner."[1]

[1]Col. iv. 10.

Paul and Silas were compelled to leave Thessalonica abruptly. We are informed that the Jews, moved with envy, incited idlers in the market-place and vicious men and created a great uproar in the city, assaulting the house of Jason, but failing to find Paul and Silas there, "dragged Jason and certain brethren before the rulers of the city, crying, These that have turned the world upside down are come hither also; whom Jason hath received; and all these are acting contrary to the decrees of Cæsar, saying that there is another king, one Jesus. . . . And having taken security of Jason and the rest, they let them go. And the brethren immediately sent away Paul and Silas by night to Berea."[1] Thus we learn that in the city of Thessalonica, as at many other places on former occasions, the Jews stirred up the people to persecute Paul. From the Acts and the first of Paul's epistles we learn that those of his own nation—the Jews—during the early part of his ministry, were his greatest enemies. From his later epistles we learn that in his closing years Judaizing Christians were his unrelenting foes."[2] He was first persecuted by the Jews for preaching Christ, he was last persecuted by Judaizers for not preaching Moses.

After the uproar had been raised in the city, and security had been taken of Jason and others, we are informed that "the brethren immediately sent away Paul and Silas by night unto Berea, who coming thither went into the synagogue of the Jews. These were more noble than those in Thessalonica, in that

[1] Acts xvii. 6–10. [2] Gal. ii. 4–14, v. 11–14.

they received the word with all readiness of mind, and searched the Scriptures daily whether these things were so. Many, therefore, believed, and of the honorable women, which were Greeks, and of men not a few. But when the Jews of Thessalonica had knowledge that the word of God was preached by Paul at Berea they came thither also and stirred up the people."[1]

In regard to the preaching of the gospel to, and its reception by, the Bereans, it will be observed that Paul went into the synagogue of the Jews and appealed to their Scriptures, as on former occasions, in proof of the Messiahship of Christ. They were commended for receiving the word and searching the Scriptures; these were the Jewish Scriptures. We have no positive evidence that any part of the New Testament was written at this time. It is important to note here that the sacred historian commends the Bereans for searching the Scriptures. Should not preachers of the gospel now profit by this example and request their hearers to follow it and thus test the truth of their preaching? Again, if it was noble for the hearers of an inspired apostle to search the Scriptures to prove his statements, would it not be still more noble or important for hearers of uninspired teachers to search the Scriptures and thus know whether the things they teach are "so"? The opportunities and responsibilities of hearers are greater now than they were then. Now, we have the New-Testament Scriptures in full to search, as well as to trace the fulfilment of the old

[1]Acts xvii. 10–13.

in the new. Again, so important did this people consider the message which Paul brought that they searched the Scriptures daily to learn "whether these things were so." If all who hear now would do as the Bereans of old, a knowledge of the Lord would soon cover the world. The important lesson learned from this is not only that it is noble to search, but that hearers by searching may find out—may know whether these things are so.

The result of Paul's preaching and this diligent search was that many believed. Here it is only stated that they believed. But that belief is put not only for the reception but obedience to the gospel is evident from the fact that we are informed that "the word of God was preached of Paul at Berea," and the Word of God, we have seen, embraces the whole system of redemption.

When the Jews from Thessalonica had come to Berea and "stirred up the people," then "immediately the brethren sent forth Paul to go as far as to the sea, but Silas and Timotheus abode there still; and they who conducted Paul brought him to Athens, and receiving a commandment unto Silas and Timotheus that they should come to him with all speed, they departed. Now while Paul was waiting for them at Athens his spirit was stirred in him, when he saw the city full of idols. Therefore he reasoned in the synagogue with the Jews and the devout persons, and in the market daily with those who met with him."[1]

Moved by the idolatry of this great city Paul sought

[1]Acts xvii. 14–17.

first to preach the gospel to those of his own nation. He therefore "reasoned in the synagogue with the Jews." Much less stress seems to be placed on the Jewish element in the city of Athens than other places. We are not even informed how he was received by the worshipers in the synagogue nor the effect of his preaching upon them. It was customary with Paul in every city which he entered, before preaching to the Gentiles, to present to the Jews the Christ of their own prophecy in whose name the Gentiles might also trust, He who alone was able to turn all "from darkness to light and from the power of Satan unto God." It is marvelous when we contrast the effect of the preaching of the Christian religion by Paul in the various cities with the preaching of the Jewish religion established in them for centuries. While for ages there were synagogues in most of the important cities of Europe, Asia, and even Africa, yet in no city of the Gentile world had this religion suppressed idolatry or heathen worship. It was not adapted to mankind—not intended to become universal. While it was intended to bring out a Redeemer for the world it seemed powerless to redeem even a single Gentile city from superstition and idolatry. But what mighty inroads were made upon idolatry by the single life of Paul, and how Christianity swept it as with the besom of destruction.

CHAPTER XXVII

PAUL AT ATHENS

Athens. Greek Achievement. Paul's Address on Mars' Hill Sets Forth the Unknown God. Their Many Gods.

THIS brings us to the consideration of Paul's single-handed combat with pagan philosophy and idolatry in its stronghold. Paul's discourse, delivered "in the midst of Mars Hill," is one of the most eloquent and instructive of his life. The Gentile world will hold it in everlasting remembrance. In this discourse and in his instruction to the Gentiles at Lystra[1] we learn how the great apostle preached to those who had no knowledge of Jewish prophecy or Jewish scripture. Viewed in this light, as well as for its facts and intrinsic worth, it becomes intensely interesting. The philosophers who called it forth, the place where delivered, the people addressed, all enhance the interest. We are informed that "certain philosophers of the Epicureans and of the Stoics encountered him; and some said, What will this babbler say? and others, He seems to be a proclaimer of strange gods; because he preached Jesus and the resurrection. And they took hold of him, and they brought him upon the Areopagus, saying, May we know what this new doctrine whereof thou speakest is, for thou bringest certain

[1]Acts xiv. 15–17.

strange things to our ears? We would know therefore what these things mean. Now all the Athenians and strangers sojourning here spent their time in nothing else but either to tell or to hear some new thing."[1]

The systems of philosophy referred to here were founded by Epicureus and Zeno at about the same period of time—some three hundred years before Christ. They largely supplanted the higher schools founded before them, and at this period were the popular systems. Pleasure was the end sought by the Epicurean system. Its highest aim was self-gratification. Being atheistic or materialistic, its final and legitimate fruits were a gross sensualism. Stoicism was pantheistic. According to their system matter was inseparable from deity. They were taught much in words that was good, but their system was founded in pride. A man living according to reason was self-sufficient, needed no higher power and cared for none. They looked with contempt on human weakness. The ultimate of the one system was self-gratification or pleasure, of the other egotism or pride. It was with representatives of these two systems Paul disputed and was called by them to discourse upon "this new doctrine" publicly in Athens, the capital city of Greece.

In regard to this advanced country it has been said that, "Nowhere on earth before or since has the human being been educated into such wonderful perfection —such an entire unfolding of itself as in Greece.

[1]Acts xvii. 18–20.

There every human tendency and faculty of soul and body opened in symmetrical proportion. That small country, so insignificant on the map of Europe, so invisible on the map of the world, carried to perfection, in a few short centuries, human art. Everything in Greece is art, because everything is finished—done perfectly well. In that garden of the world ripened the masterpieces of epic, tragic, comic, lyric, and didactic poetry—the masterpieces in every school of philosophic investigation; the masterpieces of architecture, sculpture, and painting. Greece developed every form of human government, and in Greece were fought and won the great battles of the world. Before Greece everything in human literature and art was a rude and imperfect attempt. Since Greece everything has been a rude and imperfect imitation."[1]

The Greeks were also a religious people—they were devoted to religion. While altars and idols were common to the Greeks, yet it was said that "there were more gods in Athens than in all the rest of the country." And that it was "easier to find a god there than a man." The Greeks borrowed their idea of God from man. They divined and carved him in his most perfect form. According to divine revelation God made man in His own image, but the Greeks reversed this order and made God in the image of man. This was still a higher conception of God than the worship of hideous monsters, as in India, or beasts and reptiles, as in Egypt.

[1]"Ten Great Religions," by Jas. F. Clark, page 270.

We now contemplate Paul in the capital city of this wondrous country. This great city wholly given to idolatry, or "full of idols." Here he is called upon to speak of the living and true God, surrounded by the works of art, by temples, by statues, altars, and idols. Here in Athens, the city "built nobly on the Ægean shore, the eye of Greece, mother of arts and eloquence,"[1] Paul stands alone in the home of Socrates, Plato, Aristotle, Demosthenes, inspired by the Holy Spirit, and reminded by all the great poets from Homer down, together with all the philosophers, statesmen, warriors, and the artists whose works before him commemorated their mighty deeds, kept in remembrance their laurels won on all the fields in the wide range of human ambition. Here he stands before the most cultured living and the monuments of the greatest dead. Here we see divine wisdom contrasted with human attainment, when the great apostle speaks to a race of people whose worldly knowledge had surpassed all antiquity, whose achievements were the greatest known on earth, unaided by divine wisdom, uninspired by hope of the future. Here, in such a place, surrounded with such circumstances, standing in the Areopagus where law was discussed and judgment executed, Paul shows the wisdom of this world as foolishness with God and calls their attention from created idols to the creator of heaven and earth, who has a right to call the living to repentance and the dead to judgment.

He said, "Men of Athens, I perceive that in all

[1]"Paradise Regained."

things ye are very religious. For as I passed by and observed your objects of worship I found an altar with this inscription: TO THE UNKNOWN GOD. Whom therefore ye worship in ignorance, him I declare unto you. The God who made the world and all things therein. He being Lord of heaven and earth, dwells not in temples made with hands. Neither is he served by men's hands as though he needed anything. Seeing he giveth unto all life and breath and all things; and hath made of one blood all nations of men to dwell on all the face of the earth, having determined their appointed seasons and the bounds of their habitations. That they should seek the Lord if haply they might feel after him and find him, though he is not far from every one of us, for in him we live and move and have our being; as certain also of your own poets have said, 'For we are also his offspring.' Being then the offspring of God we ought not to think that the Godhead [or Deity] is like unto gold or silver or stone, graven by art and man's device. The times of ignorance therefore God overlooked, but now commandeth all men everywhere to repent, because he has appointed a day in which he will judge the world in righteousness by the man whom he hath appointed; he hath given assurance to all in that he hath raised him from the dead."[1]

The first thing which attracts our attention in this discourse of Paul's is the compliment he pays to the Athenians on account of their devotion or their carefulness in religion. While altars were erected to the

[1]Acts xvii. 22–31.

known gods and were in great abundance on every hand, they had not failed to erect one "to the unknown God." This furnishes the theme for Paul, while at the same time it relieves him of the charge of preaching "strange gods." This compliment was just. "The whole life of the Greeks was permeated by religion. They instinctively and naturally prayed on all occasions. They prayed at sunrise and sunset, at meal-times for outer blessings of all kinds, and also for virtue and wisdom. They prayed standing, with a loud voice, and hands lifted to the heavens. They threw kisses to the gods with their hands."[1] This altar was inscribed, "To the Unknown God." Notwithstanding the Grecians had many gods, to some of whom were ascribed greater powers than to others, yet the attributes of each were limited and their passions and propensities were of human conception, as well as their form. But what was the image of Jupiter or the powers he represented compared to the unknown God. "As a work of human art the Jupiter of Phidias stands alone—has never been equaled. Made of ivory and gold, forty feet high, on a pedestal twelve feet, this greatest of human gods was seated on a throne made of cedar, gold, ebony, ivory, studded with precious stones, seated in a temple sixty-eight feet high, ninety-five feet wide and two hundred and thirty feet long, with the greatest expression of majesty and sweetness, together with the power of wisdom and goodness, ever conveyed by artist's chisel. No wonder when works of art have been admired by all

[1]"Ten Great Religions," page 301.

cultured people in all ages of the world that the Greek thought it a great calamity to die without beholding this image of their greatest god." But Paul proclaimed to them a God whom they worshiped, not knowing—a God who did not represent a passion, a propensity or a power of nature alone, but a God who had greater power, greater wisdom, and holier love than that which was ascribed to all their gods. A God whose image could not be carved, who was unknown to Greece, and for whose full revelation the world had been preparing for four thousand years—a God before whom, when all His attributes were revealed, all others were to fade away. Truly, such a God as Jesus revealed and Paul preached needed not "temples made with hands" in which to dwell when he had made the earth and all things therein. No ministration of human hands was needed by Him who had "given to all life and breath and all things." This God, great in wisdom, power, and goodness—superior to all human conception of Deity even by the wisest of earth, is now proclaimed on Mars Hill. How insignificant are altars, temples, and idols before Him who created all things, for "the heavens declare the glory of God and the firmament showeth His handiwork."[1]

From the description of this unknown God, and His great superiority over all that was known as gods or worshiped, Paul comes down to man and proclaims the unity of the human race, and asserts that God made of one blood all nations to dwell on all the face of the earth. That God made of one blood all

[1]Ps. xix. 1.

peoples is not only a revealed truth but is now demonstrated by science to be a fact.

The Grecian language, though the most perfect, had no word in it expressive of humanity—nothing to express the kinship of the race. All other people were called, by the Greeks, barbarians. As before quoted, Max Müller has stated that no such word as "mankind" is found in human language before Christ. Before Him it was Egyptian, Persian, Grecian, Roman, Jew and Gentile. Christ was the first on earth to reveal the fatherhood of God and the brotherhood of man. And Paul proclaimed here this great truth to the Gentile world.

It will be observed that Paul was interrupted before finishing this discourse to the Gentiles. Interrupted in this city of philosophers and numberless gods, when speaking of the one true God, the Creator of all; to a people who knew Him not, whose wisest philosophers had tried to discover Him by human reason but had failed. Paul asserted a truth after this which may have been inspired here when he said, "That the world by wisdom knew not God." This is a truth which can not be controverted. God and His attributes can only be known through revelation. "A proposition and its proof must be homogeneous." A superhuman proposition must have superhuman proof. "Canst thou by searching find out God?"[1] The wisest of the Greeks searched in vain to find the God whom Paul revealed. "Neither knoweth any man the Father, save the Son, and he to whomsoever

[1]Job xi. 7.

the Son will reveal him."[1] Again, this interruption of Paul and the mockery of those whom he addressed, demonstrates the truth of what he said in after years: "But we preach Christ crucified, unto the Jews a stumbling-block, and unto the Greeks foolishness." Again he says, "Not many wise men after the flesh, not many mighty, not many noble, are called."[2]

The philosophers of Greece, by reasoning knew not God, the Creator, who "giveth to all life and breath and all things." Divine revelation unfolds the design of creation and satisfies the desires of the created. The opening chapters of the Bible declare that God, when he created man, gave him dominion over the earth and all animate nature. All terrestrial creation terminates in man. He is the end. This is everywhere manifest. If man terminates in nothing, infinite design would seem to end without result—the world may grow old, fade away and die in the night of years without an eternal purpose having been accomplished by its creation, if man lives not again. No voice of nature tells the destiny of man or satisfies his longing desire for immortality. Jesus revealed and Paul preached this, giving the only solution of the problem of creation and of life and death. Revelation meets not only the design in creation but it is the only intelligent account of God known to man. "Hath not God made foolish the wisdom of the world?"[3] All the best ideas in regard to deity of the wisest of earth unaided by divine

[1]Matt. xi. 27. [2]1 Cor. i. 23–26. [3]1 Cor. i. 20.

revelation fall infinitely below the God whom Jesus revealed and Paul preached.

Paul in this discourse did not begin by referring to or quoting from the Jewish Scriptures, as he did when addressing Jews. Persons can, and many have, become Christian without having knowledge of the Old-Testament Scriptures. This new religion, while preceded by the Patriarchal and Jewish religions, is complete in itself to "save unto the uttermost." "Come unto me all ye that labor and are heavy laden and I will give you rest."[1] "Ye are complete in Him."[2] It spread over the world as an oral religion. It was the verbal story of the Christ told throughout the then known world that won for Christianity its first and greatest victories.

Notwithstanding that Paul's speech was rudely interrupted it was not without results, for, we are told, that certain men clave unto him and believed, among whom was Dionysius the Areopagite, and a woman named Damaris, and others with them. None of these, however, are again mentioned in the Acts or epistles nor was any church established in Athens in apostolic times. Yet this discourse of Paul still lives, expressing the fatherhood of God and the brotherhood of man. It grows more significant, exerts more power as the ages advance and will be proclaimed around the world in all coming time.

[1]Matt. xi. 28. [2]Col. ii. 10.

CHAPTER XXVIII

PAUL AT CORINTH

Paul in Corinth. Establishes a Church. Paul in Ephesus. His Third Missionary Journey. Apollos and The Baptism of John. Paul Arrested in Jerusalem and his Defense. Imprisoned at Cesarea. Speeches Before Festus, Felix, and Agrippa.

WE now come to consider briefly Paul's work in Corinth. We are informed that "after these things" Paul departed from Athens to Corinth.[1] It may be observed that this city, as Paul found it, was not the ancient Greek city, but it had been rebuilt as a Roman colony. In some regards it was more distinguished than the former city. Its location on the isthmus gave it great commercial advantage. It was renowned for industry, for wealth, for athletic sports, for philosophy, and noted for licentious worship. In many respects it was the most important city in Greece, and it was one of the most conspicuous cities for the early spread of the Christian religion. From this city and to this city six of Paul's fourteen epistles were written.

When Paul reached Corinth we are told that "he found a certain Jew, named Aquila, born in Pontus, and Priscilla, his wife, lately come from Italy; (because that Claudius had commanded all Jews to depart from Rome,) he came unto them and because

[1]Acts xviii. 1.

he was of the same trade he abode with them and worked, for by their trade they were tent-makers."[1] Here we learn that Paul, the great apostle, had a trade—that of tent making. This was an important industry in that age. Notwithstanding his daily toil, "he reasoned in the synagogue every sabbath and persuaded the Jews and Greeks. And when Silas and Timotheus came down from Macedonia Paul was pressed in the spirit and testified to the Jews that Jesus is the Christ."[2] But when the Jews rejected Him he said unto them, "Your blood be upon your own heads; I am clean: from henceforth I will go unto the Gentiles. And departing thence he went into the house of a certain man named Justus, a worshiper of God, whose house was adjacent to the synagogue."[3] This man was evidently a Gentile, but a worshiper of the true God. We are informed that "Crispus, the chief ruler of the synagogue, believed on the Lord with all his house, and many of the Corinthians hearing, believed and were baptized."[4] While it is only stated Crispus believed on the Lord with all his house and "many of the Corinthians hearing believed and were baptized," it can not be inferred that they did not comply fully with the terms of the gospel, as shown in preceding cases.

We will pass over briefly the remaining chapters in the book of Acts, noting any allusions to pardon, and also some of the important events in the life of the Apostle Paul.

[1]Acts xviii. 2, 3. [2]Acts xviii. 4, 5.
[3]Acts xviii. 6, 7. [4]Acts xviii. 8.

The Lord appeared to Paul in a vision by night, telling him, "be not afraid, but speak and hold not thy peace, for I am with thee, and no man shall set on thee to harm thee, for I have much people in this city."[1] How this prediction was fulfilled is shown by the fact that Paul remained there one year and a half, teaching the word of God. When the Jews made insurrection against him "and brought him to the judgment-seat," Gallio, the proconsul, drove them away, and the Greeks beat the chief persecutor before the judgment-seat. That the Lord had many people there is shown by subsequent history, and the two important epistles written by Paul to the Corinthian church. After the occurrence above named, Paul remained for some time and then sailed with Priscilla and Aquila into Syria. Afterward, "he came to Ephesus," where he went into the synagogue and "reasoned with the Jews."[2] Here we note that "he reasoned with them." Whether presenting the gospel to the Jews or Gentiles Paul "reasoned with them." It was the uniform custom with all the apostles, in presenting the gospel to the people, to reason with them—to teach them. In fact, they were commanded by the Lord to "Go teach all nations." The Christian religion is a reasonable religion. Its service is "a reasonable service."[3] It is a perfect system; perfect in its organization, in its ordinances, in its facts, precepts, and promises. It is law, order, harmony. To be a disciple is to be a learner under Christ, the great Teacher.

Paul's stay in Ephesus was brief. He sailed from

[1]Acts xviii. 9, 10. [2]Acts xviii. 19. [3]Rom. xii. 1.

there to Cesarea, went up and "saluted the church" at Jerusalem; and "he went down to Antioch." And after he had spent some time there he departed on his third missionary journey and went over all the country of Galatia and Phrygia in order, strengthening all the disciples.

Here we have the first mention of Apollos, a Jew. "Born at Alexandria, an eloquent man, and mighty in the Scriptures."[1] But he knew only "the baptism of John." While he was preaching at Ephesus Aquila and Priscilla heard him, "and they took him unto them and expounded unto him the way of God more perfectly"[2]—that is, Apollos now became a disciple of Christ and began to preach Christ. When he left Ephesus the brethren gave him letters of commendation to the disciples in Achaia, where he rendered them much assistance by his eloquent and powerful preaching. "For he mightily convinced the Jews, and that publicly, showing by the Scriptures that Jesus was the Christ."

At Corinth he was so highly esteemed by some of the Christians that he took rank with the apostles themselves. Paul mentions him, along with Cephas and himself, as one of the three upon whom the Church was in danger of dividing.[3] Some commentators put such high estimate on his character and ability that the disputed authorship of the Epistle to the Hebrews is by them assigned to this eloquent Alexandrian Jew.

When Paul reaches Ephesus, he finds there certain

[1]Acts xviii. 24. [2]Acts xviii. 26. [3]Cor. i. 10–13.

disciples of whom he inquires, "Have ye received the Holy Spirit since ye believed?" "And they said unto him, We have not so much as heard whether there be any Holy Spirit. And he said unto them, Unto what then were ye baptized? And they said, Unto John's baptism. Then said Paul, John verily baptized with the baptism of repentance, saying unto the people that they should believe on him which should come after him, that is on Christ Jesus. When they heard this they were baptized into the name of the Lord Jesus. . . . And all the men were about twelve."[1]

The question is frequently raised as to whether the disciples whom Jesus made during His earthly ministry were rebaptized or not after the day of Pentecost. Were the apostles and the one hundred and twenty rebaptized? There is no record to this effect. These constituted the charter members of the church. Why then rebaptize these twelve men at Ephesus? The twelve apostles and one hundred and twenty disciples were baptized with the baptism of John when that was an existing institution under the sanction of divine authority. But after the resurrection this institution was no longer in vogue. It was superseded by the baptism into the name of the Father, Son, and Holy Spirit. Then those who were baptized with the baptism of John after this institution had been abrogated were baptized without the sanction of divine authority and were proper subjects for rebaptism into Christ.

Paul abode in Ephesus two years: "So that all they

[1]Acts xix. 2–7.

which dwelt in Asia heard the word of the Lord Jesus, both Jews and Greeks. And God wrought special miracles by the hands of Paul." "And many that believed came and confessed and showed their deeds. Many of them also which used curious arts brought their books together and burned them before all men, and they counted the price of them and found it fifty thousand pieces of silver. So mightily grew the word of God and prevailed."[1] Demetrius, the silversmith, became very much alarmed lest his craft—the craft of making silver shrines for Diana, which brought him and his workmen of like occupation no small gain, should be set at nought; "but also lest the temple of the great goddess, Diana, should be despised and her magnificence should be destroyed."[2] Here is a most conspicuous example of the inimical clash of Christianity with idolatry—an earnest of its ultimate triumph which so soon overturned the idolatrous Roman Empire.

From Ephesus Paul revisits Macedonia and Greece, returns by way of Philippi to Troas, and observes the Lord's Supper with the brethren here on the first day of the week. Departing from Troas, Paul goes afoot to Assos where he meets his party aboard-ship and they sail for Miletus, to which place the elders from Ephesus are called to meet him and from whom he parts with a most touching farewell address. From Miletus he sailed to Tyre, where he was greeted by the disciples. Thence by way of Ptolemais and Cesarea to Jerusalem. At Cesarea he met Philip,

[1]Acts xix. 18, 19. [2]Acts xix. 27.

the evangelist, and was warned by Agabus, the prophet, that he would be delivered into the hands of the Gentiles if he should go to Jerusalem. After arriving at Jerusalem the brethren received him gladly. Before James and the elders he rehearsed his experiences among the Gentiles, and they glorified God.

Paul, as a Jew, had hurried back to Jerusalem to observe the day of Pentecost, and was willing, at the request of the Jewish Christians, to make the observance of purification in the temple. But it is here stated that "As touching the Gentiles which believe, we have written and concluded that they observe no such thing."[1] We are informed that the Jews, which were from Asia, stirred up the people against Paul, seized him and were about to kill him and were thwarted in their purpose by the chief captain of the band, who rescued him and gave him the privilege of addressing the people before taking him to prison.

Paul in his defense here relates how he had at one time persecuted the Christians, and how he himself afterward became a Christian. He had not only consented, but was an accomplice in the persecution of Stephen. Relates his conversion and call to the apostleship, a full account of which has heretofore been given. After this speech Paul was about to be scourged to exact a confession, but escaped by virtue of being a Roman citizen, and was on the next day accused by the Jews, and caused to appear before their council for a hearing. In the opening sentence of his speech, Paul states that he had lived

[1]Acts xxi. 25.

in all good conscience until this day. This is a most conspicuous example that conscience is not an infallible guide. He had the approbation of his conscience both in persecuting the Christians and in preaching the gospel. He caused division in the council by declaring himself a Pharisee, which resulted in a discussion between the Pharisees and Sadducees, and thus ended the trial. Paul was here rescued and returned to prison by the chief captain. And the night following the Lord stood by him and said: "Be of good cheer, Paul, for as thou hast testified of me in Jerusalem so must thou bear witness also at Rome."[1] Then follows a conspiracy to kill Paul, forty men having bound themselves under oath to do this. It was prevented by the chief captain, who sent him by night under strong military escort to Cesarea, with a most gracious letter to Felix, the Roman governor. Paul was here kept as a distinguished prisoner in Herod's judgment-hall, and the centurion was commanded to let him have liberty, and that he should forbid none of his acquaintances to minister or come unto him. The history of the imprisonment at Cesarea may be presented under three distinct heads:

First, the charges.

Second, the trial before Felix and Festus.

Third, his defense before Agrippa.

First, the Jews from Asia, who had laid hands on Paul, said: "This is the man that teacheth all men everywhere against the people and the law, and this place: and further brought Greeks also into the tem-

[1]Acts xxiii. 11.

ple and hath polluted this holy place."[1] Tertullus, the orator who was chosen by the high priest and elders to accompany them to Cesarea to prosecute Paul said in his discussion before Felix, the governor: "We have found this man a pestilent fellow and a mover of sedition among all the Jews throughout the world, and a ringleader of the sect of the Nazarenes; who also hath gone about to profane the temple."[2] These charges he urged eloquently, but his speech was without avail before the governor.

Second. Then the governor beckoned to Paul to make his own defense, which he cheerfully did, saying: "They neither found me in the temple disputing with any man, neither raising up the people, neither in the synagogues nor in the city; neither can they prove the things whereof they now accuse me."[3] He not only refutes the charges but implicates his accusers and makes a most memorable plea for Jesus and the resurrection. Felix deferred the case for certain days, when he appeared again before him and his wife. Upon this hearing, when Paul reasoned of righteousness, temperance, and judgment to come, Felix trembled. He was next accused of the Jews before Festus, the successor of Felix. The charges were not proven. Paul makes a brief defense and appeals to Cæsar. The case was so weak that Festus said, "It seemeth to me unreasonable to send a prisoner and not withal to signify the crimes laid against him."[4] This was the reason assigned for inviting King Agrippa to hear Paul.

[1]Acts xxi. 28. [2]Acts xxiv. 5, 6. [3]Acts xxiv. 12, 13. [4]Acts xxv. 27.

Third. This brings us to Paul's defense before Agrippa, where he makes a model speech in reason, rhetoric, and power. The manhood of the great apostle rises here to its full stature. It is not only a convincing defense of an innocent and distinguished prisoner, but is a most powerful and persuasive argument for the Christian faith. Paul's speeches here at Cesarea must ever rank with the most telling of all time. Before him Felix trembled, against him Festus could find no case, and would have set him at liberty had he not appealed to Cæsar. And Agrippa exclaimed to Paul, "Almost thou persuadest me to be a Christian."[1]

[1]Acts xxvi. 28.

CHAPTER XXIX

THE PRISONER OF THE LORD

From Cesarea to Rome as a Prisoner. Preaches Two Years and is Released. Paul's Last Days. Prayer—its Place. Terms of Pardon Divine and Unchangeable.

FROM Cesarea Paul is sent as a prisoner to Rome. On this journey, against the warning of Paul, they set sail from Crete and encountered a great storm, and were driven before the wind for fourteen days. During the storm an angel of God stood by Paul and assured him that he would be brought before Cæsar, and gave him the lives of all that sailed with him. The ship was wrecked on the coast of Melita and, notwithstanding the great peril, all reached the shore alive. After three months they took passage on a ship for Rome. When he arrived in Rome he was suffered to dwell by himself in his own hired house, with a soldier that kept him. There he called the chief of the Jews together. He told them why he was sent a prisoner from Jerusalem to Rome, and explained the facts of his imprisonment, of which they had not heard. "And when they had appointed him a day there came many to him into his lodging, to whom he expounded and testified the kingdom of God, persuading them concerning Jesus, both out of the law of Moses and out of the prophets, from morning till evening. And some believed the things which were spoken and some believed not. "And Paul dwelt two whole years in his own hired house and received all that came in unto him, preaching the kingdom of God and teaching those things which concern the Lord Jesus Christ with all confidence, no man forbidding him."[1]

Here in Rome, at the close of the history of Paul, as given in Acts, and near the close of his eventful life, we find him preaching the kingdom of God to the Jews, teaching them things concerning Jesus Christ. And we are informed that some of them believed the things that were spoken and some believed not. The burden of Paul's preaching in Rome, as elsewhere, was the kingdom of God as foretold by the prophets and as now established under the ascended, ruling, reigning Christ. Those who believed no doubt came into the kingdom upon the same terms ordained by Christ, submitted to by Paul himself, and required of all believers. It has been shown in the preceding history that these terms were uniform. Paul dwelt two years as a prisoner in his own hired house, preaching the kingdom of God.

The weight of evidence, both from some of Paul's epistles and early Christian writers, is that at the expiration of two years, or shortly thereafter, Paul was released; that he made another missionary journey, that he was again imprisoned in Rome, tried, condemned and beheaded without the walls of the city in the year 68, the last year of the reign of Nero. From the best information obtainable, seven years elapsed

[1]Acts xxviii. 30, 31.

from the time Paul first arrived as a prisoner in Rome until his execution under Nero. Besides his oral teaching there, if we include the epistle to the Hebrews seven of his fourteen epistles were written from Rome.[1]

Having called attention to all cases of pardon, giving in detail the history of the circumstances and what was required of all persons in order to enter the Church of Christ, we now observe that no man, no set of men, no ecclesiastical body since the close of this inspired history has any divine right to require less or demand more of any one in order to church membership. The requirements are full, complete, and divine, excluding all other terms imposed by man.

It is important to observe that prayer was not one of these terms. Man everywhere is a worshiper; it is not the intention to limit the mercy and power of God, when we say it was not commanded or enjoined upon any as a condition of pardon in coming into Christ. Cornelius, being a devout man, prayed, and his prayer was heard, but when Peter came to him he told him words whereby he and all his house should be saved.[2] Saul prayed for three days, and was then required to submit to the established law of pardon, as we have heretofore shown. The question may be asked in regard to the instance Christ relates of the man who "smote upon his breast, saying, God be merciful to me a sinner,"[3] who went down to his house justified rather than the other. We observe that this

[1]For an estimate of Paul's life and work, see pages 135–141.
[2]Acts xi. 14. [3]Luke xviii. 10–14.

was before Christ's death, the giving of the commission or the establishment of the Church. Also, that both men went up into the temple to pray, and were Jews, as only Jews were permitted in the temple. It is a fact that Christ lived under the Jewish economy and kept its law. This justification was under that law before it was fulfilled by Christ and taken out of the way. Prayer is neither stated nor implied in any case as a condition of pardon in coming into Christ's Church. If, therefore, prayer is not enjoined on the unconverted as a term of pardon why should such protracted scenes and sieges of prayer, as have been enacted in recent years, supplant the plain teaching of inspiration in cases of pardon?

A striking proof of a departure from the gospel by many religious teachers is that they call upon unbelievers to pray for faith and to approach God devoid of the very principle by which they are to be accepted of Him. When the apostle speaks of the efficacy of prayer he states that "the effectual fervent prayer of a righteous man availeth much," and it is when persons ask in accordance with the will of God that they are to expect an answer to their prayer, for "without faith it is impossible to please God." "Faith cometh by hearing . . . the word of God." "Hearing they believed and were baptized." "How shall they believe in him of whom they have not heard?" Therefore the order of the gospel is to hear, believe, obey, and then "to continue steadfast in prayer." To "pray without ceasing." The rule is that the right of petition belongs to the citizen and not to the alien or foreigner. This is true in society and government, and it is also true in the kingdom of Christ. The early Christians were a praying people. They followed their great Exemplar in sincere devotion and earnest prayer. In the New Testament it is most fully enjoined upon Christians. The deep and unyielding devotion of the early disciples of Christ comes down through the ages, bearing testimony to the great importance of prayer. Prayer has new significance under Christ. All Christians are constituted kings and priests to God, and can approach Him as no person ever did before—"through a new and living way," through their "great High Priest who ever liveth to make intercession for them." In fact this new religion, these new principles taught by Christ of the fatherhood of God, the brotherhood of man, of love, of humility, of forgiveness, of worship, of trust in God, and of immortality, has changed the world's destiny. Wherever taught and received it has made a more benevolent, more intelligent, greater, and better people than were known to earth. No philosophy or religion made man so happy, so great, so good; inspired such noble deeds in life and imparted such immortal hope in death.

In the Acts we see how teachers approached the unconverted, and in the epistles how they addressed Christians. These and the book of Revelation, the apocalyptic vision of John, close the Scriptures.

"The wall of separation, which forever cuts off the apostolic age from that which followed it, was built by the hand of God. That age of miracles was not to be revealed to us as passing, by any gradual transition into the common life of the church. It was intentionally isolated from all succeeding time, that we might learn to appreciate more fully the extraordinary character and see, by the sharpness of the abruptest contrast, the difference between the human and the divine."[1]

After the conclusion of the history in Acts no person or church had any divine authority to impose any new condition of pardon in order to admission into Christ's Church. After the "Alpha and Omega" of Revelation there is no divine authority to impose any new command upon any person, not a Christian, or any member of the household of God. Since the close of the New Testament nothing has come down to us, to saint or sinner, bearing the seal of inspiration. There is no apostolic succession provided therein. No infallible man or church was to succeed the Church of Christ. Paul says, "But though we, or an angel from heaven, preach any other gospel unto you than that which we have preached unto you, let him be accursed."[2] John, in closing Revelation, says: "If any man shall add unto these things, God shall add unto him the plagues that are written in this book: And if any man shall take away from the words of the book of this prophecy, God shall take away his part out of the book of life, and out of the holy city, and from the things which are written in this book."[3]

[1]See "Life and Epistles of St. Paul," Conybeare and Howson, pages 336, 337. [2]Gal. i. 8. [3]Rev. xxii. 18, 19.

BOOK SECOND

EVIDENCE OF PARDON AND THE CHURCH AS AN ORGANIZATION

CHAPTER XXX

THE ASSURANCE OF PARDON

Importance of Pardon. Different Views of Pardon. Consciousness of Sin. The Scripture the Only Evidence. Scripture Terms the Only Way of Pardon. Knowledge of Pardon. Promise Cannot Fail. Senses Versus Testimony.

IN the preparation of the chapters (Chapters xxx to xxxiii inclusive and from xxxvi to xxxix inclusive), the author in many cases has followed notes made by him for his own use years ago, and some passages may have been copied from writers of an earlier date and the quotation marks cannot now be supplied.

Having passed in review every case of pardon presented in the New Testament, and having shown, as we believe, that there is one law of pardon governing all, and that all persons entered the Church of Christ by obedience to the same law, we will now examine the evidence of their acceptance with God.

We would note the close connection between the evidence of pardon and the history of pardon, and in the consideration of this subject it will be necessary, to some extent, to repeat the terms of pardon.

To us, in the light of sacred history, a large part of the religious world seems confused both as to the terms of forgiveness and the assurance of pardon. It may be truthfully said, that no one question more deeply interests the professed followers of Christ than this: How can a person in this life be fully assured that God through Christ has forgiven his sins? To the answer of this question we now direct attention. The assurance that professed Christians have of the forgiveness of all past sins is of the highest importance.

No person can enjoy peace of mind and the real undoubted consolation of Christianity who is destitute of the proper evidence of pardon. It is not enough for persons to feel they are pardoned while at times they doubt it. We are told that "if our hearts condemn us not then we have confidence toward God." In order then to the enjoyment of Christianity there must be an undisputed evidence of the forgiveness of sins, and such evidence as shall ever be present, otherwise there will be doubt and gloom.

We now inquire for the proper evidence of the forgiveness of sins. There are three distinct and conflicting views on this subject entertained by the different denominations in Christendom. One class maintain that no person can be certain of pardon in this life. That if we are forgiven, the Almighty, in His wisdom, locks up the fact in the secret councils of His own will, leaving us in doubt and fear as long as we remain upon the earth. The second class maintain that every pardoned man absolutely knows the fact. That he has full assurance that God has blotted out his sins, and that he knows it because he has received a direct communication from heaven attesting the fact by an impression made upon his heart and that he cannot be mistaken because he feels his sins forgiven and therefore knows the fact. The third class maintain that faith in the word of God and obedience to the stipulated conditions of pardon are all-sufficient to give a man full assurance that he is pardoned, justified, and saved, independent of any other witness directly from heaven or from any other source.

We first inquire: What evidence have we that a man in an unconverted state is guilty before God and that he needs pardon? Second, what are the terms of pardon? Third, how shall we know or be assured that we are pardoned? Fourth, how shall a Christian, if he be overtaken in a fault, or commit sin, be assured of pardon?

First, what evidence have we that a man in an unconverted state is guilty before God and that he needs pardon? All agree that the information or evidence must come from the fountain of all wisdom. We must hear what the Lord and His apostles have said on the subject. Do they show that man is sinful—guilty—and that he needs pardon? They inform us we would not have "known sin but by the law"; that "God hath concluded them in unbelief, that he might have mercy upon all." Paul says: "We have before proved both Jews and Gentiles that they are all under sin." The Lord came, "not to call the righteous, but sinners to repentance." And "the Son of man is come to seek and to save that which is lost." All these passages and many more go to make man sensible of his guilty and sinful condition. In the Scriptures alone we have a definition of sin. John says: "Sin is the transgression of law." Again, we are told that "where no law is there is no transgression." Since the Lord reveals to man his sinful, guilty, and lost condition through the Scriptures we may rationally expect Him to give the knowledge or evidence of pardon through the same source. If the law declares the transgressor a sinner, why may not the same law declare the obedient righteous? If the Scriptures give evidence of man's guilt, do they not also give evidence of man's justification from that guilt through the obedience to the "Lord from heaven?" The Scriptures bear witness that the whole world (that is, those not converted), are guilty before God and included under sin, "for all have sinned and come short of the glory of God." It is Scriptural evidence alone that proves the disobedient guilty, and, therefore, it must prove the obedient justified.

Second, all who would become Christians must comply with the terms of pardon. It was shown that all persons, after the Church of Christ was established, were pardoned upon the same terms or conditions, there being no distinction made between Jew and Gentile, male and female, bond and free. All obeyed in the same manner and received the same blessings.

These terms may be briefly recapitulated here: First, all who come to the Savior to obtain pardon are required to believe on Him. This, all who have knowledge of the truth can do. And "without faith it is impossible to please God." Second, those seeking pardon must repent. "Repent, ye, therefore, and turn again." They can and must turn to God with full purpose of heart. Third, all were required to be baptized. "Go ye into all the world and preach the gospel to every creature; he that believeth and is baptized shall be saved" (or pardoned), "baptizing them into the name of the Father, and of the Son, and of the Holy Spirit." Faith, repentance, and baptism are the steps or appointed way by which persons come into the Church of Christ. Nor is there any other way appointed. Without complying with these terms there is no testimony that any one came into the Church, and all who thus came were promised the gift of the Holy Spirit, and by continuing faithful unto death were promised eternal life. To deny that persons who had thus come were pardoned and added to the believers would be to deny the sacred record.

Third, How did they know that they were pardoned? The evidence was full and satisfactory. What is the evidence? "He that believeth and is baptized shall be saved."[1] "Know ye not that so many of us as were baptized into Christ were baptized into his death?"[2] "For as many of you as have been baptized into Christ have put on Christ."[3] "For I know whom I have believed and am persuaded that he is able to keep that which I have committed unto him against that day."[4] "There is therefore now no condemnation to them that are in Christ Jesus. For the law of the spirit of life in Christ Jesus hath made me free from the law of sin and death."[5]

The kingdom of the Messiah is a kingdom which

[1] Mark xvi. 16. [2] Rom. vi. 3. [3] Gal. iii. 27.
[4] 1 Tim. i. 12. [5] Rom. viii. 1, 2.

cannot be moved, and a promise of the King is a promise that cannot fail. "Heaven and earth shall pass away, but my words shall not pass away."[1] The words then that shall not pass away are pledged for the pardon of the sins of those who obey. The stipulations made in the commission given by Christ were presented on the day of Pentecost when three thousand accepted them. They could not doubt without questioning the veracity of the Lord and His inspired apostles.

In addition to the promise that they should be saved we have the statement, "God also bearing them witness both with signs and wonders and with divers miracles and gifts of the Holy Spirit."[2] This was an additional evidence of their pardon and acceptance with God.

Paul to the Roman brethren thus speaks: "God be thanked that whereas ye were the servants of sin ye have obeyed from the heart that form of doctrine which was delivered you. Being then made free from sin ye became the servants of righteousness."[3] Here the apostle connects their being made free from sin with their having obeyed from the heart that form of doctrine delivered them.

The Lord promised penitent believers who would submit to Him in the ordinance of baptism the forgiveness of sins. This promise was the evidence to them before their obedience that they should be saved or pardoned. Upon this promise three thousand on the day of Pentecost were baptized. Did the promise

[1]Matt. xxiv. 35. [2]Heb. ii. 4. [3]Rom. vi. 17, 18.

prove true or fail? The miracles which followed them showed that the Lord had received them. But in addition to these displays of divine power the apostles repeatedly and explicitly declared them pardoned, forgiven, justified, and saved.

Some want evidence of their pardon addressed to their senses—something they can hear, see, or feel, that will give them, as they say, certain knowledge of the fact. But facts are believed on testimony. A court and jury declare innocent or guilty upon the testimony of others. Are those who have not visited the city of London just as certain of its existence as they are of the cities which they have visited and seen? We are just as certain of all the continents of the earth upon the testimony of others as if we had visited and seen them.

Again, as to certainty or knowledge, Peter says: "Let all the house of Israel know assuredly that God has made that same Jesus whom ye have crucified both Lord and Christ." We ask, in what way did the hearers know this? They knew it then only by the oral testimony of the apostles. Again, the apostle Paul says: "We know that if our earthly house of this tabernacle were dissolved, we have a building of God, a house not made with hands, eternal in the heavens." Thus, Paul speaks of this fact as known. Again, John says: "We know that when he shall appear we shall be like him, for we shall see him as he is." This is sufficient to show that the apostles speak of knowing things which they did not attest with their senses.

CHAPTER XXXI

THE PROOF OF PARDON

Feelings not Evidence. The Testimony of the Spirit. Conscience. Sanctification. Revivals. A Sure Foundation. Penalty for Disobedience.

THE Lord appeals to the higher principles of our nature. And as they are spiritual things, not carnal, for which we hope, it is proper to make the principle of faith our assurance. Paul says: "We walk by faith and not by sight." John Wesley observed that sight is here put for all the senses. This is undoubtedly correct. Hence, when a person says, "I know my sins are forgiven because I feel it," his religion is based upon the lower principle or carnal nature—upon sight and not upon faith.

It is asked, is it not the design of Christianity to make men feel well? But good feelings result from assurance of pardon and not assurance from good feelings. Religious joy is the result of religious knowledge and obedience. The joy or happiness arising after pardon is not the evidence, but the knowledge of pardon produces the joy. Are persons pardoned because they are happy, or are they happy because they are pardoned? The happiness comes from the knowledge, not the knowledge from the happiness. Some who have "gotten religion" say they are happy because they know they are forgiven, and they are forgiven because they are happy. This is circular logic, and, like the Catholic priest, when assailed by a Protestant, proved the infallibility of the Church by the Bible; and when assailed by the skeptic proved the Bible to be true by the infallibility of the Church. Making the feelings the proof of conversion, and conversion the cause of good feelings is what Paul calls "measuring themselves by themselves," and adds that such "are not wise."

But how do persons know that their sins are forgiven? Because Paul says God has sworn "that by two immutable things, in which it was impossible for God to lie, we might have a strong consolation, who have fled for refuge to lay hold upon the hope set before us."[1] They had full assurance of faith, "having their hearts sprinkled from an evil conscience, and their bodies washed with pure water."[2] That they knew they were pardoned, justified, saved, because God had pledged His immutable oath, and they had complied with the conditions and their assurance is based on God's word. They enjoy happiness then as a result of their faith, which gives them the full assurance of acceptance. This accords with the Scripture. The sacred historian informs us that after the jailer had been baptized "he rejoiced, believing in God." The Apostle Peter says: "Believing, ye rejoice with joy unspeakable and full of glory." The word contains the promise of pardon which we enjoy by obedience to the requirements.

[1]Heb. vi. 18. [2]Heb. x. 22.

This word, so far from being a dead letter, as some teach, is "quick and powerful," "liveth and abideth forever."[1]

We should remember that the Lord says, "The word that I have spoken, the same shall judge him in the last day."[2] What better evidence could any one desire than to be declared pardoned by the Judge—by His word justified on that final day?

Suppose those who want some better evidence than the word of the Lord would state some fact and we would respond, we want better testimony than your word—would we not make them liars? Can persons thus speak of the word of the Lord and believe His revelation is true? "If we receive the witness of men, the witness of God is greater."[3]

Some people speak of sin as an affair of the body rather than the soul, and forgiveness as an internal, physical sensation. Instead of such a conception sin is a transgression of the law—it pertains to the moral and religious nature, and forgiveness is not an internal operation in the sinner's heart, but is a mental act of the one who forgives. For instance, the Governor resolves to pardon a convict about to be executed. Does the convict just then feel an internal operation? No, but he still feels that death is approaching. But a message of pardon is prepared by the Governor and when he receives this message he knows that he is a pardoned man. An important change has taken place in the feelings of the convict and he rejoices, but this change was not the act of forgiveness, for that took

[1]Heb. iv. 12; 1 Pet. i. 23. [2]John xii. 48. [3]1 John v. 9.

place in the mind of the Governor before the convict knew it. But the change was effected by the message which the convict received from the Governor that he was pardoned. So the transgressor is pardoned, not in his own bosom, but in the mind of God, and has assurance of this fact in His word. But he is not required to wait after pardon, as the convict, for a message to come down from heaven to notify him of the fact, for the Word that states the terms of pardon for man also states the promise of forgiveness as soon as man obeys. "Say not in thine heart who shall ascend into heaven (that is, to bring Christ down) or who shall descend into the deep (that is, to bring Christ up again from the dead). But what sayeth it? The word is nigh thee, even in thy mouth and in thy heart: that is the word of faith which we preach; that if thou shalt confess with thy mouth the Lord Jesus and shalt believe in thine heart that God has raised him from the dead thou shalt be saved."[1]

There is nothing taught more plainly in the Scriptures than that God is ready to receive all, even those who have gone into the depths of sin, as did the prodigal son, and to extend mercy to all. We quote a few from the many passages on this subject: "And you, being in time past alienated and enemies in your mind by wicked works, yet now hath he reconciled in the body of his flesh through death, to present you holy and unblamable and unreprovable in his sight."[2] "For if, when we were enemies, we were reconciled to God by the death of his Son, much more, being

[1]Rom. x. 6–9. [2]Col. i. 21, 22.

reconciled, we shall be saved by his life."[1] "All things are of God, who hath reconciled us to himself by Jesus Christ, and hath given to us the ministry of reconciliation; to wit, that God was in Christ, reconciling the world unto himself, not imputing their trespasses unto them."[2] One of the mistakes of the religious world in praying and beseeching God to be reconciled to the sinner, is that many seem to forget that the whole remedial system proceeds upon the plan or idea that God freely offers pardon to all doing His commandments and is ready and willing to accept man immediately upon his return to Him, for "God was in Christ reconciling the world to himself." "God so loved the world, that he gave his only begotten Son, that whosoever believeth in him should not perish, but have everlasting life."[3] The world was perishing and God gave His Son to save because He loved the world. "We love him (God), because he first loved us."[4] The prodigal son did not need to stand and plead, but "when he was yet a great way off, his father saw him, and had compassion on him, and ran and fell on his neck, and kissed him," and said, "It was meet that we should make merry, and be glad: for this thy brother was dead, and is alive again; and was lost, and is found."[5] Jesus says, "Behold, I stand at the door and knock: if any man hear my voice, and open the door, I will come in to him, and will sup with him, and he with me."[6] "Whosoever will, let him take of the water of life freely."[7]

[1]Rom. v. 10. [2]2 Cor. v. 18, 19. [3]John iii. 16. [4]1 John iv. 19. [5]Luke xv. 20, 32. [6]Rev. iii. 20. [7]Rev. xxii. 17.

Again, persons often say the thief on the cross was saved. Jesus said to him, "To-day shalt thou be with me in paradise." This is all the evidence there is in the case. The word of Jesus to us is to be relied upon as much as His word to the thief on the cross. The expression, "he that believeth and is baptized shall be saved," is as true as the words, "To-day thou shalt be with me in paradise." It is conceded that the word spoken by Satan in Eden possessed power enough to ruin mankind. Why then deny that the words of Christ contain sufficient power to save men?

There is another passage relied upon more strongly than any other by those who maintain feelings as the basis of their assurance. It reads, "The Spirit itself beareth witness with our spirit that we are the children of God."[1] In what way do persons become children of God? "As many as received him, to them gave he the right to become children of God, even to them that believe on his name."[2] How do we know that the Spirit bears witness? The Scriptures say so. Thus we perceive that the Scriptures are the evidence. But the question arises, How shall we know that the Spirit bears witness with our spirit? John says, "Believe not every spirit, but try the spirits whether they be of God." Can a man try the Spirit when it bears witness whether it be of God? Again, John says: "We are of God; he that knoweth God heareth us and he that is not of God heareth not us. Hereby know we the spirit of truth and the spirit of error."[3] "Therefore by their fruits ye shall know them. Not

[1]Rom. viii. 16. [2]John i. 12. [3]1 John iv. 6.

every one that saith unto me, Lord, Lord, shall enter into the kingdom of heaven; but he that doeth the will of my Father who is in heaven."[1] The test is by hearing and obeying what is enjoined.

Paul says, "In these latter times some shall depart from the faith, giving heed to seducing spirits and doctrines of demons."[2] Trusting in the infallibility of an internal monitor and its superiority, some rely upon it altogether and neglect the testimony of the Spirit. Paul informs us, that in order to deceive the followers of Christ Satan himself is "transformed into an angel of light."[3] We should be sure that this "angel of light" is not what is called the "Light within." Persons may think they are influenced by the spirit of truth when it is the spirit of error.

All who obey the requirements of the Savior and His apostles have the witness of the Spirit because the Apostles spake "as the Spirit gave them utterance." Hence the promise of pardon by them to the obedient is the testimony of the Spirit. The testimony of the Spirit and our spirit meet in obedience. "The fruit of the Spirit is love, joy, peace, longsuffering, kindness, goodness, faithfulness, meekness, self-control."[4]

Every assurance of pardon or acceptance with God of a life after death, every divine impression or spiritual idea, either directly or indirectly, comes by the revealed Word of God, and if Christians can not trust the Lord's word as sufficient evidence of the forgive-

[1]Matt. vii. 20, 21. [2]1 Tim. iv. 1.
[3]2 Cor. xi. 14. [4]Gal. v. 22, 23.

ness of sins, they should not wonder that it is rejected by skeptics. But they can rely upon it with undoubted assurance, and all who receive it and are faithful will triumph and die in the hope of life and bliss beyond the grave.

Before feeling or impulse can be an evidence of pardon, we must have some rule imparting knowledge to us of how a pardoned person would feel. One who has never been pardoned may tell how he feels in an unpardoned state, but he knows nothing of how he would feel in a different state, and if he should experience a different class of feelings he could not determine whether they were the evidence of pardon or something else. It is like a person saying that a child is beautiful, that it resembles an angel, when he has never seen an angel and knows nothing about the appearance of an angel. But as positive testimony that our feelings are not a proper test of pardon, and conscience not an infallible guide, we have the experience of Paul.[1] He declared that after he had persecuted the saints, even to bonds of imprisonment and death for the Name of Christ, that he had lived in all good conscience before God until this day. He says, "I verily thought myself, that I ought to do many things contrary to the name of Jesus of Nazareth, which thing I also did at Jerusalem." Therefore his feelings or conscience did not prove him right. He felt that he was serving God just as well persecuting Christians unto death, causing them to blaspheme, as when preaching Christ. "And many of the

[1]Acts xxiii. 1.

saints did I shut up in prison, having received authority from the chief priests; and when they were put to death, I gave my voice against them. And I punished them oft in every synagogue, and compelled them to blaspheme; and being exceedingly mad against them, I persecuted them even unto strange cities."[1]

The heathen have the approbation of their feelings in worshiping idols and sacrificing to their gods, some even their own lives under the car of Juggernaut, and throwing their children into the Ganges to be devoured by crocodiles. If feelings can be accepted as proof, then they would be right. If a poor man should receive a large sum of money, and it was counterfeit, yet he did not know this fact, would he not rejoice and feel as well as though it were good? But when he found that the money was counterfeit there would be a great change in his feelings. Feelings, therefore, may be deceptive, and cannot be relied upon as proof of pardon or acceptance with God.

Persons who receive what they call the second blessing, or are made absolutely holy or sanctified, have no evidence that they have received such blessing, because they rely upon a sudden change in their feelings as proof. There is no scriptural rule describing how persons would feel in such a state. Ecstatic joy cannot prove that they have received such blessing.

Fourth, we inquire, How can a Christian, if he be overtaken in a fault or commit sin, obtain for-

[1]Acts xxvi. 9–11.

giveness and be assured of pardon? Will a person who sins after baptism need to be baptized again? Baptism is performed once,—"Baptized into Christ,"[1] and is not the appointment through which persons obtain forgiveness after they come into Christ. The right of petition belongs to the citizen. (See pages 232–234.) On entering the Church they are to "grow in grace and in the knowledge of our Lord." They obtain access to the mercy-seat where they can find grace and mercy in every time of need. We have the account of a man who, after his conversion, committed sin. He saw the apostles imparting the gift of the Holy Spirit by the imposition of hands and offered them money to give him this power. This was a sin, concerning which the apostles said to him: "Repent therefore of this thy wickedness, and pray God, if perhaps the thought of thine heart may be forgiven thee." This is a plain case and shows what one who has been baptized should do to obtain pardon. The language of inspiration to such is: "Repent, . . . and pray God if perhaps the thought (not thoughts) of thine heart may be forgiven thee."[2] In perfect harmony with this the Lord taught his disciples to pray, "forgive us our debts as we forgive our debtors." And John says: "My little children, these things write I unto you, that ye sin not. And if any man sin, we have an advocate with the Father, Jesus Christ the righteous. And he is the propitiation for our sins: and not for ours only, but also for the sins of the whole world."[3] "If we confess our sins, he is faithful and just to for-

[1]Gal. iii. 27; Rom. vi. 8. [2]Acts viii. 22. [3]1 John ii. 1, 2.

give us our sins, and to cleanse us from all unrighteousness."[1]

There were five of the seven churches of Asia spoken of in Revelation who were charged with immorality and sin, and also the Corinthian church, and they were told to repent. This shows that many churches were far from perfection, and that they were commanded to repent. While these give encouragement to the Christian who has sinned that he may obtain pardon by repentance and prayer, it also shows that sanctification did not mean continuous sinless perfection, even under the guidance of the apostles in the Primitive church.

The Christians, as well as the unconverted, must therefore rely upon the word of God for the evidence of pardon. They have the same evidence that there is of anything supernatural, divine, of creation, sin, redemption, the Redeemer, heaven and immortality, or of God Himself, all are known only by the revealed word of God.[2] It is sufficient "that the man of God may be complete, furnished completely unto every good work."[3] Then is not the word of God on which we rely for all divine truth sufficient to assure the Christian of the pardon of sins and acceptance with God?

We now remark, in the last place, that the worst evil attending modern revivalism, or that system which makes feeling the test of pardon, is the unstable and unsettled condition of its converts. Their feelings are excited by a revival, and their hopes are

[1] 1 John i. 9. [2] See page 217. [3] 2 Tim. iii. 17.

bright, but soon their good feelings begin to subside and they have doubts of the genuineness of their conversion. Why these sad and despondent thoughts? Because the excitement has passed and some look upon themselves as deceived, and are led to abandon religion as a scheme of deception and priestcraft. Others, not willing to give up religion, attend another revival and, in intense excitement, become converted the second time. They now declare that they never knew what religion was before, they thought they were converted when they were not. May they not be deceived this time also, for their conversion came in precisely the same way as it did before. This revival over, in a few weeks some of these doubly converted are despondent again.

Not so, however, with the man whose trust is in God and in the word of His grace. He has deliberately and understandingly complied with the terms of pardon taught by the inspired ambassadors of Christ. He can claim the pardon of his sins and adoption into the family of God by the highest authority in heaven and on earth. No one can effectually dispute his claims, for he appeals for his proof to the infallibility of the Spirit, the veracity of Christ, and the immutability of God. How sure, then, is the foundation upon which he builds. It is a foundation tried, precious, and sure, and will stand forever. Truly the poet has said:

"How firm a foundation,
Ye saints of the Lord,
Is laid for your faith
In his excellent Word."

The Christian may then rejoice for such full assurance of faith and hope as an anchor to the soul, both sure and steadfast, sufficient to keep him amid all the storms of life. With this full assurance of faith in the word, the immutable promise, no fear need find a place in his bosom, for God has promised, "I will never leave thee nor forsake thee." And when "the heavens shall be rolled together as a scroll" and the earth be renovated by fire, this confidence in the all-sufficiency of the word of the immutable God will bear him up far above the melting elements to stand as a glorified and immortal person,

"Where bliss is known without alloy
And beauty blooms without decay;
Where thoughts of grief in cloudless joy
Shall melt like morning mists away."

Retribution and Reward

Having called attention to the conditions of pardon both as to the alien and citizen, or the sinner and Christian, it is important to know what is revealed in regard to those who are not forgiven or pardoned—what shall be their condition in the future. The gospel has penalty to be feared as well as promises to be enjoyed. The penalty of the gospel is a necessary element of its perfection as a system of salvation. Being a system of law and order there must be the penalty for disobedience. Fear is an important factor in all government, whether human or divine. It is appealed to in the family, in the school and in the State, in all organizations in society. All persons must avoid violation of law and disobedience to escape punishment. No human organization ever existed without its members having fear of penalty for violating its rules or law. A person violating law or rebelling against the home, school, or nation, can not, without reconciliation, escape punishment. Law implies penalty. The penalty of human law is well understood. It is therefore reasonable that there should be penalty in divine government. Mercy and love do not bar punishment in the family, in fact they are often the incentive. Just punishment is for good. Human ideas of justice would therefore anticipate punishment on the part of the Divine for offense or crime. In fact God's dealing with man from Adam to Noah, when he destroyed the ancient world,[1] and from Noah until Moses, is most distinctly marked by punishment and reward. From Moses to Christ the history of God's chosen people shows how in a most signal manner he punished them for disobedience and rebellion, and how he awarded them for obedience and loyalty. Paul says "All these things happened unto them for examples and are written for our admonition upon whom the ends of the ages have come."[2] Every transgression and disobedience received a just recompense of reward."[3] In all the history of God's dealing with man in this life we find retribution and reward. There is therefore no warrant for a rebel against the authority of God or a violator of his law to expect to escape from the penalty and anticipate the enjoyment of the righteous hereafter, any more than he could claim immunity and honor here while

[1] 2 Peter ii. 5. [2] 1 Cor. x. 11. [3] Heb. ii. 2.

violating human law. The wicked and depraved could not enjoy association with the good and true here, and they can not expect, without preparation, to enjoy hereafter the society of the righteous and holy. "Blessed are the pure in heart, for they shall see God."

"Perfect love casteth out fear." The Christian does not live in dread but in hope and love. The gospel, therefore, is a perfect system, presenting facts to be believed, commandments to be obeyed, threatenings to be feared, and promises to be enjoyed. Each of these is essential to its completeness. The warnings of the gospel are varied and numerous and can not be disregarded with impunity. In human affairs the rewards and punishments are temporal, in Christ's rule they are eternal.

We present the contrast in the conditions of the pardoned and unpardoned, as given in the Scriptures. First there is comfort and anguish. "But Abraham said, Son, remember that thou in thy lifetime receivedst thy good things, and Lazarus in like manner evil things; but now he is comforted, and thou art in anguish."[1] Second, there is eternal life and eternal punishment. "And these shall go away into eternal punishment, but the righteous into eternal life."[2] Third, there is "Come, ye blessed," and a "Depart from me, ye cursed." "Come, ye blessed of my Father, and inherit the kingdom prepared for you from the foundation of the world."[3] "Depart from me, ye cursed, into eternal fire which is pre-

[1]Luke xvi. 25. [2]Matt. xxv. 46. [3]Matt. xxv. 34.

pared for the devil and his angels."[1] Fourth, there is light and darkness. "Giving thanks unto the Father, who made us meet to be partakers of the inheritance of the saints in light."[2] "And cast ye out the unprofitable servant into the outer darkness: there shall be weeping and gnashing of teeth."[3] Fifth, there are two places. Jesus says, "In my Father's house are many mansions; if it were not so, I would have told you; for I go to prepare a place for you . . . that where I am, there may ye be also."[4] Judas "by transgression fell, that he might go to his own place."[5] Finally, therefore, "Be not deceived; God is not mocked: for whatsoever a man soweth, that shall he also reap. For he that soweth to the flesh, shall of the flesh reap corruption; but he that soweth unto the Spirit shall of the Spirit reap life everlasting. And let us not be weary in well doing; for in due season we shall reap, if we faint not."[6]

[1] Matt. xxv. 41. [2] Col. i. 12. [3] Matt. xxv. 30.
[4] John xiv. 2. [5] Acts i. 25. [6] Gal. vi. 7–9.

CHAPTER XXXII

THE CHURCH OF CHRIST

The Church of Christ as an Organic nstitution. Its Supreme Importance. First, the Name. Second, the Officers and Their Duties. Bishops or Elders. Deacons. Ministers or Evangelists.

IN the preceding narrative we have given a history of the pardon of sin and the evidence of pardon as developed in the Christian Scriptures. We will now consider the Church of Christ as an organic institution. Paul says: "Now therefore ye are no more strangers and foreigners, but fellow citizens with the saints, and of the household of God; and are built upon the foundation of the apostles and prophets, Jesus Christ himself being the chief corner stone."[1] "For other foundation can no man lay than that is laid, which is Jesus Christ."[2] Peter said, "Thou art the Christ, the Son of the living God." Jesus' answer was, "Upon this rock I will build my church; and the gates of Hades shall not prevail against it."[3] These passages give the foundation of the church. It was organized by the apostles upon this foundation and governed by divine authority alone.

The Church of Christ, "which he purchased with his own blood,"[4] is a glorious institution, and was established by Him for the salvation of the world.

[1]Eph. ii. 19, 20. [2]1 Cor. iii. 11.
[3]Matt. xvi. 16, 18. [4]Acts xx. 28.

"Christ loved the church and gave himself for it."[1] Through the church is made known "the manifold wisdom of God."[2] "Christ also is the head of the Church, being himself the savior of the body."[3] Christians are members of the body (the church). When "one member suffers all the members suffer with it."[4] "The Lord added to them (the church) daily those that were being saved"[5] who "continued steadfastly in the apostles' teaching and in fellowship, in breaking of bread and prayers."[6]

It must be remembered that the Church of Christ is a divine institution and is the means by which God is saving the world. It is "the pillar and ground of the truth."[7] No one can claim to be a Christian and ignore "the Church of the living God" for God has exalted Christ "far above all rule and authority and power and dominion and every name that is named . . . and gave him to be head over all things to the church, which is his body."[8]

We now proceed to give a brief history of the Church of Christ. First, the name; second, the officers and their duties; third, the ordinances and their observance.

First, in regard to the name, we learn from the Scriptures that Christians were called in their collective capacity: "The church";[9] "The church of God";[10] "The churches of God";[11] "The church of the Lord";[12] "The churches of Christ";[13]

[1]Eph. v. 25. [2]Eph. iii. 10. [3]Eph. v. 23.
[4]1 Cor. xii. 26–27. [5]Acts ii. 47. [6]Acts ii. 42.
[7]1 Tim. iii. 15. [8]Eph. i. 21–23. [9]Eph. iii. 10.
[10]1 Cor. i. 2. [11]1 Thess. ii. 14. [12]Acts xx. 28.
[13]Rom. xvi. 16.

"The body, the church";[1] "The body (church) of Christ";[2] "Household of God."[3]

In their individual capacity they were called "saints," "brethren," "disciples," "disciples of Christ," "Christians," "children of the kingdom," "saints of God," "heirs"; also such figurative terms as "sheep" and "branches" were used to designate the members of the Church of Christ, and are sufficient to describe them in their varied relations.

Second, we note the officers of this organization and their duties. This is very important in giving a description of any religious body, for churches frequently differ in this regard. We learn from the Scriptures that there were "bishops" or "elders," "deacons" and "ministers" or "evangelists"; and these were all the officers. This may be thought strange in view of the multiplicity of the officers in the organizations, sects, and parties that now exist, but these three classes were all the officers authorized in the organized New-Testament church.

The term "elder," among the first Christians, meant older, or person advanced in years, of age and experience. As bishops were such men, the term was used interchangeably with the term "bishop." Paul "sent to Ephesus, and called the elders of the church," and said, "take heed therefore unto yourselves, and to all the flock, over which the Holy Spirit has made you overseers, to feed the church of God."[4] The term "overseer" which is used here, is the same we have rendered "bishop" in other places in the New

[1]Col. i. 18. [2]1 Cor. xii. 27.
[3]Eph. ii. 19. [4]Acts xx. 17, 28.

Testament. Again, Paul says: "For this cause left I thee in Crete, that thou shouldest set in order the things that are wanting, and ordain elders in every city, as I had appointed thee: if any be blameless, the husband of one wife, having faithful children not accused of riot or unruly. For a bishop must be blameless, as the steward of God."[1] Why must the elders be of the character here described? Because a bishop must be blameless. Thus the terms "elder" and "bishop" are used to designate the same office, showing that they are synonymous. Giving further the duties of the elders and bishops, Peter says: "The elders which are among you I exhort, who am also an elder, and a witness of the sufferings of Christ, and also a partaker of the glory that shall be revealed; feed the flock of God which is among you, taking the oversight thereof, not by constraint, but willingly; not for filthy lucre, but of a ready mind. Neither as being lords over God's heritage, but being ensamples to the flock. And when the chief Shepherd shall appear, ye shall receive a crown of glory that fadeth not away."[2] This expresses the duty of the elders, and promises them a great reward for their labors. And the members of the church also have duties growing out of this relationship and are admonished, "Obey them that have the rule over you, and submit yourselves; for they watch for your souls, as they that must give account, that they may do it with joy, and not with grief; for that is unprofitable for you."[3]

In the days of the apostles churches existed for a

[1] Titus i. 5–7. [2] 1 Pet. v. 1–4. [3] Heb. xiii. 17.

time without elders. We have an account of a journey made by Paul and Barnabas, in which they visited many congregations, and it is said: "When they had ordained them elders in every church and had prayed with fasting, they commended them to the Lord, on whom they believed."[1] We learn from this that they had more than one elder in each congregation, for they ordained them "elders" in every church. Here we have church in the singular and elders in the plural. Again, we are informed that Paul "sent to Ephesus and called the elders of the church," church in the singular and elders in the plural. Some of these elders proclaimed the gospel and others did not, hence we read, "Let the elders that rule well be counted worthy of double honor, especially they who labor in word and doctrine."[2] It will be observed that these bishops or elders were chosen in the individual congregations. We never read in the Scriptures of a bishop of the churches, but the bishops of the church. The New-Testament church then was unlike some modern ones, who have but one elder presiding over many churches and one bishop over a diocese. Those who are thus organized can not claim to be identical with the New-Testament church in organization.

The deacons in the church had charge of the temporal affiairs of the congregation. The first account we have setting apart persons to serve the church in this capacity is found in the sixth chapter of Acts, and they were to serve the congregation in raising, hold-

[1]Acts xiv. 23. [2]1 Tim. v. 17.

ing, and distributing material things to the needy. In regard to their qualifications Paul says: "Likewise must the deacons be grave, not double-tongued, not given to much wine, not greedy of filthy lucre; holding the mystery of the faith in a pure conscience. And let these also first be proved; then let them use the office of a deacon, being found blameless."[1]

The New-Testament church had also ministers or evangelists, whose duty it was to announce the glad tidings. Paul says: "Preach the word, be instant in season and out of season. . . . Do the work of an evangelist, make full proof of thy ministry."[2] Such were Timothy, Titus, and many others who in the days of the apostles went forth to proclaim salvation to the people to turn them "from darkness to light, and from the power of Satan unto God," and to establish churches and comfort the saints by a faithful ministry of Christ in "the desire that they may be filled with the knowledge of his will in all wisdom and spiritual understanding."[3]

As bishop and elder are synonymous, so minister and evangelist are both applied to the same person. The word "evangelist" is applied only to Philip,[4] and Timothy,[5] while minister is used three times referring to Timothy,[6] two to Apollos,[7] two to Tychicus,[8] and once each to Epaphras[9] and John Mark.[10]

Paul also once mentions "pastors,"[11] and once

[1]1 Tim. iii. 8–10. [2]2 Tim. iv. 2–5. [3]Col. i. 9. [4]Acts xxi. 8. [5]2 Tim. iv. 5. [6]1 Thess. iii. 2; 1 Tim. iv. 6; 2 Tim. iv. 5. [7]1 Cor. iii. 5, iv. 1–6. [8]Eph. vi. 21; Col. iv. 7. [9]Col. i. 7. [10]Acts xiii. 5. [11]Eph. iv. 11.

"preacher."[1] He says, "Jesus Christ was preached by Silvanus and Timothy."[2] There are many other references to persons preaching. Of the preacher, he says, "How shall they hear without a preacher? And how shall they preach, except they be sent?"[3] Again, "even so hath the Lord ordained that they which preach the gospel should live of the gospel."[4] By considering the context here, verses 7 to 13, it is evident that the minister and preacher are one and the same, and are to receive compensation for their labor.

There are no higher titles than these given to any man in the churches. However, not satisfied with these the pope and priest have used the names belonging to Deity, "Holy Lord God the Pope," and "Holy Father." The priests call themselves Father in direct violation of the command of Christ: "Call no man your Father on earth, for one is your Father even he who is in heaven."[5] This is in a religious sense and strictly forbidden. Therefore no child of God should use any of these sacred names in speaking of a religious dignitary. We note further that "reverend" is never applied to man, not even to an apostle, bishop, elder, or minister, but to God only, and used but once in the Bible "Holy and reverend is his name."[6] Therefore what right has any man to assume this title?

While such titles have no divine warrant or sanction, yet the officers of the Church of Christ were not

[1]Rom. x. 14. [2]2 Cor. i. 19.
[3]Rom. x. 14, 15. [4]1 Cor. ix. 14.
[5]Matt. xxiii. 9. [6]Ps. cxi. 9.

without honor. Paul says: "Know them that labor among you, and are over you in the Lord, and admonish you; and to esteem them very highly for their work's sake."[1] Again as before quoted: "Let the elders that rule well be counted worthy of double honor, especially those who labor in the word and in teaching."[2]

The apostle Peter also dignifies this office, saying: "The elders therefore among you I exhort, who am a fellow-elder."[3]

Thus it will be seen that the ministers and officers under Christ were to receive honor from the church for faithfulness in the important work they were chosen to do. It must be borne in mind that all members of the church without regard to office are made "kings and priests unto God"; "Children of God"; "heirs of God and Joint-heirs with Christ."

All the authority the officers have under Christ is conferred by the church of which Christ is the head. The sovereignty of the church is further shown by the statement of Jesus to the church at Ephesus: "You did try them that call themselves apostles and are not, and didst find them false."[4] This is further shown by the statement of Paul in regard to discipline. He says to the church at Corinth, "Deliver such an one unto Satan."[5] "Put away the wicked man from among yourselves."[6] Again to the Thessalonians he says: "Now we command you, brethren, in the name of our Lord Jesus Christ, that you withdraw your-

[1] 1 Thes. v. 12–13. [2] 1 Tim. v. 17. [3] 1 Pet. v. 1.
[4] Rev. ii. 2. [5] 1 Cor. v. 5. [6] 1 Cor. v. 13.

selves from every brother that walketh disorderly."[1] These passages not only show the sovereignty of the church but also the importance of discipline in the church.

Having thus called attention to the love and esteem in which preachers and officers of the church are to be held, and to the right of discipline and sovereignty of the members, we now remark that the Church of Christ was a perfect organization. In every congregation there were bishops or elders to oversee the church and labor for its spiritual welfare—to settle its difficulties, strengthen the weak, encourage the timid, seeking to restore those who had wandered away from the fold, and to build up all in the most holy faith. Also deacons to superintend the temporal welfare of the congregation and to care for the needy; and ministers or evangelists bearing news of life and salvation to the world, planting new congregations and enlarging the borders of Zion. They were "to preach the word; be instant in season, out of season; reprove, rebuke, exhort with all long-suffering and doctrine."[2]

The officers of the New-Testament church consisted of these three distinct classes and no more. It had no archbishops, cardinals, prelates, and no pope claiming political and ecclesiastical power. Thus it will be seen that no church that differs with the original one in officers and organization can be identical with the New-Testament church.

[1] 2 Thes. iii. 6. [2] 2 Tim. iv. 2.

CHAPTER XXXIII

CHURCH ORDINANCES

The Ordinances and Their Observance. The Lord's Supper. The First Day of the Week. Christian Baptism. All Monumental.

WE call attention in the third place to the ordinances and their observance. In order to give a description of any religious body it is necessary to know its ordinances. Some bodies differ materially in this regard. Some religious organizations sprinkle water upon those who would become members, while others immerse them in water, and this is sufficient to distinguish the organizations, if in other respects they are alike. The apostolic church observed one important ordinance which distinguished it from all other religious bodies. Once only, in the annals of religion or in the history of the world, was it recorded that a religious body celebrated the death of its founder. While birthdays of the great, of kings and founders of kingdoms and empires have been celebrated, never before was the day celebrated upon which a benefactor died. Such, however, was the fact in regard to the founder of the Christian Church. This important ordinance is called the "Lord's Supper," "the Breaking of Bread," and "The Communion of the Blood of Christ and of the

Body of Christ."[1] And Christ told His disciples to do this in remembrance of Him. There is one fact connected with the founder of this church that partly, if not wholly, accounts for this singular, interesting, and important ordinance, and that is, He died the great antitype, prefigured by every victim that had bled on Patriarchal or Jewish altar. He came in the fulness of time and laid down His life as a sacrifice for the sin of the world; for, "without the shedding of blood is no remission." His death, then, was the noblest act of divine love. He died that man might have life; He died that man might not fear to die; He died that death might be disarmed and the gloom of the grave dispelled, that man might rise from its dust and ashes to endless life. It was, therefore, ordained that His death should be celebrated rather than His birth; for this great work of redemption was not accomplished until from the cross He exclaimed, "It is finished." And, therefore, to His death Christians will ever cling as the foundation of their brightest hopes. For only through His death His subjects expect to live again and enjoy the mansions He has gone to prepare.

The Church of Christ celebrated the day upon which the Son of God triumphed over death. We are informed that "upon the first day of the week, when the disciples came together to break bread, Paul preached unto them."[2] But upon what first day did they celebrate His death? It was upon *the* first day. We are nowhere informed in the Scriptures that they made

[1] 1 Cor. xi. 20, x. 16; Acts xx. 7. [2] Acts xx. 7.

any difference in Lord's days; they were all alike, hallowed by the same great event and held sacred to its commemoration. When God commanded His ancient people, Israel, to remember the Sabbath Day and keep it holy, they did not remember one day in every three or four months and keep it holy, but they remembered all of them and kept them holy. If when God commanded Israel to remember the Sabbath Day and keep it holy he meant every Sabbath Day, then when it is affirmed that the disciples came together on the first day of the week to break bread, it is just to conclude that it meant on every first day of the week. The phraseology is the same in both cases. This being true, and it has not been disputed, we ask, Can any of the modern churches claim to be identical in practice with the Church of Christ when they celebrate the Lord's death only three or four times in each year? In accordance with the example of the early believers in Christ, Christians should now observe every first day of the week in memory of the resurrection of Christ.

We now observe that there is no scriptural authority for calling the first day of the week, Sabbath. The Jews observed the last day of the week, or the seventh, and Christians the first day. The Jews remembered the Sabbath Day to keep it holy as a sign.[1] And Christians met on the Resurrection Day to commemorate the death of Christ. While the Sabbath is set forth in the Fourth Commandment under Moses, it is nowhere imposed upon Christians under Christ.

[1]Ex. xxxi. 17.

The Lord arose upon the first day of the week and in the evening of the same day he appeared unto his disciples.[1] The next first day (eight days later) they were again together, and He came into their midst.[2] On Pentecost (the first day of the week), the Holy Spirit descended, and the Christian Church was founded.[3] Paul gave commandment to the Galatians and Corinthians[4] to lay by in store when they came together on the first day of the week; and Luke tells of the church at Troas, which came together on the first day of the week to break bread.[5] And we read that John, the revelator, was in the Spirit on the Lord's Day.[6] It was therefore the custom and uniform practice of the churches of Christ to observe the first day of the week, or Lord's Day, and not the Sabbath, or seventh day, and there is no commandment or teaching substituting the Sabbath for the Lord's Day. Some, however, say if Christ's death is observed every first day of the week such observance will become too common. Christ died as often as He arose. The one event cannot become more common than the other. Why commemorate His resurrection every First day and not "show his death till he come"?[7]

The next ordinance to which we direct attention is that of Christian baptism. It has been heretofore shown that this was the consummating act in entering the Kingdom of Christ or His Church. In regard to the importance of baptism we observe that it is the

[1]John xx. 1, 19. [2]John xx. 26. [3]Acts ii. 1–4, 41, 47.
[4]1 Cor. xvi. 1, 2. [5]Acts xx. 7. [6]Rev. i. 10.
[7]1 Cor. xi. 26.

final act by which persons come into Christ. "So many of us as were baptized into Jesus Christ were baptized into his death."[1] It is sacred, uniting the names of the Deity. It is the only act required to be performed in the Name of the Father, Son, and Holy Spirit—the sacred names invoked upon persons who are baptized into Christ. Again, it is the only ordinance representing both the burial and the resurrection of Christ. The early Christians were immersed, they were not sprinkled or poured. All scholars of note admit that immersion was the primitive practise, and many passages of Scripture will not make sense unless thus translated. All persons, therefore, who came into the primitive church were buried in baptism. Thus we read, "buried with him in baptism, wherein also ye are risen with him . . . from the dead."[2] Again, "we are buried with him by baptism into death; that like as Christ was raised up from the dead by the glory of the Father, even so we also should walk in newness of life. For if we have been planted together in the likeness of his death, we shall be also in the likeness of his resurrection."[3] There are some who have changed this ordinance and have utterly destroyed its meaning by instituting other things in its stead, which do not represent the burial and the resurrection of Christ. It is distressing, therefore, to see water sprinkled upon a person as baptism in the sacred names of Deity. We feel like exclaiming with Mary at the tomb, "they have taken away my Lord and I know not where they have laid him."

[1]Rom. vi. 3. [2]Col. ii. 12. [3]Rom. vi. 4, 5.

The Scripture plainly teaches that the believing penitent who is buried with Christ in baptism rises to a new life.[1] Yet some teach that the new life may come without the burial and the resurrection, and others have their converts walking in the new life first, and then bury the living instead of the dead.

There are three ordinances or monumental institutions which to-day are proof of the great facts—the death, the burial, and resurrection of Christ, which facts Paul declares to be "the gospel."[2] First, the Lord's Day, which is now kept, and has been from the first, in memory of the resurrection of Christ. Second, the Lord's Supper, which is observed in memory of the fact of His death. Third, baptism, which represents or typifies both His burial and His resurrection.

These important memorial ordinances have not been properly emphasized as an argument in proof of the facts which they represent. They are living links in a chain that reaches back to the cross and the tomb of Joseph of Arimathea. The ordinances of the church were used in the days of the apostles as proof of these facts. Paul, in writing to the Galatians, says: "O, foolish Galatians, who did bewitch you before whose eyes Jesus Christ was openly set forth crucified?"[3] How could Christ be set forth crucified among the Galatians in Asia Minor unless the fact was shown by partaking of the emblems of His broken body and shed blood? This accords with

[1]Rom. vi. 3–11; Col. ii. 12, 13; 1 Peter iii. 21.
[2]1 Cor. xv. 1–4. [3]Gal. iii. 1.

his statement to the Corinthians when he says, "As oft as ye eat this bread and drink this cup ye do show the Lord's death till he come."[1] So that when the followers of Christ partake of the Lord's Supper they show the fact of His death. When the first day of the week is observed in memory of the resurrection it shows also this great fact. When persons are immersed they show forth both facts—the burial and resurrection of Christ.[2] Divine wisdom has established them all, and they will go on together testifying to the great work of redemption, and the great facts of the gospel until time shall end.

[1] 1 Cor. xi. 26.

[2] Rom. vi. 3–5.

CHAPTER XXXIV

THE CHURCH COMPLETE

Was Infant Baptism Taught? The Church Congregational. Co-operation and Extension. Its History Complete in the Scriptures. Duties of Church Members.

WE here observe that infant baptism was not taught or practised by the Church of Christ. Jeremiah says, speaking of the new covenant: "Behold, the days come, saith the Lord, that I will make a new covenant with the house of Israel, and with the house of Judah. Not according to the covenant that I made with their fathers in the day that I took them by the hand to bring them out of the land of Egypt; which my covenant they brake, although I was a husband unto them, saith the Lord: But this shall be the covenant that I will make with the house of Israel: After those days, saith the Lord, I will put my law in their inward parts, and write it in their hearts; and I will be their God and they shall be my people. And they shall teach no more every man his neighbor, and every man his brother, saying, Know the Lord: for they shall all know me, from the least of them unto the greatest of them saith the Lord."[1]

The writer of the Epistle to the Hebrews quotes the

[1] Jer. xxxi. 31–34.

above and identifies it as the gospel covenant, and declares that it has taken the place of the old.[1] One of the distinguishing features of the new is declared to be that those in the new covenant shall not teach "every man his neighbor, and every man his brother, saying, Know the Lord, for all shall know me from the least to the greatest." In this regard it was not according to the old covenant. In the old covenant persons were members by reason of birth—they were born into that relation and, hence, when arriving at the age of understanding they had to be taught to "know the Lord." But in the gospel covenant persons become members by faith in Christ. They are taught to "know the Lord" before they become members, and hence it is not necessary that they be taught again to "know the Lord." The old was a fleshly covenant, its membership resting on a fleshly basis; the new is a spiritual kingdom whose membership rests on a spiritual basis. Membership in the old rested on the fatherhood of Abraham, in the new it rests on the fatherhood of God by adoption through Christ.

During the thirty years' history of the apostles, as given in the Acts, we read of men and women "hearing, believing, and being baptized." In no case anywhere do we read of the baptism of any but believers. It is said that the jailer "was baptized, he and all his straightway." We also read that "he believed in God with all his house." All his house therefore believed with him and then were baptized.

[1]Heb. viii. 6–13.

To insist on the necessity of baptizing persons who have no sin and do not or can not believe, is to attach an efficacy to this ordinance which is unknown to the teachings of Jesus and His apostles. It is to rob it of all its meaning—the expression of one's faith in the burial and the resurrection of Christ. It is clearly taught that baptism is the consummating act in the pardon of sin. Infants have no sin, for "sin is the transgression of the law." "Where no law is, there is no transgression." There is no law given to infants, and could be none, and no obedience is required of them. Their innocence and purity is pronounced by Christ, for He says: "Of such is the kingdom of heaven."[1] And, "except ye turn and become as little children ye shall not enter into the kingdom of heaven."[2]

The Church of Christ, as divinely established, was congregational. There was no higher organization, no synod, assembly, or ecclesiastical body placed over it or given legislative authority for it, for Christ is the "head of the church."[3] Individual Christians are made "kings and priests unto God."[4] They are called "a holy priesthood,"[5] "a royal priesthood."[6] Being sovereign they have an absolute right, under Christ, to select their own servants or officers. Until Christians realize this vital fact, many will be in servile religious bondage.

There are, however, many reasons why there should be cooperation and union among the various congre-

[1]Matt. xix. 14. [2]Matt. xviii. 3. [3]Eph. v. 23.
[4]Rev. i. 6. [5]1 Pet. ii. 5. [6]1 Pet. ii. 9.

gations, not to legislate for the Church of Christ, which is prohibited, but to promote its welfare, and by united effort to spread the gospel abroad and build up the Kingdom of God on earth. By the classification mentioned in the Scriptures it is evident that the churches were divided into districts as "The churches of Galatia,"[1] "The churches of Asia,"[2] and "The churches of Judea."[3] We are informed that "The churches of Macedonia"[4] and "Achaia"[5] joined together "in the ministering to the saints,"[6] and there was a "brother whose praise in the gospel is spread through all the churches . . . and who was also appointed by the churches to travel"[7] with Paul and Titus; and of them it was said, "They are messengers of the churches."[8] This shows cooperation of the churches in the fellowship of giving and ministration.

The Church of Christ was so ordained and established, and its simple form of government was such that it could be planted in every nation and grow under any form of government. Hence the general form of cooperation among the various churches or congregations, for its spread seemed wisely to have been left to the good judgment of Christians under their various circumstances and surroundings in different nations and among divers peoples.

The Church of Christ being a historical institution, all things pertaining to it must be determined

[1] 1 Cor. xvi. 1. [2] 1 Cor. xvi. 19. [3] Gal. i. 22.
[4] 2 Cor. viii. 1. [5] 2 Cor. ix. 2. [6] 2 Cor. viii. 4.
[7] 2 Cor. viii. 18, 19. [8] 2 Cor. viii. 23.

in the light of history. Its Author, its foundation, its terms of membership, its organization, its officers, its ordinances, the duty of its members, its discipline and its rewards can only be determined by history. This history is given in the Christian Scriptures. What does inspired history show it to be? This we apprehend to be the true ground of discussion or investigation. The past discussion has been largely on various phases of theology rather than the church as a whole. It is admitted that Christ established a church, and that He established only one church. What this church is can not be settled by discussion of the merits of any ism or schism, nor the intricate phases of divine truth. There have been reformers of churches and numerous reformers of reformed churches, but none have ever attempted to reform Christ's Church. Reforms of reforms can not take the place of the Church of Christ which needs no reform. As all terrestrial creation terminates in man, so all God's revelation terminates in the Church of Christ. It is the end. In the Church of Christ is concentrated the whole of Christian truth. It embraces the divine truth in concrete form. Being a divine institution all but divine authority of necessity is excluded. Jesus The Christ is "The Way, the Truth, the Life," so that no person before His time, since His time, or in all coming time, could or can by divine authority establish a church. This being true, believers in Christ should meet the last—the final analysis of the subject and determine by inspired history the truth concerning its establishment, and restore it again in its beauty and simplicity as it came from the hand of God through His Son. "Christ loved the church and gave himself for it."[1]

The Church of Christ was complete, and so passed into history with the close of the New Testament. So far as revealed to us there has been no change made since, by any authority in heaven or upon the earth. Why can not the Church of Christ be re-established everywhere now as it was then, in all its divine beauty and simplicity? Can not Christians build now on the same foundation, having the same Lord, the same name, the same officers, chosen in the same way, observing the same ordinances in the same way, telling the penitent believers to do the same things in order to become members, requiring the church members to live now as they lived then? If this be not the Church of Christ where can it be found? It is vain to search outside of inspired history to find the true church of the true Redeemer.

Duty of Christians

If the reader is not familiar with the following passages, it is important that they be read, as they are most expressive, both of duty and destiny.

As to the duty of church members we refer the reader to Christ's sermon on the Mount,[2] where principles are taught that were to predominate in His church or kingdom when established.

Also in regard to humility and forgiveness.[3] "Con-

[1]Eph. v. 25–27. [2]Matt. v., vi., vii. [3]Matt. xviii. passim.

tinuing steadfast."[1] See Peter as to Christian virtues.[2] Paul in regard to "charity or love."[3] Also, in regard to the "Fruit of the Spirit."[4] As to Christian equality and faithfulness.[5] Giving or liberality.[6] Duty.[7] And the "High calling."[8] In the closing chapter of Revelation it is said, "Blessed are they that do his commandments, that they may have right to the tree of life, and may enter in through the gates into the city."[9]

[1]Acts ii. 42. [2]2 Pet. i. passim. [3]1 Cor. xiii. passim.
[4]Gal. v. 22, 23; Rom. viii. passim.
[5]Gal. iii. 28; Rom. xii.; Eph. iv.
[6]1 Cor. xvi. 1, 2; 2 Cor. vii., viii.
[7]Jas. i. 27; Col. iv. 2, 3; 1 Tim. ii. 1, 8.
[8]Phil. iii., iv. passim. [9]Rev. xxii. 14.

CHAPTER XXXV

THE APOSTASY

The Corrupt Church. The Man of Sin. The Influence of Protestantism. The Fall of Babylon. False Pretenders.

First, The Man of Sin and His Influence.

HAVING described the New-Testament church from the sacred records, and desiring to aid in restoring it in its simplicity and purity, it is important to note the rise and progress of the corrupt church which was predicted by the apostles. In order to now convince the world of the true church we deem it essential to briefly consider the apostate church—an ecclesiastical and political despotism, which swayed scepter over so many nations of the world for a thousand years, and which instituted persecution, martyrdom, and the horrors of the Inquisition. If such appalling degradation and misery was the natural outgrowth of Christ's teaching and example, those who desire the good of mankind would be inclined to reject it. But we shall find that such condition was to obtain for a time, and the power causing it was to be suddenly overthrown, when the true light would shine again and the reign of the Messiah would become universal, and His pure religion would extend over all the world. This "abomination of desolation" can not, therefore, be charged to the teachings of the sinless One. While we may not understand why such a condition was to obtain, as God's ways are not our ways, we are led to accept His religion because history also shows that the true followers of Christ have led in all that is good and pure in government and in society.

The Thessalonians were troubled in regard to the second coming of Christ. Paul writes to them that, "It will not be except the falling away come first, and the man of sin be revealed, the son of perdition; he that opposeth and exalteth himself above all that is called God, or that is worshiped; so that he sitteth in the temple of God, setting himself forth as God. Remember ye not, that, when I was with you, I told you these things? And now ye know that which restraineth to the end that he may be revealed in his own season. For the mystery of iniquity doth already work; only there is one that restraineth now until he be taken out of the way. And then shall be revealed the lawless one whom the Lord Jesus shall slay with the breath of his mouth and shall destroy with the brightness of his coming. Even he whose coming is after the working of Satan with all power and signs and lying wonders, and with all deceivableness of unrighteousness in them that perish."[1]

We quote from "The Pulpit Commentary": "The prediction of St. Paul concerning the Man of Sin made a deep impression upon the early Fathers, and the references to it in their writings are numerous. There is also a comparative unanimity in their sentiments. In general, they considered that the fulfilment of the

[1] 2 Thess. ii. 3–10.

prediction was future; that the Man of Sin was Antichrist, and an individual; and that the restraining influence was the Roman Empire. . . .

"The Reformers in general adopted this opinion. Such were the views of Luther, Calvin, Zwinglius, Melancthon, Beza, and Bucer; and, among English Reformers, Cranmer, Ridley, Latimer, Hooper, and Jewell. According to them, the apostasy is the falling away from evangelical doctrine to the traditions of men and the corruptions of popery; the Man of Sin, or Antichrist, is not, as the Fathers conceived, an individual, but the succession of popes; and the restraining power is the Roman Empire, out of whose ruins the papacy arose. The Lutheran Church inserted this opinion as an article in their creed (Article Smalc., ii. 4). In the dedication of the translators of the authorized version of King James, it is assumed that the pope is the Man of Sin; and that monarch is complimented for writing in the defense of the truth, which gave 'such a blow unto that Man of Sin as will not be healed.' And the assertion that the pope is Antichrist and the Man of Sin, forms one of the articles of the Westminster Confession: 'There is no other head of the Church but the Lord Jesus Christ; nor can the Pope of Rome in any sense be head thereof, but is that Antichrist, that Man of Sin and son of perdition, that exalteth himself in the Church against Christ and all that is called God' (ch. xxv. 6). . . . Besides the early Reformers, this opinion is advocated by Hooker, Hurd, Newton, Turretin, Benson, Bengel, Doddridge, Macknight, Michaelis, Elliott, and

Bishop Wordsworth. . . . In the view of those who regard the pope as the Man of Sin, this prediction was fully verified. No sooner was the restrainer removed than the Man of Sin was revealed. As long as the Roman emperor continued heathen and resident at Rome, no ecclesiastical power was permitted to exalt itself. . . .

"Are the characteristics of the Man of Sin found in popery? Those who belong to this class of interpreters assert that the resemblance is striking and obvious. An apostasy is predicted, and there is in Romanism a falling away from the pure gospel to the traditions of men; the doctrines of purgatory, transsubstantiation, the sacrifice of the Mass, the adoration of the Virgin and the Saints, are adduced as examples. The Man of Sin is represented as opposing and exalting himself against all that is called God or is an object of worship; and this is considered as receiving its fulfilment in the pope exalting himself above all human and divine authority, claiming the title 'king of kings and lord of lords,' applying to himself the words of the psalmist, 'All kings shall bow down before thee,' styling himself universal bishop, and asserting his power to dispose of the kingdoms of the earth. The Man of Sin is said to seat himself in the temple of God, showing himself as God. The temple of God is here understood to be the Christian Church, and the pope places himself in it as its supreme head, the vicar of Jesus Christ. He shows himself as God by claiming divine attributes, as holiness and infallibility; assuming divine prerogatives, as the power of pardoning sins and the opening and shutting of the kingdom of heaven; and using such divine titles as 'Our Lord God the Pope,' 'Another God on earth.' Every pope on his election is placed on the high altar at St. Peter's, and receives the adoration of the cardinals. The coming of the Man of Sin is after the working of Satan, with all power, and signs, and wonders of falsehood. And this is considered as receiving its fulfilment in the false miracles of popery; in the impositions of indulgences and purgatory; in the wonders done by sacred images moving, speaking, bleeding; in the prodigies effected by sacred relics; in the supernatural visitations of the Virgin, and in the pretended power of working miracles which the church of Rome still claims. . . . And, besides, in the other passage where Paul predicts the falling away of the latter times, the marks which he gives find their counterpart in the corruption of popery: 'Giving heed to seducing spirits, and doctrines of devils; speaking lies in hypocrisy; having their conscience seared with a hot iron; forbidding to marry, and commanding to abstain from meats' (1 Tim. iv. 1-3). Paul represents the system as working even in his days: 'For the mystery of lawlessness is already working' (ch. ii. 7)."

So that, as Bishop Newton observes, "the foundations of popery were laid, indeed, in the apostles' days, but the superstructure was raised by degrees, and several ages passed before the building was completed, and the Man of Sin was revealed in full perfection."

"Of course, according to this view of the subject, the complete fulfilment of the prophecy is still future. The Destruction of the Man of Sin—that is, Romanism—is also predicted: 'Whom the Lord Jesus will slay with the breath of his mouth, and annihilate by the appearance of his coming' (ch. ii. 8). . . . Upon the whole, on an impartial review of the subject, we can not avoid the impression that the points of resemblance between the prophecy and Romanism are numerous, varied, and striking. Our forefathers had no doubt as to the application of the prediction, and perhaps they were nearer the truth than we in modern times, who hesitate. Such an opinion may be considered as uncharitable and unjust, and is certainly not in accordance with the more liberal spirit of our age, where popery is viewed as it presently exists, divested of its power to persecute, and as seen in the culture, refinement, and piety of many of its adherents. But when we reflect upon the abominable persecutions of the Inquisition, the monstrous wickedness of the popes prior to the Reformation, the atrocities perpetrated in the name of religion, the crimes committed by the priests, and the general corruption of the whole system; and when we think that it is only the restraining influence of Protestantism which prevents a repetition of such actions, we may see reason, if not to affirm positively, yet to suspect that such an opinion may be founded on truth, and, if so, be neither uncharitable nor unjust."[1]

[1]Pulpit Commentary on 2d Thessalonians, pages 52, 54, 57, 59, 60.

It will be observed that the above quotation shows that it is only the restraining influence of Protestantism that prevents the repetition of these crimes. This is only in Protestant nations, but what is the history of popery in papal countries, such as Spain and Spanish America and the islands in which she has held sway? What are the results of her teaching in these countries? What is the condition of the people?

Some say these crimes should be charged to the spirit or darkness of the age. But Roman despotism made the age dark or barbarous. The darkness belongs to popery and not the age, not only in the Old World but in the New. The Catholic Church has never encouraged Bible study among the people and demands that its interpretation be accepted. Where there is light it is the result of Protestant teaching and toleration, and, if Catholics have advanced it is due to the light of Protestantism. The Jews were not as corrupt at the time when Christ denounced them as hypocrites, whited sepulchres, saying, "Ye compass sea and land to make one proselyte, and when he is become so you make him twofold more the child of hell than yourselves."[1] Is not this literally true of the converts of Rome in the New World and in the islands of the sea? D. L. Leonard says:[2]

"Under the phrase Spanish America, is included the entire region lying between the southern boundary of the United States and Cape Horn. The area under view equals in size the vast Russian possessions in both Europe and Asia, or Europe twice over with

[1]Matt. xxiii. 15. [2]"A Hundred Years of Missions."

three German empires in addition, and contains a population of 47,500,000. . . .

"Spanish America was the first section of the New World to be discovered and overrun by the greedy gold-hunters from the Iberian Peninsula. In the story which sets forth their doings the truth is far stranger than fiction. In an incredibly short space of time, by an unparalleled series of tours of exploration and feats of arms, the whole coast region, both on the east and west, was visited by a mere handful of daring spirits and fell a prey to 'civilization.' . . .

"Finally, from the beginning, the entire region under view has been under the same ecclesiastical domination, and the same religious training has been bestowed. In the palmy days of the Great Discovery the privileged pope had the whole world at his disposal, and graciously bestowed the New World upon his most loyal servitors, Spain and Portugal, to wit, and a horde of priests and friars sped across the Atlantic to rescue the souls of the pagans. And ever since, in realms spiritual, the papal church has all things to its liking, has not failed to rule with a high hand, and the fruits of ten generations of the Roman regime appear in forms most characteristic, if also lamentable and heart-sickening. The outcome is even worse than that to be found in Southern Europe. The civilization is of a low grade, while the masses are left to grovel in dense ignorance and gross superstition. Too often the priesthood is scarcely above the people for intelligence and is grossly immoral, while the religious teaching and practise are a curious compound of Christianity and heathenism, and the elements of the latter preponderating. . . .

"Almost anywhere between New Mexico and Southern Patagonia, to introduce the Bible, or any form of teaching other than that of the Catholic type, is to face fierce denunciation and mob violence, if not also death. The roll of Protestant martyrs in Spanish America contains already names not a few and is a lengthening one. For practically everywhere a bigoted priesthood is supreme in the hopes and fears of the sorely benighted millions. And it is mainly on account of this universal and abject bondage to Rome that missions in these parts are of such recent origin, have as yet scarcely emerged from the estate of feeble infancy, and so South America, with strict propriety, can be termed 'the Neglected Continent.'"[1]

Second, Mystery, Babylon the Great.

The prophecy of John, the Revelator, in regard to Babylon the Great, the mother of harlots, has been considered by most reformers and commentators as referring to papal Rome. We quote a brief portion from Revelation: "And he carried me away in the Spirit into a wilderness: and I saw a woman sitting upon a scarlet-colored beast, full of names of blasphemy, having seven heads and ten horns. And the woman was arrayed in purple and scarlet, and decked with gold and precious stone and pearls, having in her hand a golden cup full of abominations, even the unclean things of her fornication, and upon her forehead

[1]A Hundred Years of Missions, by D. L. Leonard, pages 365-369.

a name written, MYSTERY, BABYLON THE GREAT, THE MOTHER OF THE HARLOTS AND OF THE ABOMINATIONS OF THE EARTH. And I saw the woman drunken with the blood of the saints, and with the blood of the martyrs of Jesus. And when I saw her, I wondered with a great wonder. And the angel said unto me, Wherefore didst thou wonder? I will tell thee the mystery of the woman, and of the beast that carrieth her, which hath the seven heads and the ten horns."[1]

Upon this we give the description found in "The Pulpit Commentary on Revelation," as follows:

"But that papal Rome is one form of this mystic Babylon we can entertain no doubt whatever. The student of history can follow out at leisure thirteen or fourteen lines of inquiry, on which we can but give a few illustrative remarks. 1. The woman was seated on the beast, as if supported by it (ver. 3). Rome has relied on the worldly power to put her decrees into execution by brute force; both in using temporal powers, and in herself claiming temporal power as well as spiritual. 2. She yet rides the beast as if to govern it (ver. 3). We know but too well how Rome has aimed at, and does still aim at, controlling the power on which she relies; claiming even to regulate allegiance to earthly princes. 3. She is seated on many waters (ver. 1). In every quarter of the world her emissaries are sent. And in many a land where the pure gospel of Christ has been preached, she sends her emissaries to undo the holy work by sowing tares

[1]Rev. xvii. 3–7.

among the wheat. 4. She rules over the kings of the earth (ver. 18). Kings are but the 'sons of the church,' to do the bidding of their 'holy' (?) mother; otherwise she may absolve subjects from allegiance to their sovereign. 5. She holds out a golden cup full of abominations (ver. 4). Papal Rome makes large offers of indulgences and absolutions, and positively lures men into sin. 6. The merchants grow rich by her (ch. xviii. 3). Many are enriched by the ungodly traffic to which she consents, in making her house of prayer a den of thieves; for her indulgences and absolutions will cover any kind and degree of sin, whether in the getting of wealth or otherwise. 7. She is presumptuous in her self-security (ch. xviii. 7). Papal Rome acknowledges no other church, and looks for the time when all will be absorbed in her, while she is to be 'a lady for ever.' 8. She is adorned with pompous array—in gold (ver. 4), purple, scarlet, and precious stones. Any one who has watched the working of papal Rome at Rome will need no words to convince him of her gorgeous display and dazzling sheen. 9. She is drunk with the blood of the holy (ver. 6). What tales does history unfold. A hundred and fifty thousand persons perished under the Inquisition in thirty years; and from the beginning of the Order of Jesuits, in 1540, it is supposed that nine hundred thousand persons perished through papal cruelty. While, although it is impossible to estimate the exact number, yet it is supposed that during the papal persecutions of the Waldenses, Albigenses, Bohemian Brethren, Wickliffites, and other Protestants, those who perished are counted by the million. The same spirit exists still. In Ireland the priests keep the people in terror, and if Rome does not persecute us, it is because she dare not. 10. She is the mother of abominations (ver. 5). Students of history and tourists in papal districts know that this is literally true. Indulgences for an indefinite number of years may be purchased with money. No viler-looking set of faces could ever be beheld than the present writer has seen surrounding the confessional-boxes in St. Peter's at Rome. 11. The beast she rides is full of names of blasphemy (ver. 3). The proclamation of infallibility is the one fulfilment of this that surpasses all others. 12. The inhabitants of the earth are led by her into sin (ch. xviii. 3). The papal church notoriously leads people into the sin of idolatry. The worship of Rome is largely the adoration of a great goddess. Papists pronounce accursed those who do not 'honor, worship, and adore the adorable images.' 13. The several kings or kingdoms into which the civil power of the beast is to be divided shall 'hate the whore, and make her desolate,' etc. (ver. 16). How true. If there is an object of imperial hatred, it is papal Rome, which is hated most of all. She is regarded as the disturber of States everywhere. 14. Yet within this great Babylon there will be to the last some saints of God who will be called on to come out of her (ch. xviii. 4). Even so. Fearfully apostate and adulterous as is papal Rome, there are in her pale many holy ones who are profoundly ignorant of the abominations done by her in religion's name. The Lord will know

His own in the day when He maketh up His jewels. But this great Babylon of harlotry, pomp, pride, and all abominations, is doomed to fall terribly, suddenly, completely, and forever. Earnestly do we press on the student carefully to follow up each of these fourteen lines on which history will be found to confirm the prophecy here couched in symbolic form. The identification is such that not one point seems lacking. . . . 'The ten horns . . . shall hate the harlot,' etc. How truly is this being fulfilled. Not one of the European powers that has not in some period or other been relied upon by Rome. And now there is not one of the main kingdoms of the world that is not 'hating' her. They are working in their own defense against papal intrigue. (See Mr. Gladstone's striking pamphlets on the Vatican.). . . . She trifled with and even trampled on the temporal powers in times past, and now of her temporal power she herself is shorn. . . . The time will come when no priests shall minister at her altars. The walls of her mighty temples will be shattered, and the shrieks of many an unclean bird shall reverberate from column to column of her dilapidated pile.

> "Thus terribly shall Babel fall,
> Thus—and no more be found at all."

"NOTE 1.—The amazing extent of the dominion of papal Rome may well fill us with wonder. It is terrible indeed to see this harlot committing fornication with the kings of the earth, seated upon many waters, intoxicating the nations with her greatness, and carrying her corruptions and abominations to the ends of the earth. But all is forewritten, that we might not be alarmed, however we may be distressed. Therefore: 2. We ought not to be dismayed, as if some calamity had unawares befallen the world. It has not come otherwise than was foretold to the apostle in Patmos."[1]

Finally, in regard to this corrupt church, we would remark that modern evolution of society began with the Lutheran reformation, when the Bible was restored to man, giving the Beatitudes of Christ, the golden rule, and man's duty and destiny. It was learned that each member of Christ's Church was a king and priest unto God, and could approach Him through Christ and be heard without the intervention of pope or priest. All who thus believe were and are freed both from political and religious despotism, for "If God be for us who can be against us?"[2] The man who believes God and one are a majority can not be enslaved. "Ye shall know the truth, and the truth shall make you free. . . . If therefore the Son make you free, ye shall be free indeed."[3] The march, therefore, of the world will be onward and upward until the pope and his power, the priest and his imposition are gone—until the Man of Sin is destroyed and Babylon the Great has fallen.

False Christs, False Prophets, and False Teachers

It is important in considering the Church of Christ to call attention to another class of scriptures referring to false Christs, false prophets, and false teachers, which were predicted. We quote:

[1]The Pulpit Commentary on Revelation, pages 420–423.
[2]Rom. viii. 31. [3]John viii. 32. 36.

"If any man shall say unto you, Lo, here is Christ; or, Lo, there; believe him not: for there shall arise false Christs and false prophets, and shall show signs and wonders, that they may lead astray if possible the elect."[1] "Beware of false prophets, who come to you in sheep's clothing, but inwardly are ravening wolves."[2]

"But there arose false prophets also among the people, as among you also there shall be false teachers, who shall privily bring in destructive heresies, denying even the Master that bought them, bringing upon themselves swift destruction."[3] "Because many false prophets are gone out onto the world."[4] "But the Spirit saith expressly, that in later times some shall fall away from the faith, giving heed to seducing spirits and doctrines of demons . . . forbidding to marry, and commanding to abstain from meats."[5] "For the time will come when they will not endure the sound doctrine; but, having itching ears, will heap to themselves teachers after their own lusts; and will turn away their ears from the truth, and turn aside unto fables."[6]

Upon these scriptures we remark that all prophecies of a coming Messiah were fulfilled in Christ. He was the end. No other Savior was predicted and there was no promise of any one to follow him. The religion of Jesus was complete in itself, and was established once and for all time. Jesus reigns over all the earth as truly as any monarch reigns over his domin-

[1]Mark xiii. 21, 22. [2]Matt. vii. 15. [3]2 Pet. ii. 1.
[4]1 John iv. 1. [5]1 Tim. iv. 1. [6]2 Tim. iv. 3, 4.

ions. He has no rival and no successor. There is no second Jesus. His constitution and laws are perfect and are binding upon all His subjects and in all time. "Lo, I am with you always, even unto the end of the world."[1]

No false prophet, no pretender, has ever conferred such honor, dignity, title, and sovereignty upon his followers as are conferred upon the disciples of Christ. None has ever pretended to promise greater rewards. They have not set such an example, taught such precepts. None ever died and rose again for the redemption of man. They have not demonstrated their power over death as He did. We search in vain the history of all recorded time, whether on rocks or rolls, on monuments or tombs, to find one who broke the bars of death save Jesus. He alone triumphed over the grave and said: "I am the resurrection and the life."[2] What have the long lists of false Christs and false prophets from the days of revelation to Mohammed and down to Smith and Young done compared with what Jesus did? All that is good in the teachings of these and other pretenders has been borrowed or taken from the law which He took "out of the way," from prophecy which was fulfilled in Him or from His own life and teaching. The scriptures we have quoted give ample warning. Beware of them, "Believe them not."

The bases of all false religions are largely sensual. Their founders set no such example, taught no such precepts, promised no such rewards as Jesus. His

[1]Matt. xxviii. 20. [2]John xi. 24.

teaching and His life, His example and His death, have no parallel in human history and can have none. As to the rewards and the final home of His subjects or followers, human language was exhausted by John on Patmos in describing their capital city, whose walls are jasper, whose gates are pearls, and whose streets are gold. There was nothing left to describe the buildings and palaces within, their furnishings, their drapery, or their scenic grandeur. As Paul knew a man, caught up to the third heaven who heard words which could not be expressed in human language, so John could not describe the mansions which Christ has gone to prepare for those who love Him where the redeemed will congregate and sing the song which angels can not sing, "Thou hast redeemed us," and listen to the heavenly eloquence of those elder Sons of God who shouted for joy at the creation of the human race, where unshackled by death and unhampered by sin, growing in knowledge, increasing in wisdom, traversing the universe, surveying the past creations of God, and witnessing the new, they shall run forever the high race of immortality.

CHAPTER XXXVI

CHRISTIAN UNITY

The Savior's Prayer for Union. The Union of Believers both Practical and Desirable. The Evil Tendency of Division. The Oneness of Believers.

HAVING given consideration to the evidence of pardon and to the organization of the Church of Christ, we now state that Christians were a united people under the guidance of the Holy Spirit. And it is plainly evident, from the prayer of Christ, that they should be united now, as they were in the days of the apostles, to convince and convert the world. We read, "Neither pray I for these alone, but for them also who shall believe on me through their word; that they all may be one, as thou, Father, art in me, and I in thee, that they also may be one in us: that the world may believe that thou hast sent me."[1]

While Protestant nations owe their advancement to the protest made against Roman Catholic domination, and Protestant Christians are the foremost leaders in civilization and religion, their work, however, is crippled, retarded, and cannot be finally successful until the churches are united, or the Church of Christ in its purity and simplicity is restored. It will

[1]John xvii. 20, 21.

be shown, from facts and figures, that Protestant churches, in their divided form, can not make the masses Christian even in Protestant lands, much less convert the world while they are divided into a multitude of sects and parties.[1] Union, then, is absolutely essential to convert the people in Protestant lands and Christianize the pagan nations.

That all the believers in Christ should be united so as to constitute but one body, one communion, one church, is a proposition clearly set forth and strongly inculcated in the Christian Scriptures.

The language of the Savior which we have quoted, exhibits very plainly His divine will on this subject. The apostles frequently enjoined it, and condemned all divisions in the strongest terms, and those who assert that there are so many different denominations of Christians that every person can be suited, take a stand in direct opposition to the prayer of the Savior, and rejoice in that which the apostles reprove.

This prayer of the Savior was uttered under the most solemn circumstances just before His betrayal. He had for some three years been developing the principles of His government, preparatory to a permanent establishment of a remedial system adapted to the nature of man, in all his varied circumstances and necessities, one which, in its perfect organization and infinite motives, could yield more happiness than all systems of religion or moral philosophy ever presented to the consideration of man. He had, by the wisdom of His teaching, the benevolence of His example, in connection with the power of God which He

[1]See pages 331, 332.

displayed in the miracles He performed, such as the expulsion of demons, the restoration of sight to the blind, and the resurrection of the dead, fully established all His claims to divine power and authority.

He selected twelve apostles whom He made the subjects of His special instruction, and to whose care He was soon to entrust the affairs of His kingdom, when the great work of redemption had been accomplished by His death, burial, resurrection, and ascension into heaven. After praying for Himself He next prayed that the apostles might be sanctified through the truth, and then for all those who should believe on Him through their word that "they may all be one, that the world may believe that thou hast sent me."

The union of all those who thus believe is not only practical, but it is an object greatly to be desired and essential, or the Savior would not have prayed for it. Those who argue for divisions among the people of God are inconsistent, for two reasons: they oppose union and preach against it and at the same time pray for it. They pray that the watchman on the walls of Zion may see eye to eye, that all may speak the same things, be of one heart and one soul, "endeavoring to keep the unity of the spirit in the bond of peace."

Second, some argue against the union of all believers in one body or church, and in support of different sects and parties in Christendom, and at the same time they preach in favor of all uniting with the particular sect to which they belong, which is, in effect, preaching against union. They will contend that the different sects are necessary to keep the church pure, by watching over each other, and especially are necessary for the accommodation of unbelievers who, if they cannot conscientiously subscribe to the peculiar doctrine of one particular church, can have the privilege of choosing from a variety of sects such an one as will suit their particular fancy. Such persons on other occasions will argue in favor of their own particular creed, and will try to make others believe as they do, which is virtually striving to do away with the very means which, according to this view, God in His wisdom designs to purify the church and save sinners. If these parties are designed to benefit the children of men, why should each one strive to have all persons believe as they do? If they are beneficial it is indeed strange that the Savior in His prayer should entirely overlook the importance and necessity of divisions among His people, and in misconception of the real interest of His kingdom pray for all believers to be one, even as He and His Father are one. And that on another occasion he should say, "Blessed are the peacemakers, for they shall be called the children of God."

Union among all true believers is both desirable and attainable. It is desirable because "in union there is strength." This is clearly shown from all the laws of nature, the history of nations and the word of God. The Almighty has always preferred union when men were disposed to do right, but disunion when they were engaged in wickedness. Thus He gave an example of sectarianism at the Tower of

Babel, when He cut the people up into sects and parties. By confounding their language they became divided, and as a consequence they were unable to carry on their project. "United we stand, divided we fall" is a maxim as true in religion as it is in the family or nation.

First, we notice the evil tendency of division.

Second, the basis upon which all may unite.

Third, the causes of division.

Fourth, the nature of the union for which Christ prayed.

Fifth, the object of union.

David says, "How good and how pleasant it is for brethren to dwell together in unity." Nothing is more unpleasant than the effects of disunion among professed Christians.

First, we wish to mention the evil tendency of division. It is the most prolific cause of the discord, animosity, contention, and ill-will so often exhibited on the part of those who profess to worship the same God and are destined to the same heaven.

Again, it is the cause of an immense waste of time in contending for and distinguishing between the peculiarities of numerous creeds and parties, which might be spent in opposing the common foe, extending the knowledge of salvation, encouraging the weak, and visiting the distressed.

Again, it wastes millions of dollars in publishing useless and worse than useless creeds, formulas, and confessions of faith, in erecting sometimes a number of houses in one village where one would meet the entire wants of the community, and in employing the same number of preachers to maintain and defend the peculiar tenets of each denomination, which money might be expended in providing for the poor, caring for orphans, sending missionaries and circulating the Bible in heathen lands. Lodges or human organizations do not commit such folly.

Again, it hinders many Christian ministers in preaching the Word by prejudicing the people and closing the doors of the church against them on the ground of their denominational peculiarities, and consequently, God having appointed preaching as the means of salvation, disunion has prevented the salvation of many souls for whom Christ died.

Sectarianism is a sin, wherever it exists and under whatever circumstances it is found—a sin of the first magnitude. It is utterly and forever repugnant to the genius of the gospel and to the Christian system. It imposes new and untried tests in church polity and government, it supersedes the divine institution—the church—by a code of laws of its own enactment, and breaks up the household of faith into many warring factions. It cripples Christian conquest, weakens the power of the gospel, hinders the conversion of sinners, lessons the force of Christian testimony, arms infidelity with its most deadly weapons, opposes the object of the prayer of the Lord, retards the increase of scriptural knowledge, calls forth and strengthens the baser passions of humanity, and robs heaven of many of its rightful inhabitants.

Can a religion which produces such effects be the

religion of Jesus Christ as it appears in the Gospel? The religion of Him who is the Prince of Peace and the author of good-will and love to man? If such be the destructive nature, ruinous effects and evil consequences of the present divided condition of Christendom, is it not the indispensable and paramount duty of every child of God to endeavor to restore to the world pure, primitive, apostolic Christianity in letter and spirit, in precept and practise?

No truth is more prominent in the Bible than the unity of the saints. No point do the apostles more often and more strongly urge, and there is no duty more solemnly and frequently enforced than the perfect oneness of believers. And they place this union on high and sacred ground.

First, the oneness of their spiritual religion. "Ye also, as lively stones, are built up a spiritual house, a holy priesthood, to offer up spiritual sacrifices, acceptable to God by Jesus Christ."[1] "But this man, after he had offered one sacrifice for sins forever, sat down on the right hand of God. . . . For by one offering he hath perfected forever them that are sanctified."[2] "For there is one God and one mediator between God and men, the man Jesus Christ."[3] "Stand fast in one spirit with one mind, striving together for the faith of the gospel."[4]

Second, the oneness of their relation. "For I have espoused you to one husband, that I may present you as a chaste virgin to Christ."[5] "That ye should be

[1] 1 Pet. ii. 5. [2] Heb. x. 12–14. [3] 1 Tim. ii. 5.
[4] Phil. i. 27. [5] 2 Cor. xi. 2.

married to another, even to him who is raised from the dead, that we should bring forth fruit unto God."[1]

Third, the oneness of their hope. "There is one body and one spirit, even as ye are called in one hope of your calling."[2]

Fourth, the oneness of the body of which they are members. "For as the body is one and hath many members, and all the members of that one body being many, are one body, so also is Christ."[3] "For as we have many members in one body and all members have not the same office, so we, being many, are one body in Christ, and every one members of another."[4]

Fifth, the oneness of the spirit which animates it. "For by one spirit are we all baptized into one body, whether we be Jews or Gentiles, whether we be bond or free, and have been all made to drink into one spirit."[5]

Sixth, the oneness of their baptism. "For as many of you as have been baptized into Christ have put on Christ. There is neither Jew nor Greek, there is neither bond nor free, there is neither male nor female, for ye are all one in Christ Jesus."[6] "Endeavoring to keep the unity of the spirit in the bond of peace there is . . . one Lord, one faith, one baptism, one God and Father of all . . . But speaking the truth in love may grow up into him in all things which is the head, even Christ."[7] This constituted, in the age of the apostles, a perfect bond of unity.

[1]Rom. vii. 4. [2]Eph. iv. 4. [3]1 Cor. xii. 12.
[4]Rom. xii. 4, 5. [5]1 Cor. xii. 13. [6]Gal. iii. 27, 28.
[7]Eph. iv. 3–5, 15.

CHAPTER XXXVII

WHAT IS IMPLIED BY UNITY

The Basis of Union. The One Confession. Inclusive and Exclusive.

SECOND, what is the basis of union? No one can doubt the ability of Christ to form a plan of union. He was supremely wise and divinely good, hence His system is perfect. The basis of union, as expressed in His plan, the word of the apostles, perfectly expressed the will of Christ. He says, "He that heareth you heareth me, and he that despiseth you despiseth me, and he that despiseth me despiseth Him that sent me."[1] "It is not ye that speak but the Spirit of your Father which speaketh in you."

This basis is authoritative, Jesus says, "All authority is given unto me in heaven and in earth. Go ye therefore and teach all nations, baptizing them in the name of the Father, and of the Son, and of the Holy Spirit: Teaching them to observe all things whatsoever I have commanded you."[2] The apostles spent their lives in compliance with this commission.

The word of the apostles contains a perfect system. Paul says, "All Scripture given by inspiration of God is profitable for doctrine, for reproof, for correction, for instruction in righteousness, that the man of God

[1]Luke x. 16. [2]Matt. xxviii. 18.

may be complete, furnished completely unto all good works."[1] James says, "Whoso looketh into the perfect law of liberty." And Peter says, "According as his divine power hath given unto us all things that pertain unto life and godliness." Again, we are told, that "the law of the Lord is perfect, converting the soul." This, then, is the basis of union—the Word of God. The basis for the union of Christians must be a Christian basis. Among all the conventions that have been called for the union of different sects and parties they have never adopted the Christian basis. They have always attempted to form a human platform on which to unite, and, consequently, have always failed. The Christian church is a divine institution, and therefore it must have a divine constitution. The foundation of the Christian church was laid by God, the Father, Himself, and it is a foundation tried, precious, and sure. Other foundation can no man lay as the basis of an enduring union of everlasting peace and unity in the family of God.

The fact must sooner or later be conceded by all that Christ is the light of the world, in a religious point of view, and that in His church He is the only sovereign and head; that He only has power to decree articles of faith and the authority thereof, and that He alone has a right to ordain rites and ceremonies and to fix the terms of union and church membership; consequently, no ecclesiastical or earthly princes or potentates have power to make laws in His kingdom which shall bind the consciences of His subjects.

[1] 2 Tim. iii. 16, 17.

All systems have centers. The sun is the center of the solar system, and God's son is the center of the Christian system. The center of the Christian system and the foundation of the Christian Church are one and the same. "Other foundation," says Paul, "can no man lay than that is laid, which is Jesus Christ." He is the chief corner-stone, and it was on the declaration of faith in His divine person and in His divine mission that Jesus said He would build His church. Hence, we read: "When Jesus came into the coasts of Cesarea Philippi, he asked his disciples, saying, Whom do men say that I, the Son of man, am? And they said, Some say that thou art John the Baptist; some, Elias; and others, Jeremias, or one of the prophets. He saith unto them, But whom say ye that I am? And Simon Peter answered and said, Thou art the Christ, the Son of the living God. And Jesus answered and said unto him, Blessed art thou, Simon Bar-jona: for flesh and blood hath not revealed it unto thee, but my Father which is in heaven. And I say also unto thee, That thou art Peter, and upon this rock I will build my church; and the gates of Hades shall not prevail against it."[1]

Here, then, is a full revelation of the Christian constitution—a full confession of Christian faith. The truth that Jesus is the Christ, the Son of God, is the foundation, the central or underlying truth in which the entire revelation from God to man centers and upon which it all rests.

When it is believed that Jesus is divine, the Son of

[1]Matt. xvi. 13–18.

God, His authority and right to rule are admitted. The prophecies of the Old Testament point down to, and have their fulfilment in, Him. The writings of the apostles, after His ascension, point back to Him. So all rest on Christ as the chief corner-stone. This central truth, that Jesus is the Christ, the Son of God, is the truth to be put before the world as the basis of union for all believers. A man coming to God must receive this before he can be received into the church. When he receives this truth he receives the whole system of which Christ is the author.

There are some who object to limiting the confession of faith to this one great truth, and have formed a variety of questions to ask a candidate before receiving him. They are not satisfied with the "good confession." To use again a former illustration: Were we to ask a person if he believed the sun to be the center of the solar system and the light and heat of it, he would say, "yes." Do you believe it lights all the planets in the solar system? "Yes." Do you believe it lights our earth? Does it light Asia, Africa, Europe, and America? Why propound such questions? He confessed all in the first proposition. If it is the center of the solar system, and its light and heat, it is the light and heat of all the planets, our world, and each division of the globe. So in confessing Christ we confess the whole system of which he is the author. "Every one therefore who shall confess me before men, him will I also confess before my Father who is in heaven."[1] Faith in the Christ was

[1] Matt. x. 32.

required of all candidates for church membership in the days of the apostles. Paul says, "If thou shalt confess with thy mouth the Lord Jesus, and shalt believe in thine heart that God has raised him from the dead, thou shalt be saved. For with the heart man believeth unto righteousness, and with the mouth confession is made unto salvation."[1] John says, "Many other signs truly did Jesus in the presence of his disciples which are not written in this book, but these are written that ye might believe that Jesus is the Christ, the Son of God, and that believing ye might have life through his name."[2]

These passages show what is to be believed and the object of belief.

First, Why do we believe? "These things are written that you might believe."

Second, What are we to believe? "That Jesus is the Christ, the Son of God."

Third, What is the object of belief? "That we might have life through his name. For this is the will of my father, that every one that beholdeth the Son, and believeth on him, should have eternal life."[3]

This is God's method of making believers, what He requires them to believe, and the object of their believing. Or, in other words, it is the will or purpose of God that men should believe through the word, that they should believe "that Jesus is the Christ, the Son of God," and that believing they should have life through His name. This basis includes God, heaven, the Holy Spirit, the entire revelation from God to

[1]Rom. x. 9, 10. [2]John xx. 30, 31. [3]John vi. 40.

man, the church, the ordinances, all spiritual blessings in Christ. It at the same time excludes whatever did not come from God. It includes all that is spiritual and excludes all that is not spiritual. This, then, is the greatest confession ever made by mortal. "Man glorified in heaven, gifted with immortality, and wrapped in the ecstacies of infinite and eternal blessedness, is but the result of a proper appreciation of, and conformity to, this great confession."

This basis of union, then, is the word of the apostles, the Scriptures of eternal truth. Christ is the rock on which the Christian institution is built. Every church founded on any other basis, or built on any other foundation, will perish from the earth. "Every plant which my heavenly Father hath not planted shall be rooted up."[1] Is not this basis broad enough, deep enough, large enough, to unite the believing world? "This institution, unlike any other, is perfectly adapted to the genius of human nature. Not to the people of one part of the world, nor one race or age, but to all parts of the globe, to all races of men and to all ages of time. It contemplates man in the light of his whole destiny, as he was, as he is, and as he shall hereafter be." Christianity contemplates the completion of one great family gathered out of all families; built upon one foundation, having "one Lord, one faith, one baptism," one spirit, one inheritance and "one God and Father of all." Everything in it is unity and harmony. Divisions are denounced and oneness is everywhere taught. It presents one book, one Savior,

[1]Matt. xv. 13.

one worship, one Judge, and one heaven. This, then, is the only basis for the union of believers, the only constitution for the Christian church.

There is a document extant in the world, in this enlightened age and nation, too, separate and apart from the Bible, having printed upon its title page, "The Constitution of the . . . Church." Now of all documents and things called constitutions there are three of which God himself is the author and finisher. He has neither given to man nor angels the liberty of making a constitution for the universe—a constitution for the human body, nor a constitution for the Church of God. Good and valid reasons can be given why man should not have been entrusted to draft a constitution for the universe, and why he should not have been permitted to form a constitution for his own body. All will find in his utter incapacity good reasons why he should not have been entrusted with such an undertaking. He is just as incompetent to form the last as either of the others. Had any individual a tolerably distinct and accurate view of the body of Christ, the Church of the living God, he would feel himself as wholly inadequate to the task of forming for it a constitution as he physically, intellectually, and morally is for his own body or the universe of God.

The church, the true church of the true Redeemer, is a glorious institution, and hence it was decreed before the Christian age began. Foretold by Isaiah, one of Israel's sweetest and most seraphic bards: "Unto us a child is born, unto us a son is given: and the government shall be upon his shoulder: and his name shall be called Wonderful, Counselor, The Mighty God, The everlasting Father, the Prince of Peace. Of the increase of his government and peace there shall be no end."[1] He is then the Founder of the Gospel Institution, "the everlasting kingdom." The noblest and most august titles in the universe surround His miter and His crown. Among these there is one to us of ineffable interest—"the author and finisher of our faith." Can man then draft a constitution for the Church of Jesus Christ? He could as easily make one for the hierarchies of heaven or for the universe of God. . . . To make for the Christian church a constitution, what a task. Had a council of the heavens been called, had Michael, Gabriel, Raphael, and all the elder sons of creation been convened to deliberate for an age they could not have made a constitution for Christ's church; they could not have sketched a system, even had it been adopted, that could have united, cemented, and harmonized in everlasting peace and unity the redeemed of the Lord. Hence, the Lord Himself was made the covenant and the leader, the law-giver, the author and founder of the Christian institution. On this and on this alone can the church be built. This constitution—this basis alone is the only basis for the Christian church. Let the Christ and the Christ alone be the basis of union, then all Christians of all nations, ages, and conditions can form one grand, holy, and happy family.

[1]Isa. ix. 6, 7.

CHAPTER XXXVIII

NATURE OF DIVISION

Causes of Division. Creeds. Are they Necessary for Discipline? Why They are Objectionable.

IN the third place we shall notice the causes of division. And here we would state that divisions have been caused by departure from Christ's church. All must return to the primitive faith and primitive practice. There are two things that are now bound on the conscience of man that are not embraced in the word of the apostles—human creeds and party names. Christ in His prayer specifies the word of the apostles as the basis, and, consequently, excludes all other bonds of union.

"A human creed or confession of faith is an ecclesiastical document, the mind and will of some synod or council possessing authority, written out as a form of union by which persons and things are to be tested, approved, or disapproved. They are called human, not merely because they are the productions of human effort, but because they are also the offspring of human authority. No one can in reason and in truth assign to them divine authority, because no man can produce a divine precept or warrant for their manufacture. No apostle, prophet, or evangelist gave any authority to any church, community, or council to furnish such a document. In order to give them any authority other than human four things are necessary: First, a divine precept commanding them to be made. Second, a selection of persons to make them. Third, a time fixed or extended during which the work is to be accomplished. And, fourth, a command to Christian congregations to receive and use them for the ends for which they were made. In the absence of such divine arrangement and enactment, they must be considered as a presumptive interference in the affairs of Zion's Law Giver and King, as an attempt to subvert His office, who has all authority in heaven and in earth. It is offering strange fire on God's altar and burning incense not commanded by Him whose right it is to ordain His own worship. It is, in fact, a reproach and an indignity offered to His living oracles and to the competency and fidelity of His ambassadors. . . . Had the Lord thought that a miniature of the Bible, an image of the whole revelation, a proper basis for church union and communion, Paul was the man, or Peter, or James or John, or all of the apostles together to give the sum of the matter and command all men to regard it as the covenant or constitution of Christ's church in general and of the congregations in particular, and then we would have had an authoritative creed—a divine rule of faith, by which to receive and reject all. His not having done this is the best evidence in the world why it should not be attempted by mortal and fallible men." Suppose the Lord himself had given a summary of His doctrine, as possibly He could have done, on a single page of the New Testament, what would have been the effect on His people? Certainly most injurious. It would have left us without any sufficient motive to study any other part of revelation. Many no doubt would have committed to memory the summary and been content to remain in profound ignorance of other divine truth. Is not this precisely the effect of human creeds? Do they not cause a great neglect of the Holy Scriptures by pretending to exhibit that which is necessary to be learned in the Bible?

Creeds retard the increase of spiritual growth and scriptual knowledge. If any gain new light there is danger that they may be regarded as heretics and treated accordingly. They are the fruits of unauthorized legislation. That creeds are legislative enactments of uninspired men no one can doubt. They are made the laws of the church. And is it not rebellion to leave the divine constitution of the Church and make a human fabrication the platform? The union of Christians can never be effected while creeds hold their place. They stand directly in the way of such union. Their unauthorized terms of fellowship can never be complied with by all. They conflict with each other, do not accord with the teachings of Christ, and, consequently they must be discarded, or the union of believers can never be effected.

It is said that creeds should be used because they are plainer than the Bible. If this be true, then man is either wiser than God or more benevolent. If God could have made the Bible plainer, and would not, then He was not benevolent. But if He would have made the Bible plainer and could not, then He lacked in wisdom. And if man has succeeded in making it plainer than God could have done, then he is wiser than God or more benevolent than He. Have uninspired men views clearer and more definite and less ambiguous than those guided and inspired by the Holy Spirit? Are they able to express themselves in terms clearer and plainer than did Christ and His apostles? If so, what is the value of inspiration? But God is wiser and more benevolent than all His children. "The wisdom of this world is foolishness with God."

Again, it is maintained by some, that creeds are necessary to a union of the Church. If this be true then Christ's church could not have been united without one. But it was. There was no human creed in the days of the apostles. It is well known that the creed called the "Apostles Creed" was formulated many years after the apostles had sealed their testimony with their blood and has no divine sanction or authority. The first important creed that was formed was made by the convention of Nice, called the Nicene Creed, three hundred and twenty-five years after Christ. Divisions commenced then and the work of forming creeds has progressed from that day to this, until in America alone there are nearly two hundred different sects of Christians. The purest age of Christianity was that in which there was no creed but Christ. If all could be united then can not all unite now on the same foundation? Instead of uniting the church, creeds tend to division. How many sects has the Westminster Confession of Faith formed? There are twelve different kinds of Presbyterians, all springing from one creed, explaining it differently. The Methodistic creed has produced seventeen different kinds of Methodists; the Lutherans are also divided into five general bodies and sixteen independent synods.[1] And so on with all other creed sects. The conclusion is, therefore, unavoidable that creeds instead of uniting believers divide them.

Again, it is urged in their favor, that they are necessary to discipline. If this be true, then discipline could not have been exercised without them, but it was. Members were excluded in the days of the apostles. "Now, we command you, brethren, in the name of the Lord Jesus Christ, that ye withdraw yourselves from every brother that walketh disorderly."[2] (For further instruction see fifth chapter of 1st Cor.) Not only were inspired teachings sufficient to discipline immoral members, but furnished the standard by which false teachers were tried. "Thou hast tried them which say they are apostles and are not, and hast found them liars."[3] And John says: "Try the spirits whether they are of God, because many false prophets are gone out into the world."[4] If there is no law in the New Testament to exclude disorderly members, how came it in the creed? Creeds may contain the doctrine of the Scriptures, if they do, then why adopt them? It is but rewriting

[1]Statistics by Dr. H. K. Carroll in *Christian Advocate*.
[2]2 Thess. iii. 6. [3]Rev. ii. 2. [4]1 John iv. 1.

them. If they do not contain this doctrine, then it is adding to the word of God. It is maintained by all that the doctrine of their creed is the same as the Bible. Then why not take the word of God and be satisfied? If the Christian Scriptures are the same as the creed, and discipline can not be exercised by the church through them, how can it be exercised through the creed?

Again, it is objected that if we had no creeds we should have no books written on religious subjects. But books are written to inform the mind, and creeds are bound on the conscience. There is then a material difference between preaching, or writing a book to give opinions, and binding such opinions on persons as conditions of church membership. We do not object to publishing opinions or books, but to the uses made of them when published—to binding them as authority on church members. Books pretend to no authority over others, usurp no power, bind no conscience—creeds do.

But again it is objected by the advocates of human creeds that those who oppose them have a creed in their own mind; that their understanding of the Scripture is a human creed; that the only difference between them is that the creed of one is written and that of the other is retained in memory. This logic proves that there is no such a thing as a written creed in the world, for all men have certain views of their respective creeds; and if this logic be true their views are the creed and not the book itself. But the primitive disciples understood the Scripture without having a human creed, and therefore we can understand it without one.

Human creeds are objectionable under any and all circumstances. First, because the Christian Scriptures are complete. Second, if a creed contains more than the Scriptures it is not right and is, therefore, objectionable. Third, if a creed contains less than the Scriptures it is not right and is therefore objectionable. Fourth, if a creed differs in any respect from Scripture it is not right and is objectionable. And, fifth, if a creed is precisely like the Scriptures it is not needed, for we have the Scriptures. Therefore under any and all circumstances creeds are objectionable.

All believers in Christ never will and never can unite on any human creed. Suppose the Calvinists were requested to discard their confession of faith and unite with the Methodists on their discipline. They would object because they prefer the confession to the discipline. Why do they prefer it? Because it more nearly accords with the Scriptures. And, again, if the Methodists were requested to lay aside their discipline and unite with the Lutherans on their confession. They would say we prefer our discipline to the Augsburg Confession. But why? Because it more nearly conforms to Scripture. Now, if all prefer their creeds because they are more in harmony with the Scripture, why not take the Scripture itself? All maintain, however, that they have taken their creeds out of the Scripture; therefore why not, then, restore them and unite?

Human creeds are positively inhibited by the word

of God. Paul says, "Hold fast the form of sound words which thou hast heard from me."[1] Jude says, "Earnestly contend for the faith which was once delivered unto the saints."[2] Again, Paul says, "Stand fast and hold the traditions which you have been taught, whether by word or epistle."[3] And God said, "this is my Son, hear ye him." These passages enjoining the Christian Scripture to be held fast in form, contended for and submitted to, most positively prohibit all other creeds. And, finally, on this point we say that their tendency is to dethrone the King, Priest, and Prophet of the Church. We are divinely commanded to hear Him. He is the supreme Head and Ruler, the Author and Founder of the faith. Every creed forms a center of government with a complete set of officers, an entirely independent body, no way connected with any other religious body or organization. Their name, their constitution, their law, their officers are unknown to the Scriptures, and they receive and exclude members upon their own authority. Human creeds must be looked upon with feelings of regret. When brought into contrast with the New Testament how insignificant they are. The creed-maker defines Jesus Christ, the Father and the Holy Spirit in a few lines, each, perhaps, in metaphysical terms, too, and calls on others to assent to this account of their God and their Savior. They learn as little of Deity by this process as they would learn of the sun by being told that that glorious luminary is a circle about a foot in diameter.

[1]2 Tim. i. 13. [2]Jude 3. [3]2 Thess. ii. 15.

CHAPTER XXXIX

DENOMINATIONALISM

Party Names Condemned. Are Denominations Branches of the Church of Christ? Statistics Show Union Essential to the Conversion of the World. Nature of Union.

IN the next place we would state that party names have a tendency to keep believers apart and cause divisions. Human names must go with human creeds. Christians can no more unite upon a human name than upon a human creed. The names of the ecclesiastical organizations condemn the bodies to which they are applied. Not one of them can be found in the New Testament. We read of the Church, the Churches of Christ, the Church of God, disciples of Christ, and Christians, but not of Episcopal, Presbyterian, or Methodist churches. Yet men will cling to such names and glory in them, as if they had all the authority of inspiration. Party names are condemned by inspiration. Paul thus reproves the Corinthians: "For whereas there is among you envying, and strife, and divisions, are ye not carnal, and walk as men? For while one saith, I am of Paul; and another, I am of Apollos, are ye not carnal?"[1] Here he not only condemns all divisions among Christians but declares that they have no right to follow men and

[1] 1 Cor. iii. 3.

wear human names. The names Calvinists, Wesleyans, Lutherans, and such like, should be discarded by every believer in the Christ. We are told that the Church is the bride, the Lamb's wife. In what a position does this figure place those who accept some other name than Christian. Suppose a married lady would take some other name than that of her husband, would this not be dishonoring and rejecting him? And is it not dishonoring the Lord for the Bride—the Church—the Lamb's Wife, to take a human name?

There are some who apologize for these different names. They illustrate the Church of Christ by a tree and call the different denominations branches. They include in these branches all orthodox or evangelical denominations. Now, it requires but little discernment to see that if all the orthodox churches are branches of the tree the tree has no trunk or body. If they are all branches of Christ's church, where is Christ's church? Such a tree is all branches and has no trunk. These churches are called branches of Christ's church, but there are no such branches mentioned by inspiration. Jesus Christ says not a word about these branch institutions. He says, "I am the vine, ye are the branches," speaking to His individual members, "He that abideth in me, and I in him, the same bringeth forth much fruit. . . . If a man abide not in me, he is cast forth as a branch, and is withered."[1] Not a "church" but a "man" is cast forth. Christ is the body, each individual Christian is a member of

[1]John xv. 5, 6.

that body. These unauthorized denominations then are not branches of Christ's church. No one of these denominations is the Church of Christ because they only claim to be branches, and His Church has no branches of this kind.[1]

It may now be asserted that the Methodist faith, the Presbyterian faith, and the Episcopal faith are not necessary to save anybody. But this does not prove that none among these parties will be saved, for those who are saved are saved not by denominational faith but by faith in Christ. All parties admit that a man can be a Christian and not a Methodist, Presbyterian, or an Episcopalian. All admit that the first followers of Christ did not belong to any of these parties, and they were Christians. The object now should be to make men Christians, disciples of Christ, children of God, and nothing more.

In the fourth place we notice the nature of the union for which Christ prayed. He prayed that they might be one as He and His Father are one. How, then, are Christ and His Father one? Certainly not one identical being or person, for two believers are not one in this sense. But Paul tells us in what sense believers are one. He says, "Now, I beseech you, brethren, by the name of the Lord Jesus Christ, that ye all speak the same things and that there be no divisions among you, but that ye be perfectly joined together in the same mind and in the same judgment."[2] In

[1] In using certain denominational names it is not the intention to specialize them, but for illustration.

[2] 1 Cor. i. 10.

Acts it is more clearly expressed: "And the multitude of them that believed were of one heart and one soul."[1] Then those who believe in Christ should be one, not in regard to personal identity but one in mind, one in judgment, one in heart and soul. In this sense God and Christ are one. For believers are to be one even as they are one.

Again, it is objected, that believers may be visibly divided yet invisibly united. But an invisible union and an invisible church is something unknown to the Scriptures. The union the Savior prayed for was of the most intimate kind—such as existed between Himself and the Father. The first Christians were exhorted to live together in union. Paul said, "Let there be no divisions among you." He would not allow the Christians to be divided unless they could show that Christ was divided. Hence he says to the Corinthians, who called themselves after different men, "Is Christ divided? Was Paul crucified for you, or were you baptized in the name of Paul?"[2] He did not say, it is right so you are invisibly united. The first Christians, then, were visibly united. They were united in feelings, desires, aims, objects, interests, under one leader and governor, and such should be the union now among all believers.

Fifth. In the last place we notice the object of Christian union. "Neither pray I for these alone, but for them also who shall believe on me through their word; that they all may be one; as thou, Father, art in me, and I in thee, that they also may be one in

[1]Acts iv. 32. [2]1 Cor. i. 13.

us; that the world may believe that thou hast sent me." It cannot be too deeply impressed that the union of believers is absolutely essential to the conversion of the world. It is plainly implied here, that if those who believed on Christ were one the world would believe. Nor is this any more plainly implied than that lack of union among believers causes unbelief. How vain, then, the thought that the existing parties of our times can ever succeed in converting the world when the structure of their own organizations weakens or destroys faith.

How comparatively futile are all missionary enterprises. How delusive the hope of saving the world when those who profess to serve the Lord are parted asunder. Can this be called an ungenerous charge when the Lord Jesus makes the faith of the world depend upon the unity of believers, and all admit that the world can not be saved without faith? The Lord implied that the world would not believe until his people were one. Hence He prayed that they might be one that the world might believe. Can Christians send missionaries to convince pagan nations? Can they print and circulate Bibles? Can they build up churches and preach with the zeal of the apostles in all the earth? Can they do all this, thinking to convert the world, while divisions are maintained? And if they do, what evidence have they that the object will ever be attained? It is true that some may be converted and saved under all these disadvantages, but what is this in comparison to the world believing? Why not, then, all labor for union? Why not remove this great obstacle that the cause of righteousness and peace may extend over the world?

What has been gained by the missionary enterprises in comparison to what might have been gained if all had been united in heart and hand, in faith and hope and love? In regard to missionary work in heathen lands in the last one hundred years, one author gives as the result of his investigation 1,100,000[1] communicants. Another author gives the number of communicants at 1,300,000[2], and over four million adherents. Of the 76,000,000 population in the United States the statistics[3] show 28,000,000 Christians and that 48,000,000 people are not connected with any church. There are 9,000,000 Catholics. This leaves only 19,000,000 Protestant Christians. Can the millions not Christian be converted by a divided church? In A.D. 1792, William Carey, the apostle of modern missions, gave the total population of the globe as 731,000,000, and the number of Protestant Christians 44,000,000, Roman Catholics as 100,000,000. In 1890, from the proceedings of the Royal Geographical Society, the total of the world's inhabitants is given as 1,487,000,000. In 1892, the *Quarterly* of the American Statistical Association for March gave the number of Protestants in the world as 143,000,000; Roman Catholics as 230,000,000. It will be seen that Protestants

[1]A Hundred Years of Missions, by Leonard.

[2]Ecumenical Missionary Conference, New York, 1900. Vol. i., page 79.

[3]By Dr. H. K. Carroll in *Christian Advocate*, 1902.

are increasing at a greater ratio than Roman Catholics. But these figures, however, show that a divided church is facing a most serious proposition which can only be solved by Christian union. Therefore it is of the utmost importance to restore the New-Testament church in order to convert the world. Not only so, but if the heathen are converted by a divided church, the same fierce, sectarian battles will be fought in those lands that have been fought in nominal Christian lands, since creed and sect and party strife began. The same indifference to church, the same infidelity will hinder the cause of Christ which has retarded its progress, weakened its influence, and prevented its triumph. While the work of conversion has been going on in pagan lands for one hundred years who can tell how many millions, on account of the unhallowed divisions and party strife, in Christian lands, have gone over to infidelity or become indifferent to the church?

How then is infidelity to be silenced and the world converted? How is Christianity to be spread from sea to sea, from the rivers to the end of the earth? It can be accomplished in only one way, in the way for which the Savior prayed. All must be united on the word of the apostles and the world will believe. A united church would have the means, the men, the ships, the Bibles sufficient to convert the whole world in less than a half century—yes, in less than a single generation. The human family might be made one in faith and to rejoice in hope of eternal life through Jesus Christ. The one great need is union. Before this is accomplished all must be united upon the foundation of the apostles and prophets, Jesus Christ Himself being the Chief Corner Stone. "The church of the Lord which he purchased with his own blood"[1] is a vital institution and must be restored in its completeness in order to save the world.

We have thus endeavored to present the divine plan of union—the principles of church fellowship, order and discipline taught in the gospel and the scriptural basis for the union of the saints. If these principles be adopted and acted upon by believers, sectarian strife, party animosity, denominational conflict and divisions would cease and a church of perfect symmetry, harmony, and beauty would arise to make glad the city of our God and bless the world. The union of all believers on the Christian basis would be both pleasing to God and honorable to His people. Such a union would bring the world to the Lord Jesus as the only Savior. Such a union God would smile upon, while the nations made glad by the sacred jubilee would sing in sweeter and louder strains than angels sang at the birth of Christ, "Glory to God in the Highest, on earth peace and good-will to men," and exultingly would shout "Hallelujah, for the Lord God omnipotent reigneth."

[1]Acts xx. 28.

CHAPTER XL

THE UNIQUENESS OF JESUS

Christianity's Great Author Contrasted with Other Founders of Religions.

WE began this volume by calling attention to the originality and superiority of the Christian religion over other religions, we close it by reference to its Great Author in contrast with other founders of religions.

Man is a religious being. Adoration of the supernatural is coextensive with the race. All peoples have anticipated some kind of existence after death. In view of this longing of the soul after immortality we may well inquire, "Is there a bright home skyward, where naught that blooms shall die?" If so, has God revealed it, and by whom? By the magicians of Egypt, the Magi of Persia, Buddha of India, Confucius of China, Socrates of Greece, Mohammed of Arabia, or Jesus of Palestine?

However old the world may be, its recorded religions are before us and have been telling upon its destiny for thousands of years. Is there one God and one religion, or one God and many religions?

Look over the history of Egypt, India, China, Persia, Greece, Rome and Arabia. What are the fruits of their religions? Is there any religion to-day lifting up the race and giving hope of future life, if so, who is its author? The answer must come back from every informed and candid man—it is Jesus. He is Lord of Lords, the Prince of Peace and Priest of the Most High God. There is stronger proof of His life, labors, death, and resurrection than there is of the life and conquests of Alexander, Cæsar, or Hannibal. His twelve apostles gave their lives proclaiming these facts and died in attesting their truth. The fact is more fully demonstrated that Jesus was crucified under Pilate than that Cæsar was assassinated by Brutus. Both are historical facts. One changed the government of Rome, the other the destiny of the world.

His life and teachings are wonderful. He spake "as never man spake." He was the first on earth who taught humility as the road to greatness. No one gave it such importance before. He first, and alone, taught mercy to the world. The Jews, Grecians, Romans, and others had ideas of justice, but mercy was untaught, as a principle, before Him. He said, "Blessed are the merciful: for they shall obtain mercy." He first taught men to pray, "Our Father, who art in heaven," and His followers are called "sons and daughters" of the Lord Almighty. He taught love to our enemies and gave the golden rule to the world. Who in this advanced age is accomplishing what Jesus did? Who has a voice like Him, heard all over the world and in the silence of the tomb?

Nineteen hundred years after His death there is, perhaps, not an institution on all the face of the world of love or mercy which He cannot claim. Before Christ and beyond Christianity where are the institutions of benevolence for the lame, halt, blind, orphans, aged and suffering? Nothing of importance before Christ—nothing in nations not Christian; nothing by infidels, no, nothing. Jesus said, "I will give you rest," and the weary and suffering repose.

He stands alone in contrast with the great of earth. He is not only the wisest of the great and the greatest of the wise, but He taught the wise wisdom and the great greatness. He towers so high above all other great men that it is easier to make Him divine than human. It would take a God to forge a Jesus.

Born in poverty, surrounded with the selfishness and bigotry of the age, yet He taught the widest philanthropy of earth. Uneducated, He uttered the wisest saying recorded on the rolls of time. While He never wrote but a single sentence in the sand, His life is told in sacred story and His words are recorded in the books of all civilized people and on the monuments and tombs of earth. He changed times and laws. The world stopped counting from creation and began at His birth, and now we write "in the year of our Lord." He is the children's friend; He blessed them and made them the models of His coming kingdom. People twine wreaths of immortelles on the day of His birth, and give gifts to their children. On the day of His resurrection they pause and think of His wondrous work. His name is first lisped in tenderness by the child, revered through life, and last spoken in death.

The greatest minds of the world are engaged in discussing His life. He lives in the finest written prose of the best writers for nineteen hundred years. The purest ideas of those who deny His pretensions are borrowed or taken from Him. There is nothing good or pure or holy which He has not uttered. Standing midway in earth's history His character is the only perfect one known to man. He is peer of the realm and commands respect of the past and will no doubt that of all succeeding ages. Nearly two thousand years have passed since His death and the world has been advancing toward His life and has not reached its perfection. When two thousand more shall have rolled away man will no doubt look up to Him with increasing admiration.

He lives in poetry. No name is so frequently sung as His. Strike it from the poetry of civilization and the dearest and sweetest songs can not be sung. The poetry of the past would be marred and the songs of the saints hushed forever. Jesus in poetry is the name chief among ten thousand and will be sung around the world till the latest ages of time. The living enjoy and the dying are cheered by its wondrous charm. "Jesus, lover of my sou "; "Rock of Ages, cleft for me"; "Jesus, thou art the sinner's friend"; "I know that my Redeemer liveth"—would not the earth be gloomier if the living lived and the dying died without these hallowed songs, more inspiring than those sung by the angels of God?

He lives in art painted by the finest artists, living and dead. How much of art relates to Jesus and His followers! After the overthrow of Napoleon III. we saw the blanks on the walls of the picture galleries of Paris where once hung the portrait of him who beautified that great city. But what blanks would be left if Jesus and His followers were taken from the art galleries of the world!

Take Jesus from civilization and you change its history, its poetry, its art, its literature, its government, its morals, its religion, and its hopes of the great hereafter. Since His death art is purer, prose holier, poetry sweeter; man enjoys more, lives better, dies happier; truth has new significance; life better objects, hope brighter prospects, and death new revelations.

The mission of His life was love. While He was poor and lone, traveling on foot without place to rest, He promised rest to the weary. "Come unto me, all ye that labor and are heavy laden, and I will give you rest." He said, "I am the way, the truth, and the life." "I am the resurrection and the life." His is the name relied on in death. He brought immortality to light. All was still, dark, silent at the tomb, and had been so for ages. No voice of comfort had ever issued from the grave. His was the first heard from its deepest gloom. Since its echoes died away on Calvary the night of death has shone like noonday, and a world more beautiful than earth has known is seen through its glory-gilded shadows. And now in every region under heaven where His name is known the wail of the mourner is less sad, and hope is breathed for the dying and the dead.

His empire is deepening and widening; year by year His cause is winning new fame and glory.

Thousands of houses erected for His worship girdle the world, and His praise is sung by millions on all the continents of the earth and in the islands of the sea. The story of Jesus was new when first told in Jerusalem, new in Antioch, in Athens and Rome; is new now and will be new in the Saturday evening of Time. Its infinite pathos will call forth tears until man shall cease to weep, the grave gives back its dead, and "Death is swallowed up in Victory."

He revolutionized the world in three years, giving it new date, new law, and new religion.

He revolutionized the empire of death in three days. With mangled feet He trod the wine-press of sorrow alone. With pierced hands he unbarred the gates of death and conquered him who had so long held its wide dominion, and "delivered them who through fear of death were all their lifetime subject unto bondage." With the prints of the nails in His hands and His feet, with the mark of the spear in His side, He arose from the grave more mighty than Samson when he carried away the gates of Gaza, with the broken shackles of death beneath his feet, "marching in the greatness of his strength . . . mighty to save," He proclaimed liberty to a captive world. "I am he that liveth and was dead, and behold, I am alive forever more, and have the keys of death and Hades."

He revolutionized heaven on the day of His ascension. Angelic hosts cried aloud, "Lift up your heads, O ye gates . . . and the King of Glory shall come in." He entered and "for the suffering of death was crowned." God gave Him the scepter and told Him to reign. From His celestial throne he now commands the ages as they roll on. "He has upon his vesture and thigh a name written: King of kings, and Lord of lords," is going forth in love conquering and to conquer, and at no distant period He will come back with the crowns of the world upon His head and the kings of the earth at His feet, Lord over all, swaying the scepter of universal dominion over earth's living and its unnumbered dead. He will gather the redeemed of all time out of every nation, kindred, tribe, and tongue to that peaceful shore where no storms beat, to constitute the one great family of God where the tenderest ties broken on earth shall be reunited, where the bright forms of human beauty, that pass so quickly from us here, leaving us to mourn their faded loveliness, will stay in our presence forever, in a celestial home where there shall be no more suffering, no more sorrow. And "I heard a great voice out of heaven saying, . . . there shall be no more death."

INDEX